THE FIBERGLASS BOAT REPAIR MANUAL

THE FIBERGLASS BOAT REPAIR MANUAL

ALLAN H. VAITSES

with illustrations by Ed Davis

International Marine
Camden, Maine

International Marine/
Ragged Mountain Press
A Division of The McGraw-Hill Companies

08 07 06 05   SB   18 19 20 21

Library of Congress Cataloging-in-Publication Data

Vaitses, Allen.
  Fiberglass boat repair manual.

  Includes index.
  1. Fiberglass boats—Maintenance and repair.
I. Title.
VM322.V35   1988   623.8'207   88-22979
ISBN 0-07-156914-6

Questions regarding the content of this book should be addressed to:
International Marine
P.O. Box 220
Camden, ME 04843

Questions regarding the ordering of this book should be addressed to:
The McGraw-Hill Companies
Customer Service Department
P. O. Box 547
Blacklick, OH 43004
Retail Customers: 1-800-262-4729; Bookstore: 1-800-722-4726

Typeset by Maryland Composition, Glen Burnie, MD
Design by Janet Patterson
Production by Janet Robbins
Edited by J.R. Babb, Jonathan Eaton, and Keith Lawrence

Contents

Preface

En route to the Bermuda Race in the pre-dawn darkness of 1974, the late Phil Weld, tacking his 40-foot fiberglass trimaran *Trumpeter* down Buzzards Bay against a prevailing southwester, struck a rock in Nasketucket Bay, a bight of the mainland shore. The main hull's forefoot suffered a violent blow, and Phil worried that the Airex-cored laminate, although not leaking, might be badly damaged. A crew from my boatshop met him at Mattapoisett Boatyard; he nosed her up to the beach, and the yard crane lifted her main hull's forefoot clear of the water. Wading out to her, we found a modest break in the outer skin, near the waterline, but she was in no immediate danger—the Airex foam and inner skin seemed intact. We decided to patch her right there, standing in water.

We were a little apprehensive about using the electric grinder, but we found a tool with a plastic casing, checked it for shorts, and I stood by, extension cord in hand, ready to pull the plug at the first sign of trouble. All went well, and in a few hours Phil was off again for Newport and the race, his boat showing no sign of her encounter with a rock.

That is just one of many examples of fast turnarounds in the life of a fiberglass repairer. Whitey, one of the two men who patched *Trumpeter* that morning, had worked with fiberglass almost 30 years, since he helped Carl Beetle build the first boats to come out of open molds.

In this book I hope to impart to you some of the many bits of know-how needed to repair fiberglass boats with similar ease and assurance. Nobody can hope to step right into Whitey's resin-spattered work shoes, but if you pay attention—if you don't just "read the pictures," rush out to the boat, and recklessly throw materials at it—you can easily learn to do a proper job. Take all the time you need at first to do it right; speed and nonchalance will come with practice.

Acknowledgments

No book is the work of one person alone, and this one is no exception. Special thanks to Arthur Potter, David Biddle, and Peter Elen; to Keith Lawrence of *Boatbuilder* Magazine, Rick Delaune of Seemann Fiberglass, Inc., Peter J. Legnos of LBI, Inc., Lee Sechler of Resin Support Systems, and to the people at Owens/Corning Fiberglas, especially Marilyn A. Tilley; to Cook Paint and Varnish Company and Detco Marine; to Fiber Glass Industries, Inc; and to Ed Davis, artist and boatbuilder, a round of applause for his illustrations.

CHAPTER 1

Materials and Construction

One of the most endearing aspects of a fiberglass boat is that any moderate-sized hole, gouge, or fracture can quickly and easily be healed by the judicious application of the same sort of materials as those from which the boat was laminated. Composed as it is of reinforcing materials glued together with resin, fiberglass is repaired by gluing—called laying up or laminating—new reinforcing materials into the area where the laminate was damaged. Done right, such repairs can make the part—the generic name for any single piece of a fiberglass boat—as good as new. Indeed, even the most disheartening damage—gaping holes or crushed topside areas—can be repaired by the willing boat owner.

To repair a fiberglass boat you need a plain and practical knowledge of what fiberglass is and how boats are built with it. You need not know chemistry, physics, or naval architecture—just what the stuff is like and how to use it. Probably the easiest way to learn would be to grab a mat knife, resin pot, brush, and roller and join a crew laying up fiberglass on a boat. Since that isn't feasible for most people, this chapter is included to give you a working knowledge of the basics. I well remember the patient and practical explanations given to me by builders with more experience, back in the days when fiberglass boats were still a very new thing. I hope the explanations that follow serve you as well.

What fiberglass is

The life blood of fiberglass is a liquid resin, which, when catalyzed, turns into a medium-hard, tenacious substance. It is not very impressive, being rather brittle, and it is hard to imagine what anyone would want with a material physically similar to amber-colored hard candy, yet unfit to eat. But when resin is used to saturate glass fibers and then cured, it binds them into a tough, flexible bundle with more tensile strength (ability to withstand longitudinal stress) for its weight than steel. This is the material in which General Electric was molding radar domes at the end of World War II. Seeing the domes, Carl Beetle, scion of a New Bedford family famous for its efficient production of whaleboats, decided that the new material was just right for the long awaited one-piece molded boat, and at the New York Boat Show in the winter of 1946–47, he introduced the world's first fiberglass boats.

Now that many problems facing early fiberglass workers have been resolved, the laminating process really is as simple as saturating glass fiber materials with a resin, in a mold or on a form. A fiberglass boat is built today as it always has been; only some details of the process have changed.

Boatbuilding resins

The two basic types of resin used in boatbuilding are polyesters and epoxies. Polyester is used in the vast majority of boat laminates—probably 99 percent of the fiberglass boats built to date—because it is cheaper; its cure time can be adjusted on the job; and it will saturate the glass fiber materials quickly yet stay in place until it cures. In itself it is not very irritating to most people, although the most common catalyst, MEKP (methyl ethyl ketone peroxide), mixed into the resin in small amounts, is extremely irritating, especially to the eyes, in its raw state. It must be handled with care, and it makes polyester resin much more irritating when added to it. MEKP should not be confused with the industrial solvent, methyl ethyl ketone (MEK).

Polyester resins can be further broken down into three categories: orthophthalic resin (ortho), isophthalic resin (iso), and vinylester resin. Although the vast majority of fiberglass boats are built with ortho resin, the use of the slightly more expensive iso resins and gelcoats is increasing, due to their higher impact strength and solvent resistance. Vinylester resin, both in terms of physical properties and cost, could be considered to be a compromise between the low-cost polyesters and the epoxy resins. At this time, the use of vinylester resin is limited primarily to the construction of high-performance powerboats, where vinylester's increased bond strength has helped to eliminate bonding problems with core materials.

Epoxy resins are, admittedly, even better "glue" than polyesters, a property that makes epoxy fiberglass stronger. Epoxies are also much less inhibited from curing by water. In fact, some of them will cure unaffected when applied underwater.

Yet only high-performance sail and power craft and special-purpose laminates have been made with epoxy resins to date, although there is, in addition, a large number of putties, glues, and other products that are based upon epoxies and are useful in boatbuilding and repair. Epoxies are much more expensive (roughly $40 to $50 per gallon in 1988, compared with $10 per gallon for polyester), much harder to handle, and incapable of cure time adjustment on the job. The polyester resin catalyst comprises only a percentage or two of the catalyzed mixture, and can be metered in greater or lesser quantity to hasten or retard the cure; the epoxy resin curing agent (which is not, in the strict sense, a catalyst), constitutes 10 to 50 percent of the volume of the two-part mixture, and its relative amount can't be varied. You must purchase a formulation that gives you the desired gel time. Finally, epoxies are very toxic, and should not contact bare skin; neither should one share unventilated spaces with their fumes.

The choice of resins

As we discuss various kinds of repairs, you will find that polyester resin is recommended for most standard patching and rebuilding of fiberglass laminates. Of the two forms in which polyester resin is supplied, *finishing* resin should be chosen for most small repair projects that can be laid up in a single operation, and for the final layer of fiberglass applied in a multilayered laminate. Finishing resin contains an additive that rises to the surface of the laminate as it cures, sealing off the air and allowing the resin to cure to a tack-free, sandable surface.

The other form of polyester resin, *laminating* resin, is said to be "air-inhibited," which means that it does not fully cure when exposed to the air. Laminating resin cures to a non-sandable, tacky surface that does not require washing or sanding before subsequent layers can be added. For larger repair projects, laminating resin and a small quantity of a tack-free additive should be purchased. The tack-free additive (often referred to as wax or TFA), when added to laminating resin, produces finishing resin.

While polyester-based resins and putties are acceptable and often preferable for fiberglass repairs, the many superlative epoxy laminating resins, adhesives, putties, and paints are of inestimable value in repair work. The epoxies play an important part where dampness would inhibit or prevent polyester's cure, and the superior strength of epoxy laminates can be used to advantage for the repair of very light, high-performance craft. Even for the repair of a heavy-displacement cruising boat, the epoxies may be helpful in areas that do not allow you to use as much polyester material as you'd like.

Keep in mind that epoxy can be used to repair a polyester laminate, but polyester should not be used for the repair of an epoxy laminate. This means that if epoxy resins or fairing compounds are used in completing a fiberglass repair, the repaired area should not be gelcoated, but should rather be finished with paint, preferably applied over an epoxy primer.

Both polyester and epoxy resins are modified by manufacturers with additives such as fillers (see below), accelerators, fire retardants, pigments, waxes, and others. These different formulations affect viscosity and cure time, among other properties, allowing the shopper to be quite specific about his needs.

Resin products: glues and putties

As implied above, there are a number of other uses made of both kinds of resin in fiberglass boatbuilding and repair. Resins are filled with various substances to make a wide range of gelcoats, putties, glues, and paints. It is only natural that the fiberglass boatbuilder should have developed products useful to his trade by mixing innumerable substances with the resin always at hand.

My first draft for this section was entitled "Mixing Putties," which is a flashback to the days when we often mixed Cabosil, talc, milled glass fibers, and microballoons into general-purpose polyester boat resin for forming, bonding, fairing, and smoothing, or purchased some polyester casting resin and thickened it with any number of good things such as asbestos, sand, sawdust, pecan shells, chopped strands of glass fiber, or even crushed rock for filling hollow keels, rudders, centerboards, lift strips, coamings, and sundry other cavities. When I began to write, however, I awoke to the fact that between but two catalogs of fiberglass material suppliers on my desk there were 26 different pastes, putties, or fillers compounded to facilitate every standard operation of boatbuilding and repair. These proprietary products are similar to the mixtures mentioned above, and anyone can still mix his own; indeed, there is an ever-increasing number of

new possibilities. But due to constant research and development and the stiff competition among today's suppliers of materials for the huge market of boat, autobody, and other plastic-product manufacturers, mixing one's own results in an inferior product and no great saving in cost to any but a very high-volume user.

I hate to let go of the independent ways of an earlier time, so if you want to get some of the above-mentioned materials—or others, such as glass microspheres, ground metal, and whatnot—you have my blessing. But if your first concern is to get the boat repaired, you'll get it done more quickly and easily and at only a little more materials cost with a proprietary product. If all you need to accomplish is a little smoothing, patching, or fairing, you will find inexpensive polyester- and epoxy-based putties in your local autoparts and discount stores that are made by the same companies that formulate boatbuilding putties.

Patching holes, radiusing corners, fairing and smoothing, and repairing gelcoat constitute one type of use for these various compounds. Bonding decks to hulls, or bonding cores, liners, beds, stringers, coamings, and other parts to main parts is another use. Filling hollow fiberglass parts, from keels to bulwarks, is still another. You must be certain you buy a product that is really suitable for its intended use. You need to know not just whether it *can* be used for a given job, but whether it does that job *well*, or if there is something else that does it much better. Some putties can be used for more than one of the above tasks—patching, fairing, bonding, or filling—but that does not mean that there is not a better putty for each job, or that *any* one putty is good for *all* tasks.

Some things you ought to bear in mind in selecting and using putties are:

1. Putties that are to be sanded, like those for patching gelcoat or fairing and smoothing a surface, need to be as easy-sanding and free-sanding (not clogging the paper) as you can get. Otherwise they will drive you crazy.

2. Putties to be applied thickly ought to be made with a casting resin, which won't

Fiberglass Boat Repair and Finishing Materials

INTENDED USE	MATERIALS	WHEN TO USE	REMARKS
Laminating resin	General-purpose polyester boat resin.	All normal building and repair jobs.	Available with a variety of specific formulations and additives. Remember the distinction between laminating and finishing resin.
	Epoxy laminating resin.	For strong, high-performance laminates.	Toxic to skin and respiration. Expensive. Provides a stronger, more tenacious, more water-resistant surface and bond than polyester.
Filling large voids, cavities, hollow keels	Casting or large-volume keel putties.	See recommendations of the various manufacturers.	There are numerous, off-the-shelf, multiuse products that fill this purpose.
	Casting resin filled with an inert material on the job.	When a laminating resin would generate too much heat of cure, but off-the-shelf keel putties are unavailable or too expensive.	For coarse, cheap filler, use washed and dried aggregate or fine crushed stone. For strength, use chopped glass fiber, talc, or milled glass fibers.
	General-purpose polyester resin filled with inert material.	When neither casting resin nor keel putty is at hand.	Catalyze moderately. Cast in layers. As each layer cools, roughen its top for a better bond to the next.
For bonding and sealing hull-to-deck joints, deckhouse-to-deck joints, and other parts	Deck-joint putties.	See manufacturers' suggestions.	Many good products. Use with through bolts or self-tapping screws.
	Glass-fiber filled polyester resin and/or two layers of wet mat.	On surfaces well sanded and fitted.	Gives "welded" hard joint, cheap and permanent.
	Polyurethane adhesives.	Anytime, for flexibility and strength.	Expensive, but flexible and durable. Recommended brands include 3M #5200 and Sikaflex 241.

Fiberglass Boat Repair and Finishing Materials

INTENDED USE	MATERIALS	WHEN TO USE	REMARKS
	Epoxy putties.	Anytime strength and flexibility are critical, or where metals are involved.	Expensive but very strong. Follow manufacturer's recommendations, and choose the proper formulation for the job. Marine-Tex is a legend of the industry.
For fairing and building out a surface; cosmetic repairs	Polyester-based fairing putties.	For easiest sanding.	Many good products available. Mor-Bond is one of the best known and liked.
	Polyester resin filled with microballoons, glass spheres, or talc.	When fairing putties not available.	Cheap for large-volume use, but best coated with free-sanding product before final smoothing.
	Autobody putty.	Anytime.	Polyester-based. Heavy. Some are hard sanding. Bondo is a well-known brand.
	Epoxy fairing putties or filled epoxy resin.	Anytime, particularly below the waterline. Cannot be coated with polyester gelcoat.	Epoxy-based putties are historically hard to sand, but some new formulations are better in this regard. Epoxy's great water-resistance and tenacious bonding makes it the preferred choice of many for filling blisters and fairing below the waterline. Marine-Tex.
Repair of gelcoat blemishes	Gelcoat putties.	For deeply gouged gelcoat.	A variety of brands available. Some suppliers will match color. Some can be polished.
	Gelcoat thickened on the job with talc or Cabosil.	When proprietary putties cannot be obtained.	Both talc and Cabosil are reasonably color-neutral. Both make a hard-sanding putty. Match your putty to the surrounding gelcoat using dispersion pigments in neutral gelcoat.

Fiberglass Boat Repair and Finishing Materials

INTENDED USE	MATERIALS	WHEN TO USE	REMARKS
	Gelcoat over autobody putty.	In lieu of mixing putty (see Chapter 2).	Requires two separate applications, but works well.
Refinishing fiberglass hulls and decks (see Chapter 2)	Gelcoat.	For best durability.	Needs most sanding and polishing.
	Polyurethane coatings.	The "next-best" choice for a durable, high-gloss finish.	Many excellent brands, including Awlgrip and Imron. Require a professional approach to preparation and application. Epoxy barrier coat over polyester resin or gelcoat recommended.
	Oil-based alkyd enamels; one-part modified alkyd enamels.	In lieu of more difficult and expensive polyurethane coatings.	Quicker, cheaper, and more user friendly than two-part polyurethane coatings. Tend to be more durable on fiberglass than wood. The one-part modified alkyd enamels are essentially oil-based enamels modified by urethanes; these may be more durable than traditional enamels, but are certainly less so than two-part polyurethane coatings.
	Epoxy paints.	See Remarks.	Proprietary formulations used as barrier coats under polyurethane coatings. Any epoxy paint (two coats) can be used as a coating on the underwater surfaces of a blistered hull, after blisters have been removed and puttied. Epoxy

Fiberglass Boat Repair and Finishing Materials

INTENDED USE	MATERIALS	WHEN TO USE	REMARKS
			paints may fade in sunlight.
Bedding hardware and trim	Polyurethane adhesives.	For a permanent bedding/adhesive that sticks to both surfaces.	Tough, flexible, very hard to separate parts without damage. Forms a more or less permanent bond. Brands include 3M #5200 and Sikaflex 241. Can be painted.
	Polysulfide adhesive sealants.	For good sealing and flexibility. For bedding teak decking and trim. The most all-purpose marine adhesive sealant.	Not as strong an adhesive as polyurethane, much stronger than silicone. Resists solvents, including fuel spills. Flexible. Can be sanded and painted. Brands include Boatlife, Life-Calk, 3M #101, Thiokol.
	Silicone adhesive sealants.	For bedding when painting not required.	Flexible. Weak adhesive. Best used under compression, as bedding under through-fastened hardware. May be used underwater. Will not accept paint.
	Oil-based mastic bedding compounds.	For quick, easily cleaned-up bedding.	Not adhesive. Not as long-lived as the above three, but durable and will stay soft when not exposed to weather. Date back to wooden boat usage.
Bedding liners and joinerwork to the hull interior	Resin-based beddings.	For fiberglass-compatible adhesion.	Some are stronger, harder, and heavier than others.
	Polyurethane adhesives.	For great flexibility, tenaciousness, durability.	Expensive but very tough. Removal of part may be destructive.
	Wet mat and/or resin filled with glass fibers or milled glass.	When off-the-shelf products not obtainable.	A much-used alternative for large jobs.

overheat during cure. This is particularly true when such large masses as filled hollow keels are involved, but there can be trouble even when a thick coat is used for bedding cores or for bonding parts with high insulating values.

3. It is very difficult to catalyze putties properly, because they are viscous and the catalyst does not readily disperse through them. Many manufacturers add pigment to the catalyst so that you can tell by the uniform color when the batch is well mixed.

The glass fiber materials

The muscles and bones of a fiberglass boat are the glass fibers embedded in the resin. They give her strength, and at the same time, flexibility. Strangely, when the brittle resin is laced with glass fibers, the resulting laminate is almost too flexible for a boat material; witness, for example, fiberglass fishing rods, or the trampolining ("oilcanning") of the bottoms and decks of small boats. You can walk up to the occasional 30-foot boat and push the topsides in a little with your hand, yet the boat may have been around for several years with no obvious signs of trouble. On such a boat, if you look closely, you may see a network of very fine cracks over the surface, or batches of them running parallel to one another where the hull has been bending over a bulkhead or where a berth butts against it on the interior. But more about such things in Chapter 2.

Types of glass fiber materials

As the name implies, glass fiber materials are composed of tiny glass filaments, or fibers, also called spun glass, which are gathered into bundles or strands. Heavy strands made of up to 100 or more continuous glass fibers, termed roving or "strand roving," are packaged on spools. Strand roving is often laid lengthwise into sharp corners and depressions which woven glass would only bridge,

and roving is also the stuff that is fed into the chopper guns used by manufacturers to spray up a boat rather than lay it up by hand, as discussed later in this chapter.

In repair work, as in much of boatbuilding, various configurations of these strands constitute the materials that you will actually lay up to patch or replace damaged fiberglass laminate. Descriptions of the most common follow. Incidentally, you may save money and avoid resins that have perhaps sat too long on the shelf if you purchase your resin and glass fiber materials from sources other than yacht supply stores and retailers. Look for outlets that sell materials in bulk as well as in small lots. Check the Yellow Pages for wholesale suppliers, who sell to the home construction industry (pools, bathtubs, etc.) as well as to boatbuilders and repairers. Many wholesalers have scattered distribution centers and will sell to individuals, sometimes at a third or less of the retail price. Among the worst bargains are the packaged repair kits for small jobs, which aren't always as good as they should be but are usually more expensive than they need to be. For small materials purchases, try a friendly local boatyard or order by mail from one of the marine discount catalog houses.

Chopped strand mat (CSM)

This is a mat of short strands laid down in random positions (not woven or arranged in any pattern), compressed into a flat sheet, and held together with a binder that is resin-soluble (Figure 1-1). It is sold in rolls, in a number of widths up to about 76 inches, and designated by its weight in ounces per square foot (commonly ¾ ounce to 3 ounces). Asking for "38-inch, ounce-and-a-half mat" will get you chopped strand mat in the 38-inch width weighing 1½ ounces per square foot. To tell the counterman or order clerk at your fiberglass materials supplier how much you want, you would ask how the rolls of his particular brand run; different manufacturers offer rolls of different sizes, which are only approximate, each roll varying a slight bit from the average. If the smallest roll offered is, say, a hundred pounds, and you have but a small repair, then you can probably

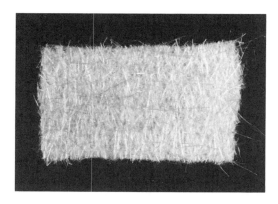

Figure 1-1. *Chopped strand mat (2¼-ounce).*

order a small number of pounds from him, or some other distributor, at a higher price per pound.

Relative to other fiberglass fabrics, chopped-strand mat is:

- *The most adhesive,* partly because of the many short strands "hooking onto" adjacent layers, and partly due to its resistance to peeling. When you try to peel it apart, or off a surface, you usually just pull a piece off it.

- *The most watertight,* because its multidirectional strands reinforce almost every drop of resin against transverse fractures and pinholes that would leak. Neither do its strands lead water anywhere by capillary attraction, as do the bundled strands of other glass fabrics on occasion.

- *The most easily molded,* simply because once the resin has dissolved the mat's binder, the mat can be stretched or compressed and its strands moved around until they conform to almost any shape, no matter how sharply curved, as long as any corners are slightly rounded—say to a radius not less than ⅛ to ¼ inch, depending on the "softness" of the particular mat.

- *Lower for its weight in tensile and flexural strength* than woven or unwoven roving or cloth. On the other hand, its strength is equal in all directions due to the random orientation of its strands.

- *The workhorse of all glass fiber components.* Many boat parts have been built en-

tirely of mat with perfectly satisfactory results.

For repair work, particularly when working alone, consider 38 inches the maximum width for ease of handling.

Surfacing tissue, an extremely lightweight mat, is often used as the first layer under the gelcoat to prevent "print-through" of the next, heavier layer of mat in the gelcoat and to ensure a complete bond with the gelcoat. With reasonable care in your repair work you should experience no such problems with normal-weight mat, rendering the tissue an unnecessary expense.

Woven roving

Woven roving is a coarse, plain weave of roving in sizable flat strands (Figure 1-2). It adds great tensile and flexural strength to a laminate. Its highest strength is in the directions of the warp and weft strands, which are oriented at 90 degrees to each other, and its lowest strength is across the bias, or at 45 degrees to the warp and weft directions.

Woven roving does not resist peeling, or shearing, of its bond to other layers very well, so it is best used in alternating layers with mat, which greatly helps to bind it against separating. Probably 95 percent or more of all fiberglass boats over 20 feet long have been built with alternating mat and woven roving laminates. Because of that, woven roving can be obtained from the manufacturer with a mat backing already in place.

The crimps in the strands of woven roving, where they weave over and under each

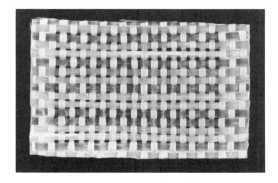

Figure 1-2A. *Woven roving (18-ounce).*

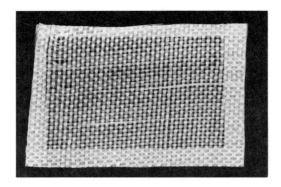

Figure 1-2B. *Lightweight woven roving (8.2-ounce).*

other, reduce its strength and cause the pattern of the weave to show up in the otherwise mirrorlike surface of the finished laminate. For these two reasons, loosely woven flat strands make the best woven roving.

Woven roving is designated by its weight in ounces per square yard, as are all other fiberglass fabrics except mat. The most commonly used weights are 18 and 24 ounces per square yard, but lighter and heavier weights are available. When backed with mat, the total weight is increased by about 50 percent. Like mat, woven roving is available in many widths, from 4 to 120 inches or more, but the most popular range for both fabrics is 38 to 76 inches wide, and for home repair work, 38 inches or less is best.

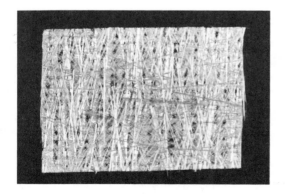

Figure 1-2C. *Bonded mat and roving. In this Fabmat, 1-ounce mat is backed with 10-ounce woven roving, the pattern of which can be seen faintly.*

Unwoven roving

Because it was recognized early on that the crimps in the strands tend to diminish the strength of woven roving, unwoven roving has long been available to those who want its greater tensile strength—approximately 15 percent greater. Unwoven roving is made up of flat strands all running parallel in any given layer, held together with rows of cross-stitching. It is available in a single layer, called unidirectional, in the warp configuration (strands running lengthwise), the weft configuration (strands running widthwise), or with the strands running at 45 degrees to the length and width (Figure 1-3). Using layers with these orientations, unwoven roving is also supplied as "biaxial" and "triaxial" composites, which give the laminator an opportunity to obtain in one material strands running in two or three directions of his choice. Alternatively, he can select appropriate unidirectional layers and use them in the way he thinks will add the most strength to the part he is building or repairing. In patching up a small damaged area, of course, you ought to consider just buying a few pounds of one unidirectional roving and turning each layer in the direction you want.

Why all of this fuss over strand orientations? Because while unidirectional roving has the greatest strength of any roving product in the direction of its strands, it has the lowest at 90 degrees to its strands. Because of this, and because unwoven roving has the same tendency to peel that woven roving has,

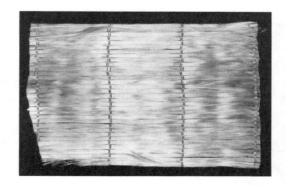

Figure 1-3. *Unidirectional roving (13-ounce).*

it is also important to use mat in alternating layers with unidirectional roving if you want better bonding of the layers and high impact resistance. Here again the manufacturers oblige, with unwoven rovings to which mat backing has been stitch-bonded.

Unwoven roving, then, can give you stronger repaired areas with minimal weight, and it is more and more likely as the years go by that the boat you are repairing was laid up with it anyway. It is also possible that you will find that some broken part such as a fiberglass mast or the amas of a multihull was built with this material and will need to be repaired with it to retain its stiffness; I built masts with it myself in the late '60s and early '70s.

Fiberglass cloth

Fiberglass cloth is a fabric, usually plain woven like common cloths of other materials, and very similar to them. In fact, a number of items, such as fireproof curtains, are made of fiberglass. The yarns of fiberglass cloth, comprising two or more strands twisted together, are much finer than the strands used in woven roving. Supplied for boatbuilding in weights ranging from a few ounces to 10 ounces per square yard and widths from narrow tapes to 120 inches and more, cloth is sometimes (though less often nowadays) used as the final finished surface on the interior of a molded hull or part, or sometimes on the exterior of a form-built laminate. It also adds tensile and flexural strength to light hulls when used in conjunction with lightweight mat. Many popular small dinghies are built with but a layer or two of mat and one of cloth.

Cloth, with its high flexural and tensile strength in the warp and weft directions and its fine weave, is an excellent material for winding tubular parts on a mandrel, such as fiberglass shaft logs, rudderports, and

Figure 1-4A. *These eight squares of mat and woven roving represent a typical fiberglass laminate with a finished thickness of approximately $^5/_{16}$ inch. Laid up in a mold, the laminate schedule reads, in order of application (left to right): gelcoat (not pictured), mat, mat, roving, mat, roving, mat, roving, mat.*

Figure 1-4B. *This laminate uses alternating mat and unidirectional roving; the two layers of the latter are laid at 90 degrees to each other. The schedule, left to right, is gelcoat (not pictured), mat, mat, roving, mat, roving, mat, and its thickness would finish $^3/_{16}$ to $^1/_4$ inch.*

through hulls to be fiberglassed directly to the hull and deck. If you are repairing a boat on which such parts cast in bronze have failed or been broken out, you might consider replacing them with tubes made of fiberglass, which can be "welded" with fiberglass right to the hull or deck and which will not deteriorate or loosen up for the indefinite future if properly installed. You can buy them or you can wind them yourself (see Chapter 8). But back to the discussion at hand.

The advanced or "super-reinforcing" materials

You will hear much about exotic materials that add properties beyond the capabilities of fiberglass. Called "advanced composites," they are not new, having been used in aerospace work for years, but they are creeping into boatbuilding slowly, as cost comes down and as high performance requirements make them essential. While you are unlikely to need them on 99 percent of the fiberglass boats built to date, the time will certainly

come for some of them. Meanwhile, if you know about them, those word droppers who always have to be one up on everybody won't make you feel ignorant by asking, "Why don't you fix your boat with such and such? It's much better, you know."

S glass is a stronger, stiffer, and tougher glass than the E glass that has been standard to date. It is also more expensive. It's easy to work with, and weighs about the same. It is only needed on high-performance boats to gain strength with light weight.

Ceramic fibers are almost as strong as S glass, but their greatest asset of resisting temperatures up to 3,000°F is of limited worth on your boat. At their current price of about $90 per pound, I doubt you'll want them anyway.

Carbon (or Graphite) fibers are expensive but very light, and worked into certain parts of an ordinary laminate they can add tremendous stiffness and tensile strength (Figure 1-5). They can improve the strength-to-weight ratio of highly stressed parts, but except for ultrahigh-performance power and

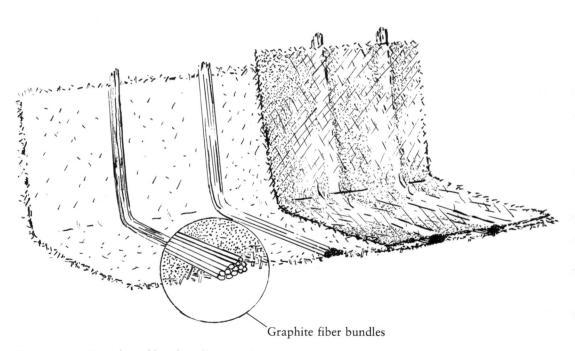

Graphite fiber bundles

Figure 1-5. *Graphite fiber bundles reinforcing a corner where great strength is needed and weight must be kept down.*

Figure 1-6. *Waxing a mold prior to lay-up.*

sailing craft, they are used sparingly because of cost.

Kevlar, which falls between S glass and graphite fibers in cost, is a remarkably tough organic fiber woven into a fabric. Besides being the most impact-resistant fiber on the market, it is probably the lightest. It's also a bear to cut and impossible to sand, because sanding raises a fuzz on it; the best way to apply it is to vacuum bag it. Further, its compressive strength is said to be poor. Nevertheless, its superior qualities are highly prized in high-performance boat construction and in small boats such as canoes and kayaks.

Constructing the fiberglass boat

Understanding the basics of how a boat is built helps one know how to repair it. In the balance of the chapter, we'll discuss building and finishing techniques, cored (or "sandwich") construction, hull-to-deck joints, and related subjects.

Molded versus form-built boats

All production fiberglass boat hulls, decks, and small parts are built in molds, except a handful that are built over a wooden inner shell or lining that is left in place in the finished part. Even some one of a kind or "one-off" parts are built in short-run or throw-away molds. The obvious preference for molding over building on a form is that once a mold has been built and polished to perfection, hundreds of mirror-image parts can be taken from it without building a finish on each one. Only regular repolishing and occasional resurfacing of the mold is required.

In molding a boat part, the gelcoat of resin mixed with pigment and some fillers formulated to resist water, wear, and weather is first sprayed onto the mold in a generous thickness (say, .015 to .020 inch, or 15 to 20 mils). This will be the outside, finish coat of the part, and if all goes well, it will come out of the mold a fair, smooth, handsome surface.

When the gelcoat has cured—it may be a bit tacky to the touch, but should not adhere to a fingertip—the lay-up of the glass fiber materials that make up the laminate is begun. Depending on the size of the boat, the laminate will range from an average of two or three to twenty or more layers of the materials we discussed in the beginning of this chapter. There may be even more layers in highly stressed local areas or in parts of bigger vessels (Figure 1-7).

If the damage you are to repair on your boat comprises a hole or shattered area that extends through the laminate, you will be able to count the layers and identify the kinds of glass fiber material with which it was built as you grind away the shattered pieces. Essentially, that is how a boat part is built in a mold: two layers at a time, almost never more than four at a time, are carried along the part, with the butts or overlaps in the different layers staggered and each piece saturated and rolled down smooth as it is put in place. More details are offered in Chapter 3.

The same boat part built in a mold can be built over a form by reversing the order of the lay-up, starting with the innermost layer and ending with the gelcoat or, sometimes, a paint finish on the outside. The only real difference will be considerable time spent fairing, puttying, and smoothing or polishing the form-built part at the end, for, as the layers are laid up, the surface of a laminate becomes ever more uneven. Even if each joint is carefully butted, rather than overlapped as one can do in a mold, and every piece rolled as flat as possible, there is no dodging the fairing, puttying, and smoothing at the end. Careful lay-up will greatly facilitate the creation of a fair and smooth final finish, but it can't eliminate all of the imperfections that creep into a multilayered laminate.

That is not merely commentary on the difference between molded and form-built parts; it is also something to bear in mind as you plan the repair of a holed part. If you can back a hole on the outside with polished, waxed material, then lay up the fiberglass

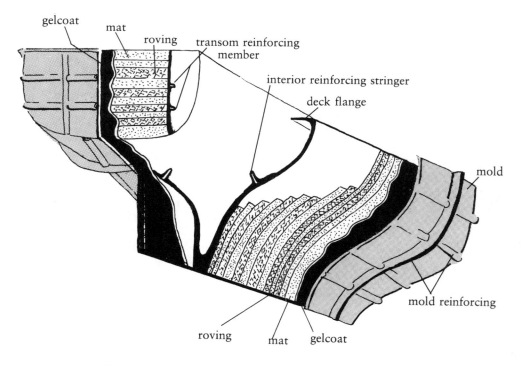

Figure 1-7. *A typical 25- to 30-footer in the mold. The hull's finished thickness ranges from ⅛ inch at the toerail to ⅜ to ½ inch or more at the keel. Note that there are progressively fewer laminate layers away from the keel, extra layers in the transom, and always two layers of mat beneath the gelcoat.*

patch from the inside of the part—starting with gelcoat, or at least resin if the exterior is so badly scratched that it needs general refinishing—the part's exterior will be largely prefinished. You won't always be able to work from the inside of a part, but you'll sure save work if you can.

Reinforcing a laminate

If the above description of building a boat part seems sketchy, it is; I know you don't want to take a full semester course in the subject, nor is it necessary. One item left out to streamline the lay-up description was the matter of reinforcing the laminate. Many boats—dinghies especially, but larger boats, too—are essentially of single-skinned, monocoque, or one-piece construction with no reinforcement of their hulls or decks other than the parts that brace them by virtue of being fastened to them. Fiberglass weighs 95 pounds per cubic foot and is relatively expensive, two excellent reasons for not using too much of it, but when a laminate is only made thick enough to have the required strength for the use of the part, such is the nature of fiberglass that it may be too flex-

ible. Indeed, large unsupported panels, though strong enough not to break, will bend in and out alarmingly, crack the gelcoat, and peel loose from bulkheads, berths, and other joinerwork.

Reinforcing members

Rather than add more layers all over such unsupported panels, it is lighter and less expensive to reinforce them with ribs, floor timbers, stringers, deckbeams, or other members whose names are handed along from wooden boat construction. Such members are often built into fiberglass boat parts to stiffen the skin locally. Usually, they are formed over a core piece of wood or foam placed against the skin, to which they are attached by turning the layers out onto it like the brim of a hat. Hence the name, "hat-shaped reinforcement" (Figure 1-8). There is another way to stiffen a laminate without having fiberglass members projecting into the interior. Sandwich construction is the solution.

Sandwich construction

The builder can place a lighter material between the layers of the laminate to give it

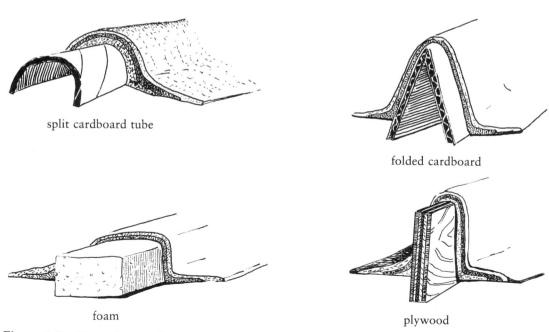

split cardboard tube

folded cardboard

foam

plywood

Figure 1-8. *Cores for reinforcing members such as ribs and stringers.*

extra thickness, spreading the strong fiberglass layers apart so that they are on the outside of a sandwich—in effect creating a deeper beam with more leverage to handle the tension and compression of the surfaces as the laminate comes under bending strains.

Such sandwich or cored laminates can very successfully provide greater stiffness to a laminate without adding the extra weight and expense of more layers of glass fiber materials. When the right core materials are used, a laminate also gains other good and useful properties. The laminate will float, which can never happen to the 95-pound-per-cubic-foot single skin. It insulates against heat and sound, making a quieter, warmer or cooler interior, and eliminates "sweating." When the core is PVC foam, the laminate becomes many times more impact-resistant, too.

The cores that have been used in sandwich construction include natural wood; plywood; end grain balsa (Figure 1-9); PVC foam (Figure 1-10); mixtures of polyurethane foam and PVC foam; poured-in-place polyurethane or polystyrene foam (see below); expanded paper, nylon, or metal honeycomb (Nomex is a nylon honeycomb—ultralight, very strong, and very costly); preformed steel mesh; and a number of composite cores, including glass fiber–reinforced foam and fiberglass ribs or corrugations formed around or filled between with foam.

These are not all the cores possible, but they're the most common and enough to give you the idea: any material that is light, that is reasonably firm in compression, and one that can be glued to the laminate. In current practice, you will find more balsa, PVC foam, and PVC/polyurethane foam than all the others put together.

A special case I should mention is that the lighter, weaker cores are sometimes replaced with solid fiberglass laminate, aluminum plate, or steelwork where the structure needs extra local support, as under a deck-stepped mast or in the way of chainplates and stem-

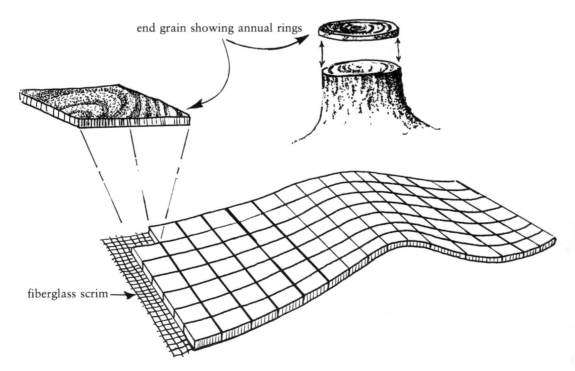

end grain showing annual rings

fiberglass scrim

Figure 1-9. *End grain balsa core material. In the Baltek Corporation's Contourkore, end grain panels are cut into 1-inch by 2-inch squares and glued to a loosely woven fiberglass scrim.*

Figure 1-10. *Airex sheets fitted on the building form for a 50-foot ketch show the flexibility of this "rigid-elastic" PVC foam, which is also resilient and has excellent impact resistance. Foams blended from PVC and polyurethane, such as Klegecell, are stronger in compression and stiff but brittle. Both are closed-cell foams and will not absorb water. (Courtesy Torin Inc.)*

head fittings. Under stanchion bases, winches, genoa tracks, and other deck hardware, small squares or strips of marine plywood are frequently used to replace the core material.

Installing core

The proprietary core materials are sold in sheets, either of small blocks stuck to a "scrim" (an open-weave net-like cloth) or, in the case of a flexible material such as foam, of unbroken expanse, unscored for slight curves or deeply scored for hard and compound curves. In molded parts, the core is weighted down into wet mat for the best adhesion to the outer skin, then the inner skin is built up over it (Figure 1-11). For a form-built one-off part, PVC core is sometimes temporarily fastened directly to the form and the outer skin built over it, as in Figure 1-10; then the part is removed from the form and the inner skin laid up inside it. When the one-off is started on a form with a "starting" material such as C-Flex (fabric "planking" reinforced with glass rods), the foam might be saved for the boat's interior (after the starter laminate is popped off the form), or it might be weighted down in wet mat outboard of the starting material. But if the one-off part is being built on a male mold (and

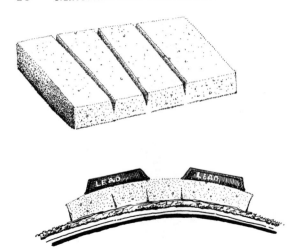

Figure 1-11. *Core foams, deeply scored to take compound curvatures. The core material is pressed into the wet mat with weights. For sharp curves the scores would be placed on top.*

usually only small parts such as centerboards and tanks are built this way), then the core is always put on in the middle of the laminate the same as in a female mold. And that reminds me of one more detail you might want to know: The two skins are close to the same thickness in many boats, but the outer skin will always be thicker when there is a difference, for the obvious reason that it takes more abuse.

Where cores are used

After this section, we'll drop the subject until the chapter on "Core Problems." While any part of a fiberglass boat can be and probably has been cored, the parts most often cored are decks, house tops, cockpit soles, and hatches. These parts need sandwich construction most because they are usually quite flat, gaining little stiffness from shape; some are quite wide and unsupported; and their weight is critical because it is high in the boat. Moreover, these parts are subjected to the concentrated impacts of active crewmembers who might weigh well over two hundred pounds. Few walking areas on the decks of boats over 20 feet long are built without sandwich construction today.

The use of sandwich construction in hulls is not nearly as universal as it is in decks, but still it is used in the hull of just about every fast powerboat and in large multihulls. There are many builders still using a single skin in fairly large sail and power boats; the smaller the boat, the less likely she is to have sandwich construction of the type we're talking about.

The foam-filled double hull

A landmark in fiberglass boatbuilding was the now-ubiquitous Boston Whaler, developed and manufactured by Dick Fisher. Molding an outer and inner hull, or hull and deck if you prefer, fastening them together around the rail, then filling the space between with lightweight foam was an inspired concept, which has since been adapted to the construction of myriad other small craft. At first polystyrene foam was used. Now polyurethane foam is used more frequently. Not the least benefit of this type of coring is that it can make a boat unsinkable. Board boats and all other foam-filled craft are safer because of that, but also tend to be thin-skinned or heavy due to the great mass of foam. These cores are not intended to provide structural stiffness in the manner of those we discussed above.

Joints in fiberglass boats

The inevitable deck joint

Without a doubt, the best boat would be one whose hull and deck were all one piece. It has been tried, the idea being to spin settable plastic materials in a closed hull and deck mold until the plastic sets. Once the plastic cures, you would have a one-piece boat, but either a suitable plastic hasn't been found, or perhaps the system has other unresolved problems. Anyway, almost all fiberglass boats still have at least one joint—that of deck to hull.

The deck joint is not such a bad feature if the builder takes the trouble to join the two fiberglass parts with some stout layers of fiberglass, but only a few of the better builders do this. Most use overlapping flanges on hull and deck; smear the interstice with an ad-

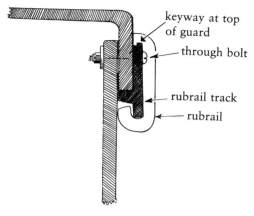

Figure 1-12. *Common hull-to-deck joints: the shoe box.*

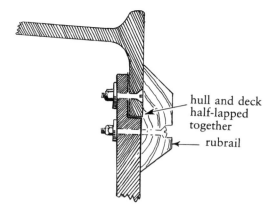

Figure 1-14. *Common hull-to-deck joints: the coffee can.*

hesive putty of filled resin, a polyurethane or polysulfide adhesive sealant, or an oil-based mastic bedding; and then mechanically fasten the joint with bolts, self-tapping screws, or even pop rivets. We have all in our time sworn that it's a good enough joint, but you may be one of those asking some years later, "Then why is it leaking?"

Centerline and other hull joints

It can be very difficult to do good fiberglass work reaching into deep, narrow keel and skeg recesses in a mold. In contrast, if the mold is split down the fore-and-aft centerline and laid open, laminating these parts

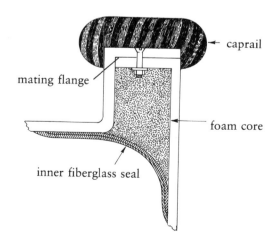

Figure 1-13. *Common hull-to-deck joints: the bulwark.*

becomes very simple, and incidentally, so does the laminating of the entire expanse of both sides. What wonder, then, that some boats are at least partly laminated in two halves, then joined down the centerline with more layers after the mold is bolted together again.

Do boats so joined ever split open along the centerline? They certainly have, if poorly tied across with too few layers, as some foolish builder occasionally does. But some models which were well joined with many strong layers have given no trouble in 30 years.

One thing: Not every boat with an offset line or ridge along the centerline was built in two halves. She may be just a boat built in a split mold that is designed to be taken apart after lay-up because the building is too low to lift the hull clear of the mold, or because the tumblehome of the hull locks it in the mold. In time, the bolt or "key" holes wear oversize, the split halves of the mold refuse to mate precisely, and the workers will not bother to erase the resultant slight offset where it won't be seen, as on the bottom of the keel.

Another type of hull joint is made by cutting a window in the mold, which allows workers to better reach a tight place. When the lay-up in that place is well along, the window is closed and the laminations are carried over it.

Still another hull joint results when a keel,

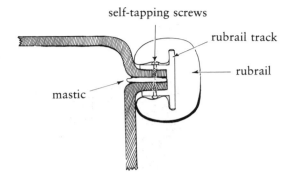

Figure 1-15. *Common hull-to-deck joints: the pout.*

skeg, or other part is made in a separate mold and then fastened to the main hull with bolts, usually with a filled resin adhesive putty or other bedding between.

In fiberglass sailboats, the ballast keel takes two basic forms: In the first, a metal casting is bolted to the exterior of the hull or to a partial fiberglass keel called a stub. In the second, metal in one or a number of pieces is installed and sealed over inside a hollow fiberglass keel that is molded as an integral part of the hull.

The external ballast is most used for the short, deep keels (fin keels) on the canoe-bodied hulls that are currently popular; internal ballast is most used on longer-keeled tradi-

tional models. The main difference in construction of the boat is that short, deep, metal keels often need reinforcing members inside the hull or stub to spread the strains of the bolts over a large area. This used to be taken care of by individual athwartship members called floor timbers that were copied from wooden boat construction. Now, they more often take the shape of a waffle-like grid molded in one piece of fiberglass and then fiberglassed to the laminate of the hull (Figure 1-17).

In contrast, the pressures imparted by inside ballast on the hollow keel are absorbed by a thickened keel laminate and a web of sealing fiberglass laminated on top of the ballast and a short distance up the deadrise (Figure 1-18).

Chop versus hand lay-up

"Spray-up" is the euphemism, but "chop" is the more widely used name for those layers of fiberglass laminate made by spraying chopped strand roving and catalyzed resin on the mold with a "chopper gun." After chop is rolled down flat, it becomes about the same end product as saturated chopped strand mat, except for two variables: The length of the chopped strands can be varied by chang-

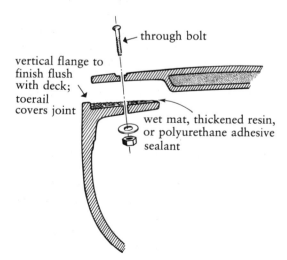

Figure 1-16. *Common hull-to-deck joints: the flange.*

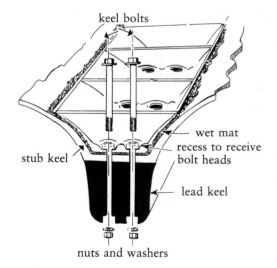

Figure 1-17. *The waffle-like "floor timber" subassembly becomes an integral part of the hull.*

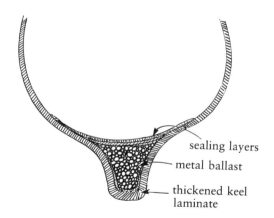

sealing layers

metal ballast

thickened keel laminate

Figure 1-18. *Inside ballast keel.*

ing the gun's setting, and, while the thickness of chopped strand mat is uniform as manufactured, the uniformity of chop depends upon the conscientiousness and skill of the operator.

Chop is used alone or with minimal layers of the fabrics to quickly construct noncrucial parts, especially small or very busily convoluted parts for which it is difficult to cut, fit, and saturate the fabrics. A number of boatbuilders use chop in lieu of mat between the layers of woven or unwoven roving in a standard alternating mat-and-roving laminate. The resin sprayer, without a chopper throwing glass into the spray, is also used to wet out the fabrics as they are laid up.

The proponents of chop claim greater efficiency and a big saving in labor, meaning more boat for the money and the same quality in the boat. Those who prefer hand layup say chop is too susceptible to under-catalyzation, incomplete saturation, and uneven thickness. As their advertisements say, "hand laid-up fiberglass" is generally regarded as the standard for high-quality fiberglass laminates.

Gelcoat and paint finishes

Gelcoat

Almost from the beginning of fiberglass, practically all production boat parts and many one-off parts, too, have been gelcoated. It is a very efficient thing to spray gelcoat on a highly polished, waxed mold and to release, at the end of lamination, a part with an equally highly polished, pigmented finish that, barring damage or chemical stains, has proven likely to remain almost as flawlessly beautiful for 10 or more years.

Gelcoat is, essentially, pigmented resin compounded with other additives to make it more weather- and wear-resistant. It is applied in a thickness of 15 to 20 mils, which gives it the depth to survive considerable water sanding, compounding, and repolishing. Over the years it stays put very well, for the resin base makes it truly a part of the laminate.

Not that gelcoat is perfect: If not compounded properly, or if applied too thickly, it can craze or crack like dried mud. If not backed up with fiberglass everywhere, the air bubbles under it will "break out" when pressured or struck. If the laminate under it bends too far, it will crack. But perhaps the greatest indictment against it is that, if it is porous, if the water is warm, and especially if the underlying fiberglass is not thoroughly enough cured, it can contract a case of "boat pox" (see Chapter 2).

But despite all of the above, there is no coating or paint known that has more than half the cosmetic and protective life expectancy of gelcoat.

Paint

In the past decade, a number of production companies that have not been able to protect their boats' gelcoat on the production line, and who felt that they were spending too much money on gelcoat repair, have tried molding the boat without it and painting her when construction is completed.

Painting is currently the usual way to finish a form-built one-off boat. It is also the way to refinish one whose gelcoat has worn out or has been extensively damaged. Some very slick and durable paints such as Awlgrip and Imron, which are hard to distinguish from gelcoat, have made it unnecessary to spray on thinned gelcoat, then water sand and compound it by hand to a high gloss.

When properly handled, these super paints are self-leveling, and they dry with a perfect surface. So far, no gelcoat with comparable characteristics has been available for use as a paint to be applied on exterior surfaces. A more complete discussion of gel-coating versus painting follows in Chapter 2.

Interior parts

Slowly, over the past decade or so, fiberglass boats have acquired more fiberglass interior parts to replace or complement those being made of wood. Not that all fiberglass boats were built with wooden interiors until lately: it's not that simple. In their enthusiasm for the speed of fabrication and the promise of durability with minimal maintenance of

molded fiberglass parts, some of the earliest builders brought out models that were almost 100 percent fiberglass inside and out. But when boat buyers snubbed the "bathtub look," even the open boats went back to the shop to have their fiberglass coamings cut off and replaced with wood, while, belowdeck, builders turned to extremes of burying fiberglass under wood, Formica, vinyl, and fabric.

But lower costs for essentially similar products are unstoppable in the long run, and an all-teak interior is as tiresome as any when you've seen too many of them. Today, some very pleasant interiors have fiberglass overhead liners and fiberglass hull liners, which, between them, take care of the basic interior joinerwork and finish. Two or three large, one-piece molded units can reduce the finishing off of the overhead and the construc-

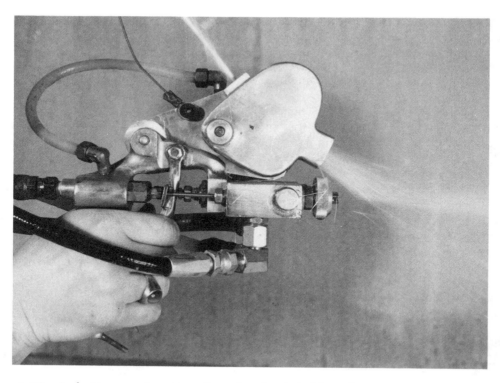

Figure 1-19. *A chopper gun in action. Strand roving is fed into the gun at top and sprayed as chop. Catalyst and resin are injected separately, mixed in the gun barrel, and sprayed from the nozzle below. (Courtesy Owens/Corning Fiberglas, Inc.)*

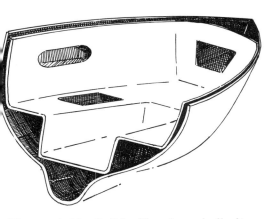

Figure 1-20. *Solid fiberglass hull liner, showing limited accessibility of the hull for repair. Sometimes the liner is made up of sub-assemblies, particularly in the head area; these can ease access. The headliner is almost always a separate molding.*

tion of soles, berths, counters, and lockers to a fraction of the labor involved were these all to be done in wood, plywood, or sheet plastics.

From the boat repairer's point of view, the older boats with wood and plywood joinerwork often suffer from loosening of the fiberglass tabbing that joins the wood to the hull or deck. Fiberglass never did stick well to wood, and never will.

In comparison, fiberglass liners stick better to the hull and deck. But when it comes to repair, the greatest complaint is that they often cover huge areas with blank fiberglass, through which only tiny scattered hatches give any access (Figure 1-20). All too often, it is necessary to cut open fiberglass soles and berth tops or fronts to reach parts of the hull needing repair. Builders just won't make two parts if they can get by with making one.

Other fiberglass parts

Because fiberglass is gas- and liquid-tight and immune to attack by gasoline, oil, LPG, and battery acid, it is used to build all manner of parts, some integral with and some just installed in a fiberglass boat. A partial list of such fiberglass parts includes hatches; companionway slides and weather covers; deck and cockpit gear lockers; LPG gas bottle lockers; flush deck lockers for anchors and lines; deck drain and through-hull tubes fiberglassed to deck and hull; shaft logs; rudderports; exhaust mufflers and tubing; battery boxes; engine beds with integral oil pan; tanks for water, gasoline, oil, and lube oil; refrigerators; and freezers.

These items speak for themselves as highly practical money-saving parts, so compatible with the base material that they can easily be made integral with, or fiberglassed to, the main parts or interior liners.

Integral tanks

At the same time, I would point out what you may already have found out if you have had trouble involving a liquid storage tank that is integral with the hull: This particular stunt is not the best of all arrangements. Fiberglass makes an excellent tank. I have built and installed many of them, most of them metal-lined by the way, which have never given a bit of trouble. But when tanks are integral with the hull, the difficulty of repairing hull damage in the way of them is compounded, and they themselves are very difficult to repair if they should start to leak into the boat. The least troublesome are freshwater tanks, because they do not have to be steam cleaned before you can repair them—not on the inside, at least, although there may be bilge oil on their outside surfaces.

Other integral parts

Although integral tanks are not the great improvement some thought they would be, many of the other parts mentioned above are, in that they replace parts of wood, rubber, plastic, and metal that were carried over from wooden boat building. These traditional parts were fine in their time, and they had to be mechanically fastened to the wood no matter what. But when one can make parts of fiberglass, which can be integrated into the larger fiberglass structures or at least glassed to them, it replaces a mechanically fastened joint with one that will never deteriorate into a leaker. Like wooden-spoked wheels on an automobile, many parts made from other materials had a tenuous place in fiberglass boats only as long as habit blinded us to the greater suitability of fiberglass for their construction.

CHAPTER 2

Restoring the Surface Finish

In this chapter we begin with the more superficial problems that can occur on the surface of a boat, and proceed to the more serious.

Gelcoat dullness and fading

The standard treatment for gelcoat that isn't as brightly colored and shiny as it ought to be is a good cleaning, waxing, and polishing. When this is done regularly, boats with a good gelcoat have been known to remain extraordinarily new-looking for as long as 10 years, and not bad enough to necessitate refinishing for more than 20 years.

When not so well cared for, boats build up a film of dirt, stains, and faded color at the surface of the gelcoat. That degree of deterioration goes deeper than cleaning can reach, and the surface will need compounding, at least, to be rid of it.

Compounding

Compounding is polishing with a paste containing a fine grit, like the paste used on automobile finishes. In fact, you can use compounds bought in an auto parts store, and the same electric polisher with soft pad and polishing head that an autobody shop might use. You shouldn't start compounding the whole boat right away. Before you do any-

thing else, make sure the wax is cleaned off the surface. On a boat with well-cured gelcoat, acetone is good for removing wax. The most troublesome to remove are waxes containing silicones. Before compounding (or painting) gelcoat that has been treated with a silicone product, wipe down the surface with an automotive silicone-remover containing toluene.

Next, using a fine grit, try compounding a patch in one of the more dulled or faded areas. If that doesn't cut through to better color, try a coarser grit, and polish two or three square feet until you have uncovered fresh, shiny-looking gelcoat. Multiply the time it takes to do a square foot by the total surface area to be done, and you'll know the full extent of the job you face. If compounding doesn't work well within a reasonable time, you may have to resort to water sanding with fine paper or dry sanding with somewhat coarser paper.

Water sanding

Water sanding involves sandpapering with waterproof emery paper, which is repeatedly dipped in water to rinse it off and to keep the surface wet. Called "wet-or-dry" paper, it is widely available in grits from less than 100 to 600. The lower the number, the coarser the grit. Start with the finest grit that will take off the dulled surface in a reasonable time, since the use of a coarser paper than necessary will leave deeper scratches, which might penetrate any thin spots in the gelcoat. Even if the gelcoat is amply thick, it will take unnecessary work to eradicate deep scratches, for once the faded layer is sanded away, the surface must be brought back to a highly polished condition with a series of progressively finer grits, then with compound. Wrap the paper around a sanding block or pad, or simply hold it against your fingers if you wish. With 400 to 600 grits, you don't have to worry about creating bumps and hollows. Of course, like compounding, wet-or-dry paper might be too slow in removing a badly deteriorated surface in the grades from the low hundreds to 600 that are most often used. In that case, provided the gelcoat is thick enough to stand it, you might want to use dry paper.

Dry sanding

Dry paper is cheaper than wet-or-dry paper. It is sold in grits from the very coarsest up to about 400, but I can't imagine the gelcoat on a boat being thick enough to suffer a grit coarser than 80 or 100 without risk of abrading through; neither would I start a conversation with anybody while holding the sander in one place with these grits on it. So start no coarser than 80 or 100, and if hand-sanding, use a block or pad to avoid digging grooves in the gelcoat. At the top end of the grit numbers, perhaps at one or two grits before 400, you will probably want to switch to water sanding to avoid clogging. When the grit of the paper clogs, or fills up with fiberglass dust, it won't cut anymore. "Open grit" papers, and some papers that are coated with a fine, powdery coating, have a reduced tendency to clog, but clogging is aggravated by power sanders, which heat up the material they are cutting and cause it to coalesce into hard, glazed streaks or clots on which the paper skids without cutting. As you might suspect, the unidirectional machines such as disk and belt sanders are most likely to clog paper, and the faster they turn up, the worse they are. Orbital sanders, which change direction constantly, and even reciprocating sanders are better. Remember that washing off the wax first will alleviate clogging problems, and remember that what you're looking for is the finest paper that will cut away the deteriorated surface of the gelcoat in a reasonable time. You don't want to cut any deeper than necessary, lest you go through the gelcoat, but if this should happen in a few small spots, the area can be gelcoated over and polished along with the rest of the part.

If you can't polish or sand away fading or stains because they are too deep in the gelcoat or the gelcoat is too thin to allow it, then your only choice is to apply a new finish, as discussed at the end of this chapter.

Scratches, dings, and breakouts

Scratches and dings need no introduction to anyone whose boat's topsides have ever been abused at a crowded fuel dock. A breakout starts its life as a void under a thin layer of gelcoat; it is a place where, during lay-up of the part in its mold, the first layer of laminate failed to bond with the gelcoat. This is particularly common in inside corners of a mold (which the glass fiber materials are prone to bridge) and thus on outside corners of the part. The corners of a cabin trunk or cockpit coaming are common locations. The skin of gelcoat is like thin ice over a depression, just waiting for a sharp impact from an anchor or winch handle to become a breakout. Breakouts indicate no weakness in the part; they are simply troublesome and ugly.

Depending on their depth, scratches, dings, and breakouts may more profitably be repaired either before or after a general compounding or sanding. Those flaws that are shallow could be obliterated, or nearly so, by the surface removal process, but those that are deep are better filled first to overflowing with gelcoat putty, smoothed down until they are flush with the surrounding surface, and then polished along with the rest of the part's surface.

Naturally, it is always possible to fill a single gash or breakout and polish it locally, and that's a good thing, for a lone blemish is most obtrusive when the surrounding surface looks good. To fill any hole in the gel-coat that does not involve serious damage to the underlying fiberglass, you need gelcoat putty.

Gelcoat putty

Gelcoat, you'll remember, is polyester resin with pigment and fillers added to impart color and resistance to wear and weathering. You can paint it on as it comes from the man-ufacturer, after catalyzing it, provided that it has the ability to dry in the air. Some gelcoats have to have wax added to keep the air off until they cure completely; others don't. You can obtain the wax additive from the gelcoat supplier, who also should know whether wax is necessary. If in doubt, you could dissolve some shaved or grated paraffin, such as Gulf Wax, in a little liquid styrene, or wait until the gelcoat has cured enough not to move around and either coat it with paste wax or cover it with Saran Wrap. For more details of gelcoat application, see Chapter 3.

Gelcoat as supplied in a viscosity for spraying or brushing will not stay where it's put in any bulk, so for deep dings and break-outs you will need to buy a gelcoat putty or thicken some gelcoat to make your own. You need only mix a filler into it until it reaches the consistency you want, the most com-monly used filler being a finely ground pow-der of talc, also called talcum or soapstone. Long a staple in the paint industry for thick-ening paints and putties, talc is sold in bags specifically for the purpose, suitably cleaned and dehydrated. Use no more filler than nec-essary for sufficient viscosity; excessive use of filler might alter the gelcoat pigment and could reduce its water resistance.

That's the general idea. Now to put it into step-by-step form:

1. *Match the gelcoat.* Begin with a gel-coat that matches the original as closely as possible. It is best to get the same gelcoat if you can, but this grows more difficult as a boat grows older, and staining and fading over the years can make the original and a local patch a mismatch anyway, unless, through compounding or sanding the entire surface, one can uncover the original hue.

Starting from scratch by mixing dispersion colors into neutral gelcoat, however, one can match almost any surface. Inorganic pig-ments mixed in polyester resin are available for this purpose. Some colors are very ex-pensive; if you can't obtain small tubes of them, it might be less expensive and less trou-ble to have a supplier or a fiberglass boat builder or repairer mix the color for you.

2. *Thicken the gelcoat.* For deeper digs, mix in some talc to thicken the gelcoat into a putty that will stay where you put it. Be sure to mix the talc and gelcoat well, and make a bit more than your present need de-mands. One always finds other places to patch sooner or later, and the shelf life of gelcoat and gelcoat putty is from many months to a few years if stored away from air, heat, and sunlight.

3. *Catalyze thoroughly.* When you cat-alyze gelcoat or gelcoat putty prior to use, the catalyst must be stirred or kneaded into it very thoroughly; it is not easy to disperse it evenly throughout a liquid as thick as gel-coat, and harder in a putty. If you don't mix it well, portions of it may remain undercured, or even uncured, when spread on the boat.

Catalyze small batches until you get a feel for how much catalyst it takes to make the putty begin to cure within a reasonable time. It should not gel too soon, and never in less than a half hour, lest it lose its adhesiveness and workability before you apply it all; nor should it withstand gelling longer than 1 to $1\frac{1}{2}$ hours, lest it hold up your work or fail to cure completely.

4. *Combat shrinkage.* It may come as a surprise, but when polyester resin–based products cure, they shrink. Thus, if you fill depressions flush with the surrounding sur-face, they will still be depressions, however slight, when the putty has cured and shrunk.

There are two ways to handle shrinkage: You can overfill depressions and sand them flush after they cure and shrink, or you can putty them flush with the surface at least twice.

It would seem that overfilling a depres-sion once is the more efficient way to allow for shrinkage, and many boat repairers do slap an overflowing dab of putty on every flaw, then sand it down flush with the surface when it is cured. Unfortunately, it doesn't always work out quite that nicely. In cutting down a lump of putty that projects above the surface, you are more than likely to dig into that surface—particularly since, to expedite the job, the temptation is to use relatively coarse grit paper and a fast-cutting power tool. If you're not careful, you will have to polish out scratches in the surrounding surface, and the end result is inevitably a large, shallow dimple where the smaller, deeper depression was.

With the fairness of the surrounding surface in mind, then, it is not necessarily being overly cautious to fill depressions flush and clean off any excess putty with the putty knife, then refill as needed after curing. This approach at least keeps the problem confined within the outline of each flaw.

5. *Sand and polish.* After filling the gouges in the surface, repolish the surface as needed to blend in the repair.

Substituting autobody putty

For good reasons, you may decide to use ordinary polyester body or fairing putty, such as Bondo, rather than gelcoat putty, there being actually very little difference between these resins mixed with filler, as they all are in use, and gelcoat putty, except the lack of pigment and the easier sanding qualities of the plain putties in most cases:

1. In the first place, there may not be enough gouges to make it worth your while to mix a gelcoat putty, in which case you can fill the depression(s) with body putty almost but not quite to the surface. Then, to match the surrounding color, you can fill the gouge flush or a little more than flush with a coat or two of the appropriate gelcoat. If you make the mistake of letting the plain putty come up to the surface anywhere, you will surely uncover it when you sand and polish the gelcoat flush with the original surface. I once watched two grown men smear gelcoat on the same spot and go through it twice with their wet sanding, because they had puttied a hole flush to the surface with plain putty

and didn't realize that by the time the gelcoat was perfectly fair they *had* to be through it.

2. Another reason for not wanting to use gelcoat putty would be many large, deep gashes in the part to be repaired. Not only is gelcoat putty too expensive to use for filling large depressions, it is also relatively brittle and weak, and you would be better off to use a tougher, more resilient body putty. Remember, if you want gelcoat over it, don't bring it quite to the surface anywhere.

3. Then again, if the gelcoat on the part is destroyed and you intend either to regelcoat or paint the part, you can use body or fairing putty and bring it up flush with the surface everywhere. Then you can sand and refinish the entire area or part to prepare it for the new finish.

Substituting epoxy putty

Epoxy putty is stronger, forms a more tenacious bond with the underlying surface, lasts longer, shrinks much less on cure, and is more water-resistant than any polyester putty. It is also two to four times as expensive and much harder to sand. Although epoxy bonds extremely well to polyester, a polyester resin, gelcoat, or putty applied over cured epoxy will *not* bond well; also, epoxy is not in itself a good gelcoat (even if you could color match an epoxy putty patch to the surrounding polyester gelcoat), because it fades with time in sunlight. These factors limit epoxy's use in cosmetic repairs to underwater areas, which are covered with bottom paint, and to topsides and decks that are about to be coated. In these uses it excels.

Gelcoat cracks that won't stay puttied

There are some cracks in gelcoat that are not likely to remain sealed if merely filled with gelcoat or gelcoat putty. These cracks go by names such as "crazing," "star cracks," or "stress cracks," which are descriptive of their causes.

Star cracks

As one can readily appreciate, a star crack is an array of cracks radiating from the point of an impact or from the center of localized, intense pressure. A common example of such pressure is that exerted on a deck laminate by a lifeline stanchion when deflected under the weight of, say, a falling crewmember. Star cracks spreading outward from the bases of stanchions are frequent. Recently I found a star crack in each side deck of a boat at the aft outboard corners of the cabin trunk; the trunk ended abruptly at the cockpit, its girder effect continued only by a teak coaming lightly screwed to deck and trunk. A star crack made by such ongoing if intermittent forces will surely reappear if you repair the gelcoat without taking steps to stiffen up or bolster the underlying laminate. If the laminate is being bent enough to crack its more brittle gelcoat, then the repaired gelcoat will only crack again.

It's another matter if you create a one-time star crack by dropping an anchor on deck or by ramming the topsides with a small boat's stemhead fitting. You can grind open such cracks and fill them with gelcoat putty that can be expected to stay, provided the underlying laminate is not seriously fractured. Should the laminate be damaged, then, of course, you should repair the damage first. See Chapter 4.

Stress cracks

We have mentioned that a star crack can emanate from a center of stress, but there are other configurations of stress cracks that assume their various shapes from the pattern or nature of the stress causing them. It is not unusual to see fine parallel cracks along the juncture of a seat front with a sailboat's cockpit sole. Such fine, closely spaced cracks are caused by forces that bend the underlying fiberglass farther than the gelcoat can stand. When a 200-pound person jumps down onto the cockpit sole, the sole is bent downward and cracks the gelcoat along the corner where it turns up onto the seat front.

In another common case, a batch of parallel cracks may appear on a molded toerail and on the side deck adjacent to it. Probably when the boat slammed against a piling, the force of the blow actually rippled through the deck like a wave and wrinkled the laminate a bit more than the gelcoat could accommodate.

Will these kinds of cracks reappear if filled with gelcoat putty?

The cockpit cracks could come back the first time someone landed heavily on the sole, unless, of course, some supporting structure or more layers to stiffen the laminate are added below deck. It is obvious that the part as built flexes too much.

The repairability of the side deck and toerail cracks is a different matter. As long as the laminate under them was not seriously fractured by the blow to the deck edge, they should not return once ground and filled. Of course, another blow to the area would replicate them, but unless the helmsman is a slow learner, that is not too likely. If the laminate sustained damage that would allow the slightest movement or opening and closing of fractures under stress, repair of the laminate must precede repair of the gelcoat. Otherwise, one could open cracks again just by stepping on it.

Cracks on thin-skinned parts

Sometimes a hull with a single skin will develop very fine cracks in its topsides gelcoat, so fine that one easily overlooks them. A close inspection may reveal whole groups of them, some aligned in parallel vertical or horizontal bundles while others take seemingly random curved paths across the topsides. Parallel cracks running vertically are caused by the topside laminate bending over bulkheads, and horizontal cracks are due to bending over the edges of berths or counters fastened against the hull on the interior. As for those random, curved cracks, they are probably created by the buckling of a large unsupported panel of the skin as it is pressed inward by waves at sea or by support pads or Travelift straps ashore.

I do not mean to imply that this sort of gelcoat cracking stops at the waterline. Indeed, small boats especially are likely to have as much in the underbody as in the topsides. I point out those in the topsides because it is there that one can examine them best. Except on "dry sailed" craft with unpainted bottoms, the bottom paint tends to obscure such fine cracks, although, after a boat has been hauled out and the majority of the paint has dried, one can often see a spidery trace of wet lines where water that has entered the cracks is still working out.

Why on your boat?

In most all boats, but particularly in high-performance power and sail boats, the topsides are built as thin as designer and builder think safe, in order to save weight and improve performance. When the laminate is single skin, the result can be so much flexibility that the gelcoat is, as we said, hard put to follow the flexing without cracking. Although in most hulls the underbody is strengthened with additional layers, and often with fiberglass reinforcing members as well, the strains to which the bottom is subjected are also more severe. That's why you are likely to find stress cracks in the bottom that are very similar to those found in the topsides.

Extreme cases of stress cracks

My eyes were opened to stress cracks when I was asked to examine an aging fleet of centerboard racing sailboats that had been used in competition almost daily by a prep school. These lightly built craft had stress cracks on either side of the centerboard trunk at its juncture with the bottom, on the side decks, and everywhere between, inside and outside: the bottom, the topsides, the air tanks, the centerboard, the transom, the rudder. If it was a fiberglass part, it had stress cracks. The maintenance crew of the school had done a lot of patching, mostly by adding layers of fiberglass wherever the laminate beneath the cracked gelcoat was also fractured or leaking. Short of grinding off all gelcoat and adding an appropriate number of layers to each part to make it more stress-crack–resistant,

that was all they really could do. Considering the age of the boats, it was time to just keep on sailing or sell the fleet and get a new one.

I mention that experience so you won't get the idea that stress cracks appear only in special places. They can appear in the gelcoat or paint on any fiberglass part not built like a brick wall, and they are as likely to show up on thin-skinned parts as crabgrass in a lawn.

Summary of stress crack repair

It should be obvious that stress cracks cannot be eliminated with fresh gelcoat, or putty, unless they stem from a one-time overbending of the laminate which is not likely to be repeated. If they *are* a one-time affair, they can be ground out and filled with gelcoat putty or another polyester or epoxy putty and refinished in the manner of any scratch or gouge as described above. Otherwise, the only sure repair is to stiffen or brace the part so that it can't be overbent as easily as before.

Suppose your boat's forward topsides are stress cracked—perhaps parallel to the outboard edges of the V berth, along the athwartship bulkheads of that compartment, or in the midst of the unsupported panel of topside above the berth. Couldn't you grind out the cracks, fill them with a tough epoxy putty, then paint over the entire topsides, perhaps with a really flexible polyurethane paint?

It wouldn't do a bit of good, because the gelcoat is going to crack again as soon as it is overbent again. How about taking all the gelcoat off and then repainting with an elastic paint?

The trouble with that is that the very flexible polyurethanes have a primer under them, which, unfortunately, is not so flexible. Sorry, but stress cracks are trying to tell you something: The laminate is bending too much. When you get that message, you are well advised to stiffen the laminate first; then there won't be so much of a problem as to how you refinish the surface.

Going back to your stress-cracked topsides, there are three routes to a permanent repair:

1. You could grind off the gelcoat, add layers of glass materials to the topsides to stiffen them, then refinish. If the stress cracks are bad and widespread, this might be the best approach, especially if working on the interior is going to require a great deal of disruption, or even destruction of joinerwork, liner, or finish. It's a lot of work to refinish topsides, but at least it's outside work with plenty of elbow room, light, and air.

2. If working on the interior seemed best in your boat's case, you could build fiberglass ribs on the topsides, fiberglass stringers, or both. The easiest way to build such members is to glue PVC or polyurethane foam to the topsides, then cover them with the laminate of glass fiber materials. See Chapter 3 for details.

Of course, while very effective at stiffening a panel, ribs and stringers don't make very good bedfellows; for our hypothetical case of a forward compartment with V berth they are probably the worst method of stiffening the topsides, unless the berth is so wide that you can afford the space to sheathe over them with a smooth wooden ceiling after they are in place. While not so good above a berth, ribs still might be best below it if you are faced with built-in joinerwork and cramped access to the area. In building a few ribs you are not compelled to reach *every* far corner of the space through impossibly small locker doors, drawer openings, or hatches in the berthtop—only the particular path that each rib or stringer takes. Further, there is less time and material involved in each member, so that you can spend minutes on each rather than a much longer time for each layer if you were to add more layers to the whole area (see below).

3. The other approach to stiffening forward topsides from the inside, and the best one for saving space, is to add more layers to the laminate over the whole area. If this is the preferable method on your boat, you should, after covering all uninvolved areas and woodwork with drop cloths, heavy paper, or pasteboard, grind the surface all over, cut pieces of material to fit, then lay them up two layers at a time. Chapter 3 dis-

cusses laminating in detail. Unwoven roving materials build up stiffness most quickly; orient their strands so that most of them run across the stress cracks.

Bubbles, blisters, and boat pox

Sometimes the need to restore the finish of a boat arises from blisters growing in her hull or, more rarely, in other parts. When blisters are mentioned, nearly everyone suspects a case of "boat pox," and it is true that most outbreaks of blisters are due to that ailment. There are other causes of blisters, however.

Bubbles

When production builders spray gelcoat on the mold before laying up the rest of the laminate, they catalyze it heavily so that it will cure quickly and allow them to begin lamination with a minimum of delay. Then they try to get one to three layers of the laminate over it right away, partly to keep anything from happening to the gelcoat, which is a relatively fragile coating clinging to a polished wax surface. One can't blame them after having once seen the problems that undercatalyzed gelcoat or gelcoat sitting around unprotected can bring, but a gelcoat that cures and then is quickly overlaid with laminate can trap tiny bubbles of gas. When, later in the boat's life, someone sands the gelcoat, opening many of these tiny bubbles, and after washing or wiping water or solvent into them coats them with a nearly impervious polyurethane paint, the coating may bubble. If a somewhat porous paint such as ordinary marine alkyd enamel is used, there is often no problem, but the painter is well advised to apply an epoxy barrier undercoat before coating with a polyurethane.

The most common type of gelcoat bubble, which may appear on any fiberglass part, has a similar cause—moisture trapped beneath the gelcoat. This sort of blister tends to show up when the part is heated, as when the boat sits in the hot sun. It is similar to those that appear on wooden boats when moisture is trapped behind paint or varnish. Eliminating them locally is always a matter of grinding out and filling each one, while eliminating the problem as a whole is always a matter of removing the gelcoat or paint and recoating the entire surface.

The good news about moisture bubbles is that they may be isolated cases confined to one part or one small area of a part. But not always. The worst case I experienced was with a one-off boat my shop built by the form method. When we got through laying up the glass fiber materials from the inside outward over the form, we faired the entire hull with body putty, sanded her smooth, then sprayed on several passes of gelcoat, which we sanded and polished to a pretty nice finish. Well, all went well for a few weeks, until we got her deck on and moved her outdoors for final finishing and rigging. When the sun hit her hull, bubbles began to appear, and they kept on appearing—not for weeks or months, but years. Looking back, the hull was built upside down under an open-sided, metal-roofed shed in the spring, in wet weather, and, not too surprisingly, moisture must have been trapped under the gelcoat. When the sun heated up the laminate, the water vapor blew bubbles in the gelcoat up to 1½ inches in diameter. Grinding out the bubbles and filling them with gelcoat putty worked fine, but it was an expensive, ongoing nuisance, which, in the long run, could only be laid to rest once and for all by grinding off the entire surface and refinishing it. Naturally, any such happening is something most builders would wish to correct. We did.

Boat pox

Boat pox is the aptly named blistering of gelcoat on the underwater surfaces of a boat. While it is hardly ever a serious threat to the structural integrity of the hull, it can be an ugly nuisance.

Boat pox gets underway when porosity in the gelcoat allows water to penetrate it, and the water dissolves any unbound chemicals—such as solvents, accelerators, and other additives—in the first layer beneath. The resultant acidic solution has a higher solute concentration than even seawater, and thus induces more water to join it through the gelcoat by the process of osmosis (the tendency of ion-poor liquids to diffuse through ion-rich ones). The solution may also attack resin, particularly any local pockets of undercured resin.

Incredibly, the continuing reaction, fed by the osmotic increase in volume, presses outward and upward, raising the gelcoat over it into a dome or blister. Puncture the blister, and you get a liquid that smells like styrene or uncured resin. Because these small independent reactions are the product of water penetration at spots with different degrees of porosity and different degrees of vulnerability in the underlying laminate, one never knows whether, when, where, or in what number and size they'll show up. A boat might come down with the pox in her first six months or not until she is six years old or older. There are myriad boats 25 to 30 years old that have never had it, and if you ask me (an optimistic, cold-climate, saltwater boatman, not a pessimistic warm-climate, freshwater one), probably never will. Why?

Causes of boat pox

The first requirement for boat pox is porosity in the gelcoat, which develops in some kinds of gelcoat more readily than in others. Isophthalic gelcoat resin is said to be less vulnerable than orthophthalic resin. But porosity is also caused by the way in which builders apply the gelcoat, and some degree of undercure or the presence of unbonded additives in the resin of the layer adjacent to the gelcoat also seems to be a requirement. The onslaught and severity of the disease also varies directly with the amount of time the boat spends in the water each year and the temperature of that water, and inversely with the water's salinity.

Can you get repairs on warranty?

You should try. Some builders won't admit any responsibility for boat pox, but others will help you to varying degrees, right up to resurfacing the entire underbody free of charge. So, it is worth a try.

The short-term repair of boat pox

As long as your boat does not have an overwhelming number of blisters, it is a simple matter to grind them out, dry them, and fill the craters with body putty. An epoxy-based putty is more adhesive and much more water-resistant, but polyester body putty is much less expensive when you need a large quantity, and it seems to work well enough. On the other hand, having been burned once by blisters, you could hardly be blamed for wanting the most-likely-to-succeed-over-the-long-haul repair, which would mean epoxy. If you should be so lucky that only a manageable number of blisters show up each year, perhaps because the boat has a short season in the water, then you could continue with this sort of repair indefinitely. But when you get tired of patching blisters, or when you get hit with a great number of them all over the bottom, it is time to try to cure the disease once and forever.

A cure for boat pox

At this time, the treatment considered most likely to permanently succeed begins with grinding or sandblasting all of the gelcoat off the underbody, up to the waterline.

After smoothing any unfair places with body putty (again, epoxy putty is best) and finer sanding, the bottom is painted with no fewer than two coats of epoxy paint to seal it watertight. Finally, for saltwater use, you would spread antifouling bottom paint over the two coats of epoxy paint.

Preempting boat pox

Can you do something to preempt boat pox?

Yes, you *could* coat the bottom of your boat with at least two coats of epoxy paint recommended for that purpose *before* any boat pox shows up. To do this would entail removal of all antifouling bottom paint, some grinding of the gelcoat (at least enough to roughen it and give the epoxy paint a good grip), and any other preparation of the surface, including the application of a primer, that the epoxy manufacturer might recommend.

But unless you know that your boat's make and model is very likely to come down with boat pox—or unless you are preparing to cruise or live aboard in the tropics or in fresh water year-round for some years, perhaps where hauling and performing the work would be difficult to do or have done—it would not seem to make a great difference whether you took action now or waited until the first blisters appeared. Without some of the predisposing conditions mentioned above, the average yacht, living in temperate to chilly salt water less than six months out of the year, has almost no chance of acquiring boat pox for some 30 years or more, which is as long as I have been watching them.

Boat pox complications

Can boat pox cause more damage to the laminate than raising blisters in the gelcoat?

We know that it is possible, because of one highly publicized case of a boat in which the breaking down of the resin didn't stop at the interface of the gelcoat and the layer adjacent to it. Instead, water worked its way into the interior of the laminate, perhaps wicking along some not entirely saturated strands, found more resin to reduce to liquid, and left the glass fibers involved with it delaminated and limp.

I hasten to add that, as far as I know, this has very rarely happened. It would certainly be abetted by undercured resin, but fortunately, very few boats have much undercured resin in their laminates, and even fewer boats are likely to have a porous gelcoat, undercured resin somewhere in the laminate, and built-in access from the outer layer to the undercured one(s).

Slim as the chances of such a frightening complication of the disease would seem to be, if you have found it in your boat, what should you do?

Again, you ought to contact the manufacturer. Almost invariably it is a manufacturer's fault if there is undercured resin in a laminate. It could *possibly* be the fault of a supplier of materials to the manufacturer, but the manufacturer would still be the one to whom you should look.

If help from the manufacturer is not forthcoming, and legal action produces no immediate redress, my suggestions would be, after grinding off the gelcoat, to grind out the layers found to have been delaminated by the incursion of water, then lay up fresh layers with well-catalyzed resin in the hollows thus created (Figure 2-1). If the delaminated areas are small, some body putty might be a more practical way to firm them up. Whether the undercured areas are determined to be extensive or quite local, I would not trust the laminate as it was. Before putting on the two coats of epoxy paint, I would cover the entire bottom of the boat up to the top of the boot-top with additional layers of fiberglass. These should consist of a minimum of two layers of chopped strand mat, because mat makes the most watertight laminate. Two layers enable you to butt each layer's pieces and cover the butts of the first layer with the next layer, making your work smoother, eliminating the grinding of overlaps, and ensuring at least one sealing layer everywhere. *Always* use two layers of mat at the end of any laminate facing weather or water. They can be thick or thin; they can be covered with cloth that is rolled out smooth; but always, two layers of mat.

Whether you should also add some stiffening or strengthening layers such as unidirectional, biaxial, triaxial, or woven roving will depend upon the extent of the undercured resin, as near as you can estimate that. When you have added enough layers to re-

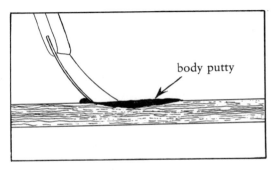

Figure 2-1B. *Small areas can be filled with body putty.*

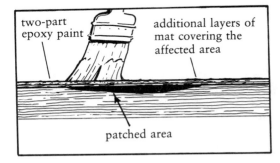

Figure 2-1C. *A filled and patched area, top-coated with two additional layers of mat and two-part epoxy paint.*

store your confidence in the hull's laminate, then you can fair and smooth as necessary and apply the two coats of epoxy paint followed by boottop or antifouling bottom paint, and finally, hopefully, begin to enjoy your boat again.

Regelcoating versus repainting fiberglass

When the gelcoat on a fiberglass part becomes cosmetically hopeless or has to be materially destroyed in making repairs, it raises the question of what method to use in refinishing that surface. The choices at present are to regelcoat the part (as described in Chapter 3), to paint it with one of the polyurethanes,

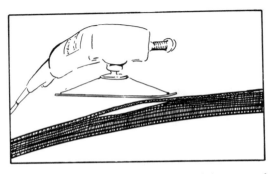

Figure 2-1A. *Grinding out delaminated areas.*

which rival the high gloss and smoothness of gelcoat, or to paint it with a marine paint such as an alkyd enamel, a modified alkyd enamel, or a one- or two-part epoxy.

Regelcoating

There is nothing at this time that makes a better protective coating for a fiberglass part than gelcoat—not surprising when one considers the nature of this material. Gelcoat is resin-based, which means it bonds chemically with the fiberglass of the part. It is applied many times thicker than most paints, which means that it can be worn and gouged much more deeply without loss of its physical protection; neither will there be an unsightly change of color at the base of every slight scratch. It has been known to resist weather and still look alright for over 20 years. It is relatively easy to use in patching areas of modest size, either as supplied for brushing or spraying or filled to make a gelcoat putty, and it is relatively nontoxic to most people.

All these wonderful attributes notwithstanding, gelcoat is not most repairers' choice for recoating an entire part whose gelcoat has been destroyed or removed. Not that it won't be the best possible coating after you get it on and polish it; it's just that the amount of labor involved in getting it on and polished is too great. Nobody makes gelcoat that is self-smoothing or that dries to a glossy finish; it's probably not possible, considering the nature and consistency of the material. Spray or paint it onto a highly polished mold, and it mirrors that polish beautifully. But no matter how adeptly you apply it to an exterior surface, or how perfectly smooth that surface is, gelcoat will cure with many surface imperfections that must be sanded and polished out if you want it smooth and glossy.

This sanding and polishing process is worthwhile on a minor area, the patching of which returns the huge majority of a gelcoated part to its original cosmetic viability. When the area to be refinished involves a larger percentage of the part's surface, however, the labor to polish it increases exponentially, and the use of gelcoat is abandoned as too "labor intensive."

The polyurethanes

If you are an owner who wants a highly polished refinishing job on your boat that rivals gelcoat in slickness, yet one that doesn't have the requirement of endless sanding and polishing to put the shine on it after application, the polyurethanes may be for you. These amazing paints, such as Awlgrip and Imron, were used on aluminum airplanes before they spread into the boat-painting business. When applied and allowed to dry in a dust- and moisture-free atmosphere, they develop a handsome sheen. Their durability, or ability to maintain that cosmetic excellence, while less than half that of gelcoat's, is better than most other paints. At the same time, the cost of applying them, while much less than the cost of putting a polish on gelcoat, is pretty stiff: much more than the cost of regular boat paints, which we will discuss shortly.

What do you get in a polyurethane paint job? A relatively tough and elastic, nearly nonporous, high-gloss surface. If all goes well, it will be difficult to distinguish it from gelcoat in tiptop condition. Sometimes only careful inspection of an edge that had to be masked, such as the waterline, boottop, or sheer, will reveal the ridge that betrays an applied coating. Because of this cosmetic excellence, polyurethanes are often employed to revive the topsides of shabby-looking fiberglass boats, or even just to change their color at the whim of an owner to whom money is less important than the appearance of the boat. At current prices of over $100.00 per foot of boat length for a professional polyurethane job, that's either very expensive taste or very disposable income. But then, few objects man has created are cherished as much as a yacht.

It should be noted that all of the outstanding properties associated with polyurethane paints come from the use of two-part *coatings* rather than one-part *paints*. The two-part systems form a cross-linked polyurethane plastic coating on the surface as they cure. The one-part paints contain some suspended polyurethane polymer, but they are simply modified alkyd enamels which dry by solvent evaporation.

Can you paint your boat with urethane?

That is not a question to which I can give an unequivocal yes or no. In truth, I was so worried about this question that I appealed to the man among my boatbuilding friends and acquaintances with the most knowledge about the use of these paints, one who for some years represented a polyurethane-paint manufacturer in the boating field. He agreed that painting one's own boat with these products ought not to be attempted by all owners in all circumstances. Briefly, this is how he put it:

"The polyurethanes are extremely sensitive to contamination and moisture. At the same time, once set, they are exceptionally gas- and liquid-tight. So, to achieve the most perfect finish with them, and indeed, to avoid disastrous results, a very strict and fairly involved set of instructions must be followed. Some of these are:

1. The job must be done in a clean, dry atmosphere, since dust, of course, but also moisture can turn a sparkling job into a drab one.

2. If you are applying polyurethane over gelcoat, you must be aware that sanding the gelcoat opens up tiny bubbles in it, created when it was heavily catalyzed to cure in a hurry, and that dust, solvents, or water will

Figure 2-2. *The 87-foot* Yelad *being coated with polyurethane dockside in San Diego, California. The aged gelcoat's many surface defects were glazed with epoxy putty before being recoated. The finish was applied with a foam roller, followed by a brush to tip the still-wet paint into a smooth film. As you can see, the brush/roller method provides results comparable to those obtained with a spray gun, but is significantly easier (and safer) for amateurs. (Photo courtesy Detco Marine)*

be trapped in these opened bubbles. Body putties, too, are porous and tend to harbor contaminants. Depending upon the nature of the contamination, lumps or bubbles will be created sooner or later in the pristine surface you had hoped for. Unlike the usual boat paints, which have some degree of porosity, the polyurethanes will not let even the tiniest of contaminants escape. An epoxy barrier is therefore recommended.

"Fish eyes," too, can be a problem. Fish eyes are created almost immediately upon application of the paint due to wax or silicone on the surface, which prevents adhesion. Fish eyes, however, are easily eliminated with a dedicated additive available for all two-part polyurethane systems. Again, an epoxy primer-sealer will solve most adhesion problems; fish-eye eliminator and the same care that a good painter uses with alkyd enamel will solve most of the rest.

3. There is also the matter of toxicity and the need to use a mask that brings fresh air to the operator and excludes the fumes of the paint.

Considering the hazards and controls involved in achieving a good polyurethane paint job, it is hardly a project to be undertaken lightly. I know of several persons with no particular training who are putting out excellent polyurethane paint jobs. It's not so much a matter of education as it is faithfully following instructions. Anyone who will sit down and read the instructions provided with these paints, who will believe what they read and follow it, can do a good job of painting a boat with polyurethane paint.

I like to sum it up this way: A high school science teacher who is handy and has the summer off is many times more likely to succeed in painting a boat with polyurethane than a college chemistry professor who heads down to the boatyard to do it over a weekend."

It is not my intention to discourage you from refinishing a boat or a part with either gelcoat or polyurethane paint. They're each wonderful in their way, but it does seem necessary to point out that regelcoating is labor-intensive, which makes big jobs a real drag, and using polyurethane is fraught with restrictions, controls, and hazards. But cheer up, there is one way to refinish a boat or part that is almost as well adapted to weekenders as to the pros. That way is with the common, everyday marine paints.

Marine paint

Sometimes it's an advantage to have been working in the trade, building wooden boats, before fiberglass came along. Having practiced the old-fashioned ways as well as the new-fashioned ones, not to mention those that came between, one is freed from the notion that the prevailing way is the only way. That's how this boat refinishing business appears to me: There are people who seem to believe that the only choices for finishing fiberglass are gelcoat or polyurethane paint, that the material somehow requires them. That notion is far from the truth; in most situations fiberglass is *much* more easy to protect than wood.

To put the finishing of fiberglass in perspective: A good gelcoat job is the best, most durable protection and most high-gloss finish known, while the polyurethanes are the next best and are much less labor-intensive except when gelcoat is applied in a mold. At the same time, it is the stable, grainless, virtually impervious surface of fiberglass that allows these coatings to remain in such beautiful condition for periods measured in years, not months. What most people don't seem to realize is that the nature of fiberglass also promotes greater durability in the more traditional types of marine paint, and there are excellent marine paints on the market: one- and two-part epoxies, modified alkyd enamels, and traditional alkyd enamels that will put a nice finish and excellent protection on a fiberglass part. Neither do people seem to realize that these paints will also last years, not months, on fiberglass, although not as many; that these paints are relatively easy to apply, self-smoothing, and less finicky about ambient conditions; and further, that they can be water sanded to heighten their shine, waxed to preserve it, and retouched with ease.

Using marine paint on fiberglass

It would only be confusing to rehash the recommendations and instructions of marine paint manufacturers. There are too many quite different products, some requiring their own primers, special thinners, etc. Nevertheless, I ought to remind you that preparation of the surface is the most important part of any paint job. No paint will smooth up a rough surface, and most paints will bead right up on a dried surface that is too slick. Those that don't may peel off later.

Therefore, after physically repairing your boat if necessary, her surface must be well sanded, filled with polyester body putty, fairing putty, or epoxy putty where needed, and finally brought down to a fine sanded surface. Even if the part needs no repair to the laminate and if the gelcoat is in well-preserved condition except for scratches and fading, it will need sanding all over and possibly some "surfacing" with fine putty to perfect its smoothness before painting. From that point on, it's a matter of what primer, if any, the manufacturer requires; more fine sanding; then on with the paint.

When painting the topsides of all except the smallest boats with quick-drying paint, it can take some of the tension out of the project if two people work together on the side of the boat, one following along below the other or one putting the paint on with a roller and the other brushing it out.

Don't underestimate marine paint

For years I have been recommending that clients for whom I surveyed boats or consulted on repairs use marine paint for refinishing, but when I came to the subject in this chapter I decided to check out the current thinking of the painter in a local boatyard. It only took minutes for him, escorting me through the sheds, pointing out boat after boat that had been refinished with marine paint, to reconfirm in my mind that this approach is still very much appreciated among professionals and some of their customers. Though I had passed most of these boats many times on my way to survey others, I had never noticed that they had been refinished with marine paint. Just as with the polyurethanes, about the only way you could tell was to look for a scratch or an edge that was painted against masking tape.

I don't mean to imply that marine paints are going to recapture the boat-finishing field. In a world where most boats are one of a very large series of look-alikes, it seems to bring great satisfaction to many owners to have the shiniest one, or at least one of the shiniest ones, at all times; and to that end, if you don't mind the cost, the other ways are still the best.

CHAPTER 3

The Art of Fiberglassing

Gelcoating

So many repairs to fiberglass boats and boat parts involve gelcoat that every boat repairer ought to have a working knowledge of how to apply this unique material. The matters of when and where to use gelcoat or whether to use a paint instead were discussed in Chapter 2. With those questions behind us, we can concentrate in this chapter on *how* to use it.

Gelcoating against a mold

A repairer will only occasionally use gelcoat as the builder does, applying it to the highly polished surface of a mold before laying up the fiberglass against it. The most frequent such occasion is when he backs up a hole in the part with a polished (and waxed) material on the outside and fills in the hole working inward from that backing. In effect, the backed-up hole is a mold. Of course, a repairer who needs to replace some part that is no longer available from the manufacturer may elect to make it in a temporary mold that he builds or in a mold taken off a part of another boat of that model, both of which processes involve gelcoating before starting the laminate.

Whether gelcoat is brushed or sprayed onto a mold and how smooth its interior surface (the one facing you) is when it gels are not important, within reason, for its exterior surface will be as smooth as the surface against which it is applied, and its interior surface will be obscured by the laminate laid up over it. The thickness of the gelcoat and its thorough catalyzation are, however, most important.

"Pease porridge hot . . . ," and thick

By "gelcoat," I mean orthophthalic or isophthalic polyester gelcoat. Epoxy is not appropriate for gelcoat, and vinylester is too expensive. The primary advantage of vinylester gelcoat is high-temperature resistance. It's still a polyester and is not significantly more water resistant than ortho or iso—not enough to justify its cost, anyway.

A generous gelcoat thickness (see manufacturer's recommendations for the particular product) will give excellent protection against wear and weathering even while allowing for a modest smoothing or polishing with wet-or-dry paper and compound to blend the edges of the patch with the surrounding original gelcoat or to eliminate minor imperfections. In general, it is the purpose of gelcoat to supply a thick protective coat—much thicker than paints (except for "high-build" paints)—and one which can be disfigured, patched, and repolished for many years before it is considered worn out and in need of replacement. It is shortchanging oneself to apply only a thin, enamel-like layer.

When catalyzing gelcoat you should be generous, adding an amount near the top of the manufacturer's recommendations, and, as the manufacturer may or may not remind you, *be very sure to mix it thoroughly*. It is not easy to disperse catalyst to every last dollop of gelcoat, because of its very high viscosity. Failure to do so, however, creates undercured areas and invites wrinkles in the gelcoat, or alligatoring, when the catalyzed resin of the first layers of laminate laid up over it cure and shrink atop its undercured patches.

In the early years of my boatshop's ventures into fiberglass building, I found out about alligatored gelcoat the hard way. Now and then one of those ugly spots, like a heavy dose of poison ivy, would be there in the midst of an otherwise sleek skin as we removed a part from its mold. On one occasion we made three tries at building a mold over a double-diagonal wooden prototype, only to have the first two layers of mat laid up over the gelcoat attack and shrivel the gelcoat so badly in places that, fortunately, the wrinkles showed through. We hurriedly removed the mat and the gelcoat. Letting them harden would have made removal difficult and, if the wax on the prototype had been penetrated, might have damaged its surface even to the point of taking some bites out of its planking.

The owner of the prototype was screaming for his new boat—already long delayed, as usual—and I was afraid we might ruin her highly polished finish, thus violating one of the contractual inducements to let us take a mold off her. Suppliers and manufacturers of gelcoat were sympathetic but vague about probable causes of the alligatoring. I finally had the men use resin, not gelcoat, on their fourth try. With it they got a perfect mold, albeit one without the desired contrasting color and tough mold surface of tooling gelcoat.

For counsel on the causes of alligatoring, I then turned to my friend, neighbor, and mentor on fiberglass lamination, Bill Milne, vice-president of Beetle Plastics. Sifting through our case history, Bill concluded that we simply weren't mixing the catalyst thoroughly enough. My men claimed they "always" did, but Bill was adamant. To settle the matter, I undertook the catalyzing and stirring of every bit of gelcoat myself for the next several jobs. To the chagrin of some and the amazement of all except Bill, there was not a trace of alligatoring on any of the parts involved. We never had another serious alligatoring problem, although once in a while some cavalier new worker did need tutoring in the art of catalyzing gelcoat.

Gelcoating outside the mold, on a part's exterior

Applying gelcoat to the exterior of a part after patching or adding layers to the laminate is quite a different matter than applying it to a mold or mold-like backing material. There is no polished surface here that will be mirrored in the gelcoat. Rather, the gelcoat will dry with much the same surface configuration that it assumes when sprayed or painted on. If sprayed, there are likely to be "orange peels," "blops," or "curtains," and if brushed, there will be "runs," "holidays," or "brush strokes" adorning its surface. At best, if thinned and sprayed by a fairly expert man with a special gun, it will need wet sanding and polishing to give it a highly polished finish, for the material simply is not self-leveling, nor are most gelcoats compounded to dry with a high-gloss surface. At worst, if brushed on as it comes from the bucket or blurted on with a coarse sprayer such as production builders use to apply it to molds, it will need considerable sanding with dry paper before it can begin to be polished with wet-or-dry paper and compound.

This is not to say that care in applying gelcoat does not improve its fairness and smoothness. Rather, it is a forewarning that gelcoat is not paint and, until someone manufactures a new kind with special qualities, doesn't do much to complement a painter's efforts. This is why most repairers shy away from regelcoating entire large parts as too labor-intensive compared with using paint. Nevertheless, there is nothing better as a finish on fiberglass than a good coat of gelcoat, and the refinishing of a repair always comes down to the degree of polish wanted versus the expense of achieving it in gelcoat or the other available finishes.

As examples of how some repairers work out this problem in different situations in my town: When Elen Boat Works covers wooden fishing boats with fiberglass, it uses gelcoat rolled on with a roller (after fairing and smoothing the laminate with a putty made for that), and the fishermen are quite happy with the handsome, colorful, wear-resistant finish, albeit no mirror, that careful rolling leaves. "Can it be polished to a high shine like yachts have?" some will ask.

"Sure, for . . . thousand dollars [the number depending on the size of the boat], or you can do it yourself."

"Forget I asked," is the usual rejoinder.

Phoenix Boat Works uses a special sprayer made to apply gelcoat as smoothly as possible on yachts, but it also offers Awl-gripping as an alternative, for there is still wet sanding and polishing to be done to the gelcoat if a highly polished surface is wanted. Currently, at about fifteen hundred dollars, the cost of the yacht-quality gelcoat sprayer makes it impractical for occasional use, nor does anyone rent them as far as I know. Still, a repairer that wants a large part gelcoated could have it sprayed by a yard and then do his own sanding and polishing. Not many boatyards will insist on doing that portion of a job, for few workers are wild about the prospect.

Rules for gelcoat application

1. *Wax any mold or backing surfaces* with several coats of mold release wax, allowing these to dry for at least an hour between coats and before applying gelcoat. This is especially important the first time a mold or backing material is used, or until the surface is well saturated with wax. It is a real disaster if the wax is penetrated and the gelcoat along with the accompanying laminate becomes inseparably glued to the mold or backing surface; nothing but grinding every trace of the latter away can salvage the newly created part. In many cases where a large part is stuck to a mold, the two become one unwieldy piece of landfill. When a piece of hardboard or Formica is used to back a hole, it can be ground away, alright, but the operation is at best a waste of time, and stressful, too.

To add extra protection against sticking, a coat of PVA, polyvinyl alcohol, can be applied over the waxed surface prior to the gelcoat. PVA is water soluble, but impermeable to resin or gelcoat. It is sprayed on and dries quickly, forming a film between the surfaces that is easily washed off when they are parted.

If any doubt exists concerning the compatibility of the material from which the mold or backing is made, or of any paint or other coatings on the surface, make a small sample application of the gelcoat and two layers of 1½-ounce mat about a foot square before you try the whole job. Once in a while one runs into a material with which polyester resin reacts in strange ways, perhaps turning the interface into a gooey mess, a mass of wrinkles, or one insoluble chunk that seems to ignore the presence of the wax or parting agent. *If in doubt, always make a test.*

There are materials with coatings to which polyester resin will not stick, two of the most commonly available being ordinary waxed paper and melamine-coated wallboard. With a little testing to make sure, you can use these to avoid embarrassing attachments, cutting waxing down to a coat or two for "insurance" should you rip the waxed paper. When working against melamine-coated material, wax may be needed to seal joints, uncoated edges, or fastenings, and it may be used to fill and put a higher polish on the surface.

2. *Mask off any adjacent areas* to which you do not want gelcoat to adhere if it runs down or is oversprayed onto them. If masking is not practical, waxing them will enable you to clean away the unwanted gelcoat easily.

3. *Use enough catalyst,* well mixed in, to assure a complete and even cure, but remember that thin coats and cool temperatures or ambient dampness all tend to slow the cure of polyester resin, while thick coats develop exothermic heat, heat given off by the reaction, which tends to hasten the cure. Cure is also hastened by external heat and radiant heat and light sources, especially bright sunlight. All such factors are more good reasons to try a sample area before doing a very large one, then adjust your catalyst amount to suit. You may laminate over gelcoat that is

slightly tacky, but not to the point of sticking to a finger.

4. *Before using a gelcoat on the exterior* of the laminate—as opposed to brushing or spraying it on a mold and sealing it from the air with layers of glass fiber materials—find out from the supplier or manufacturer whether it will cure completely in air or whether it will need a wax additive to keep it from remaining tacky for a long time after gelling. If it needs protection from the air, either use the additive or, after applying it, spray its surface with PVA to keep out air until it has cured hard. Some gelcoats are waxfree yet will harden in air to a free-sanding state (in other words, one that will not clog the sandpaper).

5. *To polish up gelcoat that was molded* against a smooth, shiny surface, you should need only to clean off any mold-release wax or PVA residues, perhaps compound the surface, and finally wax it with boat wax. If the gloss is not high enough for you in a sample of such treatment, you might have to go to heavier compounding or even to wet sanding.

6. *Thinning gelcoat* with acetone, which quickly flashes off into the air, will enable you to get it through an ordinary paint sprayer. Then, given patience and some even-handed dexterity with the sprayer, you can build up a relatively smooth, thick coat over large areas, perhaps even a whole hull or deck. Spray the hardest-to-reach, most convoluted part of your repair first, working outward from there in long (1½- to 3-foot) parallel passes, each one overlapping the one preceding. Maintain a wet edge to your work. When you finish the passes in one direction, go back over them with another set of passes diagonal or perpendicular to the first. Three sets of passes, each depositing a thin but continuous film, should provide a total gelcoat thickness in the recommended range of 15 to 20 mils (thousandths of an inch). Do not let gelling advance between passes.

Although there is not yet a gelcoat on the market that will dry to a beautiful, self-leveled gloss as the enamels and polyurethane paints do, a good spray gun operator can at least minimize the water sanding and compounding required to achieve a high gloss. Meanwhile, sanding and compounding *can* put a gloss on gelcoat, creating a finish that is shinier, harder, thicker, and many times more durable than any other. Applying gelcoat to the exterior of a laminate is labor-intensive, but the result can be the best finish possible.

7. *Here is another tip to consider when you apply gelcoat to the exterior* of a part: Given but a small patch to coat, you can afford to catalyze it and apply it by brush or roller just as it comes from the bucket. When cured, it will possibly need some general fairing or "leveling" with rather coarse paper on a block, and it will certainly have brush strokes (unless you remember that a roller is better) or other surface imperfections to be sanded down before it is fine sanded and polished, but the time and trouble these require in a small area could be less than would be required to set up for spraying on a smoother coat.

8. *If you don't want the laminate to surface* through your new gelcoat, grind down all its high spots until they are below the level of what will be the faired, finished surface. That might seem too obvious a warning, but if the surface were uneven, you might believe your thick application of gelcoat had buried everything until sanding suddenly exposed the top of a high spot that was only thinly covered. Another way to put this same bit of advice is: never gelcoat a rough surface thinking that the gelcoat will level it. Even 15 to 20 mils, the maximum thickness usually recommended, is thin relative to bumps in a laminate surface.

A similar problem is encountered when gelcoating a repair in the midst of the original gelcoat. If you bring the surface of the repair laminate up flush with the surrounding older coating, or putty and smooth it flush, then, when you apply your new gelcoat and sand it down, you will not get it perfectly flush around its edges without striking through it to the laminate. True, if you lap the new gelcoat a long way over the old you can taper the patch until it seems flush, but the right approach is to leave, or grind, the top of the patch's laminate as a depression like a shallow pond around whose edges the original gelcoat is sloped like a beach (Figure 3-1). Then, when you fill the depression with new gelcoat and sand it down flush with the old, you won't be so likely to sand through either of them.

A related problem is encountered when the original gelcoat adjacent to a patch is worn very thin. One has to be careful not to sand too much past the edges of the patch lest the thin stuff be broached, and it often saves time in the long run to grind out the old gelcoat in such areas, especially if the shadow of the laminate is already showing through. If the thinness is too extensive for grinding to be practical, a different approach is to extend the new gelcoat application a long way past the borders of the patch—after sanding the original gelcoat lightly to assure a good bond, of course. With a long overlap and careful sanding, one can get the patch's gelcoat smoothed, polished, and blended into the original surface without striking through it.

9. *Matching the color of the original* gelcoat is not a problem if the boat being repaired is relatively new; "gelcoat repair kits" are now made up and supplied by manufacturers. As mentioned in Chapter 2, however, it becomes more unlikely that the same color will be available as the boat's age increases, and it becomes more likely that fading and staining will have made the original color a mismatch anyway.

The routes to mixing a color that matches the one currently on a boat are:

- Buy a gelcoat of the closest color available and adjust it by the addition of other colors. A word of caution about mixing two or more ready-made gelcoats of different colors: sometimes they won't stay mixed. If you let the mixture stand awhile after much stirring, and the two colors begin to separate, you can be sure they'll do the same on the job, and the marbled or spotted pattern that results won't match any existing gelcoat.
- Buy neutral gelcoat and color it with dispersion colors, which are pigments prepared for this mixing. Such pigments can be bought in small tubes from retailers of fiberglass materials, and in larger quantities from wholesalers.
- If you don't wish to get involved in mixing colors, some suppliers will match a sample, and so will some local boat repairers and refinishers.

Hand lay-up

Laying up a fiberglass laminate can be messy and frustrating, or it can go along as smoothly as a squirrel on a rail fence. Practice helps, for it teaches (the hard way) neatness and planning ahead. Even if you are a complete novice, however, you can avoid a number of pitfalls as well as the massive cleanup that unsuspecting workers often make for themselves. Just keep in mind the following simple but important points:

1. *Protect* the areas not involved in the repair from spills, drips, and runs of resin. The surest way is by covering adjacent areas with newspaper and masking tape. You can also wax nearby fiberglass as well as other nonporous materials such as metal or glass, which will keep resin from getting a grip.

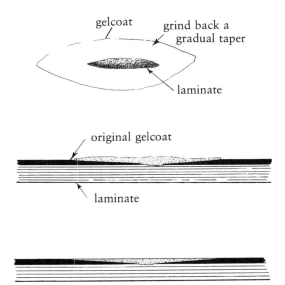

Figure 3-1. *Grind a gradual taper surrounding dings in the gelcoat; fill, and sand flush.*

Safety

Fiberglass repair tools and materials are capable of great things, but they are also hazardous. Be circumspect. Treat them with the care they deserve.

- When grinding fiberglass, wear goggles and a toxic-dust mask, if not a respirator. Direct the debris stream away from you.
- When grinding or laminating, consider using disposable Tyvek suits. These can be difficult to find, but disposable clothing is usually no farther away than a Salvation Army or Goodwill store, or the back of your closet.
- Wear disposable gloves at all times. Gloves don't get dermatitis. Use drip guards (such as half of a hollow rubber ball) on tools. Barrier creams provide an extra layer of protection.
- Styrene, which comprises 40 percent of polyester resin by weight, is a strong skin and mucous membrane irritant and has exhibited long-term neurotoxicity among fiberglass workers, leading to premature senility. Compared with epoxies, polyester resins are relatively benign, but don't take chances. Wear a respirator when laminating.
- Acetone, the solvent most commonly used by fiberglass workers to clean hands and tools, causes severe dermatitis and, in large quantities, causes nervous system dysfunction. In addition, the vapors are explosive. Do not smoke; tolerate no open flames; do not use electric tools around acetone.
- Catalysts, such as MEKP, can splash when poured. Keep them away from your eyes, preferably with goggles. If you're unsuccessful, flush eyes immediately with cold water.
- Accelerators have no place in an amateur boatshop. Buy a resin with the correct formulation, and adjust cure times with catalyst.
- Although epoxy smells less formidable than polyester resin, it is actually more toxic, causing skin irritation, headaches, and nausea. In addition, the side effects are cumulative. The more you use it, the worse the effect.
- Keep fire extinguishers handy; use big fans to ventilate; closely follow manufacturers' safety recommendations.

2. *Your setup should include:*

— A convenient table for cutting the glass fiber fabrics. A plywood or corrugated pasteboard top is best to withstand the marking by mat knife and shear.

— A place to dispense, catalyze, and stir resin. A piece of disposable corrugated pasteboard makes a good mat on which to place the containers and do the mixing. *NOTE! Have clean water, at least a gallon jug if not a hose; an eye cup with eye wash; cotton swabs; and a mirror nearby this station and near the job in general in the event that anyone splashes resin or, worse, catalyst in his eyes.*

— A place to wash one's hands and clean tools, and a five-gallon bucket with cover in which to store tools temporarily. Acetone is often used for all these functions. Lacquer thinner is cheaper, and works just as well for cleaning up uncured resin, but its fumes take longer to dissipate.

3. *Cut the fiberglass materials first*—all of them—and have them piled neatly in the order in which they will be used *before* you catalyze any resin for the job. Cut the pieces from 38-inch-wide rolls. This width is the easiest to handle.

4. *Small pieces are best.* Use pieces that can be easily handled, completely wet out, and neatly rolled down before rolling is

New Materials for Cleanup

Until recently, acetone, lacquer thinner, and other solvents, but particularly acetone, have been the accepted agents for removing resin from hands and tools. But they have problems: They cause severe dermatitis; because the dissolved resins are held in solution, they present hazardous waste disposal problems; and they are extremely flammable. More than 3000 boatshop fires have been directly attributed to acetone.

A new product, Res-Away, developed by Lee Sechler of Resin Support Systems and marketed by Norac Co., Inc., promises to replace acetone in many applications, and has already done so at, among other boat manufacturers, Bayliner, Boston Whaler, and Thunderbird.

Res-Away (and similar products such as Thermo-Clean) is a nonflammable, nontoxic, emulsifying detergent mixed in water and approved by the EPA as a nonhazardous substance. It effectively removes resin from tools and hands, allowing the residue to be polymerized and discarded as solid waste.

Res-Away isn't *quite* as effective or fast as acetone, and must be kept warm (100°F) to work effectively, but the reduced insult to health and the environment and the elimination of the fire hazard make this an efficiency trade-off worth pursuing.

More information is available from:

Norac Co., Inc.
405 South Motor Ave.
Azusa, CA 91702
    818-334-2908

---

rushed or stopped by incipient gelling. Until you become adept at hanging them (it *is* a little like wallpapering), pieces for vertical or near vertical surfaces should be no larger than two square yards for one worker or four square yards for two. Slightly larger pieces are permissible on horizontal surfaces; pieces for overhead surfaces should be much smaller.

5. *Butt all pieces laid up on the outside* of the part (Figure 3-2), lest you build up ridges in the laminate where edges overlap. Any such ridges would have to be faired out before finishing.

6. *Overlap those pieces laid up against a mold or backing;* overlaps make the layer stronger, and ridges on the interior surface of the part are of little consequence.

7. *When the thickness of a laminate is to be tapered* to nothing at its outer edges, always put on the shortest pieces first, so that each succeeding piece will cover the edge of the one under it, and each will get a new grip on the underlying surface along its outer edge. By so doing, you hedge the bond of the new laminate to the surface beneath it, whereas laying down the biggest piece first

leaves the entire laminate dependent on the first layer's bond. To compound the problem, as the shorter pieces shrink they tug at the bond of that one piece.

8. *Always use mat for the first layer*

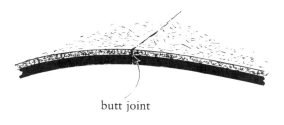

butt joint

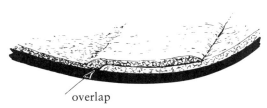

overlap

Figure 3-2. *Butt all laminate pieces laid up on the outside of the part. Overlap those pieces laid up against a mold or backing.*

against any other material for best adhesion; mat between layers of roving materials to minimize peeling and shattering; and mat at the outside face of the part to best seal it against water penetration (Figure 3-3). How many layers should you apply? There are too many variables to permit a hard-and-fast formula, even one that takes into account the size of the boat and the location and function of the part you're laying up. This is a question

we'll explore in more detail where appropriate in the chapters that follow. As a starting point, however, look at the laminate thickness in the part you're repairing, and give your repair as many layers or, if the part was too weak to begin with, a few more.

9. *Never laminate over fiberglass* or gelcoat that hasn't been sanded recently, unless it was laid up within the preceding 24 hours.

10. *Always paint a surface with resin* be-

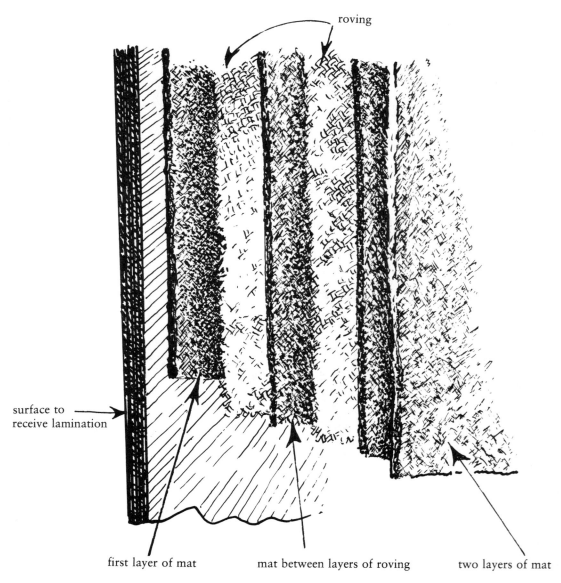

roving

surface to
receive lamination

first layer of mat   mat between layers of roving   two layers of mat

Figure 3-3. *A typical laminate, laid up against a core material such as plywood. Two layers of mat provide an effective seal against water.*

fore putting the glass materials on it, unless it is already quite wet with resin of the previous layers.

11. *Catalyze only small quantities of resin* at a time in 2½-quart non-waxed paper containers. This allows you to take your time without losing too much resin due to gelling in the pot. Small batches also facilitate more frequent adjustment of the amount of catalyst as the work proceeds; you can use more catalyst if cure is too slow, or less if cure is too fast.

12. *Use throwaway tools* for applying resin: cheap bristle brushes for small jobs, and fluffy paint rollers for wetting out large areas.

13. *Use hard, knubbly paint rollers,* or grooved aluminum ones (Figure 3-4), for rolling down the material. Rolling compacts the laminate, works the resin through it, and wrings the air bubbles and excess resin out of it, all at the same time.

14. *Presaturate small pieces or strips of material* by laying them on a disposable piece of pasteboard and wetting them with a few quick, gentle passes of the brush. Then, when they are saturated and softened by the resin, you can fit and form them easily to the job without tearing them to pieces or balling them up by trying to "wet them out" in place.

15. *Two layers at a time* are usually laid up on large areas. This results in a more efficient use of labor, and because the second layer sponges up some of the first layer's excess resin, there is an overall reduction in the amount of resin needed. Furthermore, under adverse conditions a single layer may be agonizingly slow to cure, whereas two layers curing together have sufficient thickness to permit a buildup of exothermic heat, which accelerates the reaction.

Conversely, too many layers carried together over a large area build up too much heat, which, especially in hot weather or bright sunlight, will "cook" the resin, rendering it weak and brittle. Even if the reaction does not become too hot, there will be a very fast cure with excessive shrinkage of the laminate, which tends to distort its shape.

16. *More layers* can be laid up simultaneously in cool conditions, on small areas, or in narrow strips—in other words, whenever the concentrated mass of the laminate is slight or the heat it gives off can be expected to dissipate into the surroundings. For instance, you might well pack eight or ten layers simultaneously into a small hole, or build up a smashed toerail with four to six layers, or wet out as many as four layers in a backed hole the size of a dessert plate, but under the same ambient conditions you would be likely to warp the top of a hatch cover if you tried to lay up more than two layers at once.

17. *Wash your tools regularly* with acetone, then wash your hands, too, unless they are protected with gloves, which also ought to be washed. Do not leave resin-covered tools lying around, for if anything distracts or delays you from cleaning them, they will inexorably "turn to stone" and become worthless. Get into the habit of washing the tools every time you break from work for any reason. Keep a five-gallon bucket with a reasonably tight cover and a half gallon to gallon of acetone or lacquer thinner in it (depending on the size of the job or number of tools) in which to store your tools during breaks, lunch, or overnight. Always change the acetone before a weekend or longer downtime. To be safe for extended periods, wash tools thoroughly and store them dry; given time enough, any resin left in them or settled to the bottom will harden even under acetone.

18. CAUTION!!! *Acetone and MEKP (catalyst) are very volatile and flammable, and polyester resin is also flammable.* Read the labels and take precautions to keep flame away from them.

19. *Water ruins green fiberglass.* Don't fiberglass in the rain or on a wet surface, and do cover uncured fiberglass from rain and dew with a polyethylene or Mylar sheet.

20. *Don't try to fiberglass over a leak dripping out of the boat.* It won't work. The water will simply ooze through the uncured resin, leaving a path that will not heal. Either dry out the boat or staunch the flow of water with hydraulic cement, which goes by such brand names as Water Plug and Water Stop. Then your patch will work.

21. *Work on many-faceted or detailed*

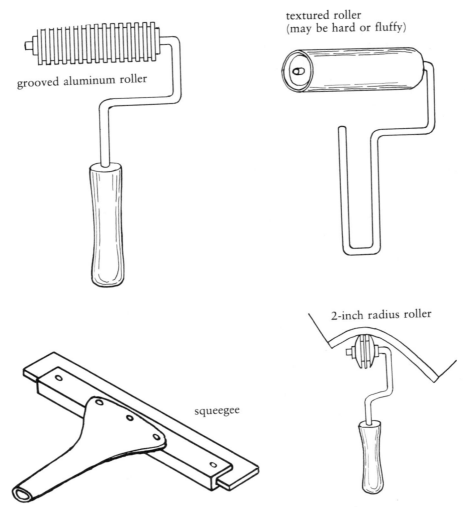

Figure 3-4. *Grooved aluminum or hard, knubbly rollers (having the texture of a short-nap industrial rug) are used for rolling down wetted reinforcing materials to get out the air bubbles and compact the laminate. Seven-inch rollers are the workhorses, 9-inch rollers may be used for big jobs, and very short rollers (1- to 3-inch) work well in corners and concavities. Thick, fluffy rollers are used for applying resin. In my opinion, a squeegee is no better at compacting a laminate and working out excess resin than a roller or a brush, dragged toward its heel. There are many times, incidentally, when the best way to use a brush, particularly to avoid tearing out mat strands, is to jab or "stipple" rather than drag through the work.*

Figure 3-5. *A hand lay-up laminator's tool kit: catalyst measuring pump, paper pot (wax-free) and stirrer, brushes, roller, and shears.*

Figure 3-6. *Using a roller to apply catalyzed resin. The worker is wearing gloves and a respirator. More protective clothing would be better.*

parts separately from large uncluttered surfaces. If you try to cover toerails, hatch coamings, guardrails, or skegs while you are laying up large pieces you will be too rushed to do a good job on the fussy work, too preoccupied to keep ahead of the curing of the big pieces, or both.

22. *If a detailed part contains sharp corners* you will find it easier to form with an all-mat schedule, or by turning unidirectional roving to run along the corners (Figure 3-7). You certainly will not want to try to bend the roving in an adjacent plane surface over or into corners, for it will persist in bridging them, will take the crispness right out of them, and will frustrate you no end.

Even when a detailed part calls for the great strength of roving, as where a skeg attaches to a hull, you are better off to cut and fit the roving in pieces, applying them so that they taper out onto the plane surface. Blend the corresponding pieces of the plane surface into these small pieces with, at worst, some of the plane surface laminate lapping a short way onto the base of the detailed part (Figure 3-8).

23. *Don't forget* when fiberglassing inside a boat to blow out the fumes and bring

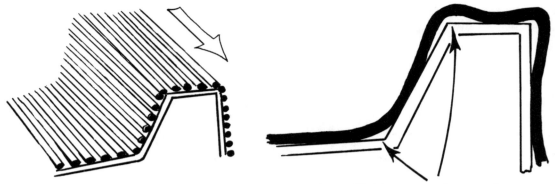

unidirectional roving *will* lie down lengthwise . . . but will bridge corners that cross it

Figure 3-7. *Unidirectional roving will readily conform to sharp curves or corners along the line of the strands, but turning corners will stop any roving configuration cold. Use mat to cover complex shapes.*

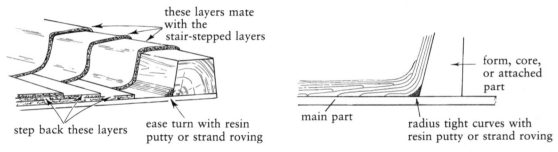

these layers mate with the stair-stepped layers

step back these layers

ease turn with resin putty or strand roving

main part

form, core, or attached part

radius tight curves with resin putty or strand roving

Figure 3-8. *Bonding an attached part to a plane surface: The layers of roving should interleave for greatest strength, and to provide a smooth surface. The laminate of the attached part may be laid up over (left) or under (right) the main part's laminate.*

in fresh air with a good big fan. A portable space fan in a rectangular case lying flat over the forward hatch does a great job, exhausting fumes and the dust of grinding up through the hatch and dragging fresh air through the boat.

Laying up core materials

There is a chapter devoted to core problems and repairs; here we discuss how you can avoid creating some such problems in the first place by properly installing core materials when making repairs.

A core is a bulky, stiff material interjected in a laminate to separate the fiberglass layers into two sublaminates. The good things a core brings by way of stiffening the laminate and adding sound, vibration, and heat insulation are well known, but these highly desirable properties, and especially the stiffness, depend upon the bond of the fiberglass layers to the core. As long as the sandwich retains its integrity, you have a superior laminate, but if delamination occurs, the result is no longer as good as a single skin.

A good bond of the fiberglass layers to the core depends on a large area of contact.

Resin has good adhesion or gluing properties, but a thick layer of it between the stronger materials is a weak and brittle one. In other words, laying core into a puddle of resin does not make a strong bond; *pressing it into wet mat does.*

Whenever possible, core materials should be weighted or pressed into place with shores and wedges, clamps, screws or bolts through sheet materials (insulated from the resin by waxed paper of course), or any other practical means. Unfortunately, this is easiest to do on flat horizontal surfaces where it is least needed, and most difficult on the curved vertical, or even overhead surfaces often encountered by the repairer. Be resourceful, for good contact is important.

You should always set a core material in wet mat, and if the laminate against which you are setting it is uneven, two layers of wet mat will be better than one. When you lay up fiberglass on the other side of the core, the first layer should again be mat; whenever adhesion is important, mat is best. To obtain a good bond to a porous core such as balsa or softwood, wet the core well so that the resin will penetrate, then press the glass fiber materials flat with the roller. Thorough rolling is useful also in that it eliminates air bubbles and increases the strength of the laminate by squeezing out excess resin. Cores made of such comparatively nonporous materials as hardwood or a closed-cell foam require less resin to achieve a good bond.

The special cases comprise such materials as PVC foam and honeycomb, the latter being a collective name for core materials made by gluing up strips of paper, metal, nylon, or other sheet materials to create a sheet of hexagonal cells. Any PVC foam core—Airex is a popular brand—is actually attacked or dissolved by resin, so that the bond is chemical. It is thus neither necessary nor desirable to use a large amount of resin, for the excess would eat away some of the body of the foam. Thinner sheets can be virtually destroyed in this fashion. The Airex manufacturer now coats the surface of the foam with a cobalt solution, which accelerates the cure of catalyzed resin and prevents it from penetrating too deeply.

The problem with honeycomb cores is that the paper-thin edges of the hexagonal cells provide precious little surface area for the resin to grip (Figure 3-9). For a better bond the resin needs to flow a short distance into the cells, curing against the walls, and this is best accomplished by thickening the resin with a filler. Consider the consequences of a thin resin: If the honeycomb is set down into wet mat, the resin is likely to drain away from the cell walls before it can cure; if wet mat is laid up on top of the honeycomb, the resin may run all the way down the cell walls to collect at the bottom. In either case the bond of glass fibers to honeycomb will be weakened, and in the latter instance the core will become heavier besides. Remember to thicken the resin and catalyze it well, for you want it to stand up like slush around the edges of the cells and lock them in its frozen grip.

Milled glass fibers, Cabosil, talc, microballoons, and microspheres are all used to thicken resin. The first three are somewhat heavy but should work for a small patch or where weight is not critical. The last two are much lighter. With a little experimenting you ought to be able to make a slush that will get a good hold on the honeycomb without either draining away or loading up the cells. When in doubt, don't bull ahead, do a little testing. If you prefer, you can purchase premixed bonding putties suitable for honeycomb (and balsa, too) from suppliers of

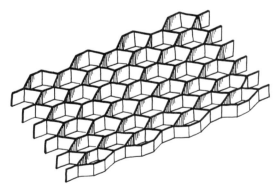

Figure 3-9. *Expanded honeycomb core. The walls of the hexagonal cells may be made of Kraft paper, metal, aramid fibers, etc.*

fiberglass materials. A putty using micro-balloon filler is a good choice.

Repairing or applying reinforcements

After centuries of development in wooden boats, it is not surprising that ribs, stringers, floor timbers, sole beams, deck beams, carlins, knees, bulkheads, and half bulkheads are useful in reinforcing fiberglass boats. Of course, their use contravenes the pure concept of one-piece, stress-bearing fiberglass hulls, decks, and other parts. As a practical matter, however, except in small sandwich-constructed and very small single-skinned boats, reinforcing members add great stiffness and strength for very modest costs in materials and weight. Pleased as we who assembled them are to have put the "bundles of sticks" of the past behind us, there is no need to ignore the great body of wooden boat building wisdom in our preoccupation with monocoque (one-piece) boat parts.

In repairing boats, our concerns with reinforcing members are that we be able to repair them and that we be able to construct and install them if the boat has areas that are too flexible, as many do.

Hat-shaped ribs, stringers, and deck beams

When a boat is built these continuous members are created by gluing a core or forming piece to the inner skin of the part, often while it is still in the mold, then covering the core with fiberglass. The sides of the core are often slanted about 30 degrees from the vertical to soften the angle of the corners. The top corners are also rounded a bit, and the ones at the bottom where the member meets the skin of the part are radiused, or filled in. The resultant soft bends allow the glass materials to drape more easily over the core and out onto the inner skin of the part, forming an attaching flange on each side not unlike the brim of a hat—thus the term "hat-shaped."

Floors, engine beds, and deep stringers

A number of other members, such as floors (or what are called "floor timbers" in wooden boats), engine beds, and the deep stringers in powerboat hulls, are sometimes built in place over a core or former. These, because of their greater depth, are often less flaring or hat-shaped, and the core is more likely to be wood or some other relatively rigid, dense material so that it will add strength and stiffness to the member and will hold fastenings applied into or through it.

Repairing and applying cored members

Cored members are relatively easy to repair or to apply as new parts against a too-flexible skin. The core, acting as a male mold, makes them so.

To repair a cored member, you have but to cut out the damaged area, taper the fiberglass well back from the edge of the break or missing portion, replace any damaged section of core, and patch in the missing fiberglass (Figure 3-10). There's just one more detail that you must see to: If the core around which this particular member is built is contributing strength to the whole, it should be repaired with a tapered, glued and/or mechanically fastened joint, *not* with a butt joint. For wood the rule is a 12-to-1 scarf (thus, a scarf 6 inches wide for wood ½ inch thick) to make a full-strength glue joint, but if the core is a laminated wood with the butts of the layers staggered, you can use similarly staggered butts in the repair. If the core is PVC foam, resin will glue it very strongly, even in a butt joint. Low-strength cores, which are only there to give the fiberglass its shape, need only be glued in place well enough to stand up under the laminating process. Once the reinforcing member is built, they just go along inside it for the ride.

To fasten formers or cores to the skin of a part until they are glassed over, hot-melt

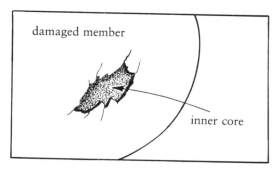

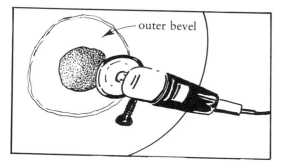

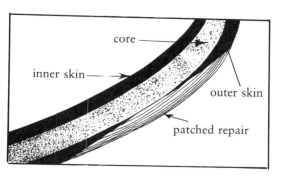

Figure 3-10. *Repairing the damaged outer skin of a cored member. Taper the fiberglass well back from the damaged edges, and make long, tapered joints between the new and original laminates.*

glue—the kind that comes in a stick that you squeeze through an electrically heated gun—is just the right, handy adhesive. Cores too stiff or too massive to hold in place with hot glue can be shored or braced in place with sticks of wood and nails or screws until fiberglass tabs or angles or sections of the covering can be deployed to secure them for the balance of the laminating.

Two general rules pertaining to laminating reinforcing members might save some problems: First, watch out for the insulating property of cores, especially the foams. By preventing the dissipation of heat, they can cause a too-thick or too heavily catalyzed laminate to overheat and "cook" the resin. With foams, one should go a little more slowly, laying up fewer layers simultaneously and using a bit less catalyst. Second, be sure to seal up the members so that they are watertight. There's not much likelihood of their not being sealed along their sides, but one might neglect to cover the core ends. Some people used to think that a wood or balsa core would rot when encapsulated in fiberglass, but the fact is, if air and moisture are sealed out, this simply won't happen. On the other hand, given access to the end grain, moisture, air, and the fungi responsible for rot will get some going. Once it starts, it will be abetted by the fiberglass wrapping, which prevents the core from drying out. Another reason for sealing reinforcing members entirely is the ever present danger of entrapped water splitting the fiberglass by causing the wood to swell or by freezing in winter.

Application of new members to weak skins

Unfortunately, as discussed in Chapter 2, some fiberglass boats are too thinly built, the result being an overly flexible hull, deck or other part that cracks its gelcoat. In such an instance you will want to reinforce the part, for, if it has not already cracked, the laminate could be next. Should you decide that reinforcing members are needed (you will remember that the alternatives are adding fiberglass layers to the whole laminate or adding a core to it), you can build them in place just as the manufacturer might have done, but didn't. The reinforcing members will do the most good if they are normal to (at right angles to) the stress cracks. Think of the cracks as hinges or folds in the laminate, and think of your ribs or stringers as stiffeners crossing them so that the laminate can no longer fold.

Make up a core the size and shape of the

member with the thickness of the laminate deducted. Precision is not terribly important unless the member being installed is an engine bed or stringer—in which case you must watch its height—or a hatch, especially the bottom surface of a sliding companionway hatch—in which case you must preserve sufficient clearance. Incidentally, it is not far-fetched to talk about reinforcing hatches, for hatches are probably broken more frequently than any other part of a boat. But we go into hatch problems in Chapter 9.

When the core is shaped and set up in place, cover it with the laminate you feel is most suited to the job the member has to do. The following details are good to keep in mind:

1. The inner skin of the part should be cleaned of grease, paint, and other foreign materials and sanded in the way of the reinforcing member in order to provide a good grip for the new materials.

2. Alternating layers of mat and roving make the best laminate in a reinforcing member.

3. Unidirectional roving laid with its strands along the axis of hat-shaped members will adapt to the corners best and will impart the greatest resistance to bending, which is what one typically wants in a rib or stringer. It is a different matter, however, with members bearing loads in a variety of directions: engine beds twisted, thrust, and vibrated by the engines bolted to them; motorboat stringers pounded from the bottom at high speed and from the top by crew tramping over them; or floor timbers, which must distribute the strings of a hung ballast keel in a sailboat and the pressures of sitting on the keel ashore in all boats. Such members need biaxial or triaxial rovings, whose strands give strength in two or three directions, both over the core and where the fiberglass is turned out onto the hull to grip the inner skin. The connection or tabbing of parts to other parts will be discussed shortly.

Repairing premolded reinforcements

Not all reinforcing members are built in place around a core. Indeed, fewer and fewer of them are so built, as, in their quest for efficiency, manufacturers have taken the fabrication of the more moldable reinforcements such as floor timbers and engine beds out of the boat and into the mold room. Nor did they stop at molding such members individually and gluing or tabbing them into the boat. Early on they turned to the next logical step, the molding of a single grid or waffle containing a number of related parallel or intersecting parts in one piece. We now have motorboats with one large grid of engine beds, stringers, and tank foundations, which also stiffens both the cockpit sole and the bottom, and we have sailboats with a waffle of floor timbers and stringers through which the keel is bolted from below while the cabin sole rests on top. That's what fiberglass and its moldability do best: make one part, and one operation, out of many.

But these members, too, can get broken or dislodged when a boat is damaged, and as repairers, we have to put them back together. Naturally, the first thing to do is to grind away any shattered areas of the member. The next move is to realign the member, making sure that the hull, sole, liner, or other parts that may have been knocked out of place are also restored to their proper shape and locations, or that they can be returned later if they have been removed for access to the area.

With the damaged parts realigned and held in place with any temporary shores, wooden cleats, and fastenings you may need, you can begin to rebuild the member. If it has a core, and any of that is missing, it will have to be patched before the laminate is rebuilt (Figure 3-11). Of course, many premolded reinforcements don't have any core. They don't need one for a form when they are built in a mold, nor do they need one for strength if the laminate is strong enough to do the job alone. This is of no particular advantage to the repairer, however. A core in a damaged member offers a form over which to lay up the patching laminate, whereas, when no core is present, the gaps left after grinding out any shattered material and tapering back the edges of holes or breaks in the member will have to be closed with some sort of backing on which to rebuild.

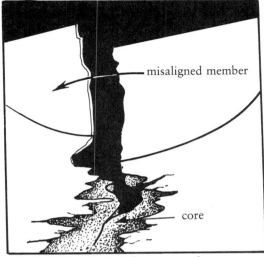

Damaged reinforcing member

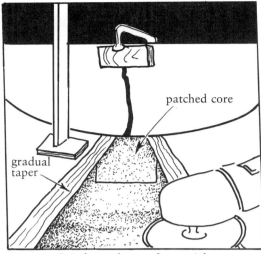

Grind out shattered material,
back to undisturbed laminate

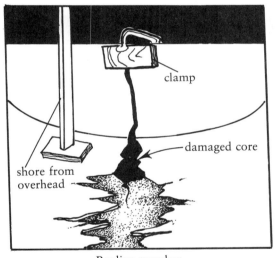

Realign member

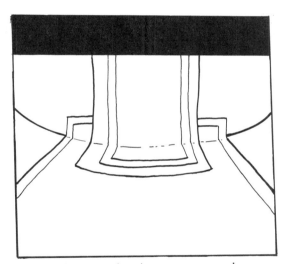

Laminate repair using generous overlaps

Figure 3-11. *Realign damaged parts and devise brute force methods to hold them in position until the repair has sufficient strength to stand alone.*

Various ways to do that are discussed in Chapter 4.

Finishing reinforcing members

Usually, since they are most often located under the sole or in the engine room, the repair of premolded reinforcing members is not a fussy job requiring a handsome finish. Builders sometimes gelcoat them anyway, simply because it is so easy to do so in a mold and because it makes the members so easy to clean of engine oil and bilge water. A strong laminate should be your prime concern, for these are strength members. To get maximum strength from a given number of layers in members that will not exactly be "on display," why not, for instance, overlap rather than butt all joints of the glass fiber materials?

The second concern is neatness. If the area is normally accessible, you don't want to tear your hands or have debris become entangled in icycles of glass fibers not flattened out, ground off, or filled in with putty. Except for such concerns, the amount of cosmetic finishing on premolded members is certainly optional.

More often than their premolded relatives, built-in-place ribs or stringers will be in plain view for at least part of their length. This calls for more care to make them fair and smooth, and to finish them at least as well as other members in the same region of the boat. This could mean that you should use butted joints to avoid lumps in the surface of the laminate, and possibly do some fairing with polyester putty as well as some painting or coating with gelcoat.

Tabbing parts to hull and deck

The list of parts that may be tabbed to the hull, the deck, and even to each other is long. Sometimes called "taping," the process involves laying up wide tapes or strips of glass fiber materials, more or less centered on the intersection of the two surfaces, to form a connecting angle of laminate with one leg attached to each part. Bulkheads, soles, joinerwork, and, of course, reinforcing members are the parts most often tabbed in place. In addition to holding the minor part in place, tabbing prevents the major part's skin from bending.

Before going further, I should mention again that there are two divergent practices for attaching minor parts and stiffening major parts. One way is to tab individual parts, the greatest number of which are wooden, to the boat. The other way is to combine a number of parts in one molded fiberglass piece, the liner, which is then fastened into the boat by tabbing its perimeter, by setting it into a mastic or bonding putty, or both. Often the two methods are combined: One model might have a fiberglass overhead liner with all plywood and natural wood bulkheads, sole, and other joinerwork. Another might have sole, berths, and counters molded in fiberglass, but with wooden bulkheads tabbed in between the molded parts, or fitted and fastened to a rabbet in the fiberglass liner, or both.

However the interior parts of your boat are configured, you are quite likely to find them bounced loose from the skin of the major parts when the boat is damaged, if you are lucky; in a worse case they may be damaged themselves. Furthermore, it does not always take an accident to loosen tabbed parts from the skin of hull or deck, for they are often worked loose by the bending of the major part's laminate as the boat crashes into seas or, if a sailboat, is distorted by the opposing forces of the rig knocking her down and the heavy ballast keel trying to keep her upright. I have sometimes surveyed boats with entire bulkheads in the way of the rig adrift, so that the only things holding them in place were bolted chainplates and contiguous joinerwork. Sometimes the owners seemed only to be aware of the chainplates leaking or a door through the bulkhead jamming.

Your task as a repairer is to reattach tabbing that has come loose. If the part that is adrift is wood or plywood, almost certainly the leg of the tabbing that is loose is the one against the wood (Figure 3-12). Wood shrinks and swells as its moisture content changes, and glass that is laid up on it does not; they therefore simply won't stick together through many shrinking and swelling cycles. This is a plain, hard fact that I have been trying to explain to boat people for about 25 years with only moderate success. Wood that has fiberglass laid up on it may function a long time without changing its moisture content drastically enough or moving far enough to break the fiberglass bond, and people often don't believe separation is inevitable—until it happens. What do you do if the fiberglass tabbing comes loose from wood or plywood bulkheads or joinerwork in your boat? Don't just reglue it, and don't grind it all away and lay up new tabbing. Refasten it mechanically.

Figure 3-12A. *A new bulkhead tacked in place. The white strip between the hull and bulkhead is a wedge of Airex foam that both prevents building a hard spot into the hull, and eases the right angle between hull and bulkhead.*

Figure 3-12B. *Bulkhead tabbing of mat/ woven roving/mat completed. Mechanical fasteners into the bulkhead would ensure that the tabbing doesn't come adrift from the wood.*

Suppose you find that the fiberglass tabbing has let go along a bulkhead or along the outboard edge of a berth, but the leg attached to the fiberglass of the hull is still as solid as the day it was laid up. You can feed the gap between the wood and the fiberglass with a little bit of tenacious polyurethane adhesive sealant such as 3M #5200 or Sikaflex 241, some bonding putty, or just some catalyzed resin, which will seal the gap if not reglue it. Before the adhesive sets, however, fasten the errant flap to the wood with a row of flathead stainless steel or bronze screws, countersunk flush with or below the surface of the fiberglass (Figure 3-13), then either cover the screwheads with a layer or two of fresh fiberglass, or putty and paint over them.

At the risk of being tiresome, I repeat: Never expect wood and fiberglass to stick together without mechanical fastening. Use nails if you wish—especially ring nails but also flatheaded shingle nails—or use staples, bolts, or rivets. If you are replacing the tabbing or laying up new tabbing, you can also hook the fiberglass into a rabbet in the wood—especially one made with a dovetail or flaring router cutter—or you can bore holes into or through the wood, fill them with disks of fiberglass, then lay the tabbing up over them. But probably the handiest way is with the flathead screws.

Should the tabbing be adrift from the fiberglass of the hull or deck—and it is just as likely to be as not if the part tabbed in was either fiberglass or very well-fastened wood—you must choose your repair carefully. You won't want to try regluing and mechanical fastenings in the loose flap if the hull or deck is of single-skin construction, for

Figure 3-13. *Despite what many manufacturers continue to think, bare wood and fiberglass just won't stick together for long. Add sealant to tabbing that has come adrift from the wood but is still solidly attached to the hull (top). Mechanically fasten the loose leg of tabbing as well (above).*

fear that the fastenings might pierce the laminate and show up outside the boat. Given sandwich construction, however, you could use self-tapping screws through the inner skin and into the core.

Some rules for tabbing

If you find the loose tabbing such a mess due to a sloppy initial installation that you will have to grind it all away, or if it is in need of replacement along with other ruined portions of the craft, the following rules will help you do it right:

1. Mark off what will be the edge of the tabbing on the hull or deck and on the part being tabbed, taking care that these edges parallel the axis of the intersection between the part and the hull or deck. To assure a really neat edge to the tabbing, and to avoid all sloppiness, cover the surrounding area with masking tape and paper. When laminate buildup on the surface of a wooden part is objectionable, you can rout a rabbet into the border of the part and lay up the laminate flush with the part's surface. It is not necessary to make all layers of tabbing the same width, so that they build up a pronounced step at the marked edge. By starting narrow and making each layer a little wider than the one previous, you taper the thickness of the legs into the surrounding surface. Starting with the narrowest strip gives each succeeding strip a new grip on the surface, while building a taper with the widest strip first would not only leave all the edges exposed, but would force all the layers to depend on the adhesion of that first strip even as they dry, shrink, and place considerable stress on the bond.

2. Be sure to grind all surfaces against which fiberglass will be applied, to remove foreign materials that might interfere with good adhesion.

3. It helps to run a small fillet of thumbed putty or triangular section of foam in the corner where the parts intersect, to make the bend easier for the fiberglass materials.

4. Another way to achieve a softer bend, and take care of a different problem at the same time, is to fit a thin piece of foam under the edge of a bulkhead or other stout part which might imprint a ridge in a single-skinned hull or deck when squeezed against it during the curing of the tabbing. By making the piece of foam wider than the tabbed-in part's edge and sloping the projecting portion like the edges of an old-fashioned threshold, you will be softening the bend, too (Figure 3-14). As stated, such a pad is only needed against a single skin.

5. What glass fiber materials should you use in tabbing? All of them have been used in some boat at some time. Mat is by far the easiest to work with. Cloth is thin and smooth, but *peels* easiest, so most builders only finish off with it. Roving is strongest by

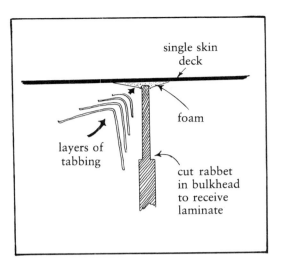

Figure 3-14. *Use a fillet of foam between the bulkhead and the hull to prevent a ridge from printing through the hull, and to ease the curve for the tabbing.*

far, and unwoven roving in its biaxial configurations—especially the 45-degree biaxial—takes the bend well enough. Don't forget to use alternating layers of mat and roving for the best combination of adhesion and strength.

6. For a neat job, cut your materials cleanly, presaturate them on pasteboard or a similar surface, and smooth them gently into place with a bristle brush or short roller.

7. The proper width of a tabbing leg calls for a judgment of how heavy its work will be and whether or not it is tapered, but common widths start at 1 inch in small boats and range up to 6 inches in a 50-foot workboat, with 2 to 3 inches being typical for a 30-footer.

8. The number of layers is again a judgment call, but you might try one layer of mat and one of roving for every inch of leg width. If in doubt, look at other boats similar to the one you are repairing, preferably older ones, and see how their tabbing has survived. A common rule of thumb states that tabbing should equal half the local hull thickness, or be equal in thickness to the inner skin in cored construction.

In truth, the design and construction details of boat models vary so much that a precise rule or chart of tabbing scantlings would be too complicated to be worth attempting. There are few reasons other than inertia not to use a little extra width or a few more layers when in doubt.

10. As a parting observation on the subject, tabbing parts to the interior of a hull or deck is like welding steel: It's a skill dependent on the conscientiousness of the repairer, but when it's done right its strength in pounds per linear inch can be tremendous, and the good things it does for a boat are of utmost value.

CHAPTER 4

Fractures, Small Holes, Delaminations

This chapter deals with the repair of areas that are not so extensively damaged as to distort the shape of the structure or completely destroy significant parts. To rebuild large holes and shattered areas, see Chapter 6. In essence, all proper fiberglass repair must go through three phases: grinding, rebuilding, and refinishing.

Grinding and cutting

Safety precautions for grinding

The very mention of grinding fiberglass makes some people's skin crawl with memories of the itch that particles of fiberglass can cause. Nevertheless, abrasion is the most efficient way to remove fiberglass material from a laminate. Like splitting wood, cutting metals with heat, or shearing fabric, grinding fiberglass takes advantage of the material's peculiar weakness—its poor resistance to abrasion. That is why the first move in making a fiberglass repair is to bring out the grinder. The best type of grinder for cutting away damaged fiberglass and preparing the damaged area for rebuilding is a disk grinder with an open or unguarded disk—which, unfortunately, throws out dust and particles more than any other tool.

Just how much protection one will need from the products of grinding depends upon the sensitivity of one's skin, the magnitude of the repair, and the ease or difficulty of avoiding contact with the dust. To be on the safe side, make it a rule: NEVER GRIND FIBERGLASS WITHOUT WEARING GOGGLES. Not only will the fine dust make one's eyes sore, but coarse disks can throw large particles into the eye at high speed.

Another danger—unseen, insidious, and alleged by many to result in fibrosis of the lungs, or silicosis, is the longtime inhalation of this insoluble dust. I've known several stubborn individuals who have ground fiberglass regularly, sometimes for several successive days, wearing either no mouth-and-nose protection or only a bandit's kerchief or surgical mask, and haven't wheezed or coughed in 20 to 30 years. But why take chances? Why not make it a rule: NEVER GRIND WITHOUT WEARING AT LEAST A TOXIC-DUST MASK, which, unlike a surgical mask, molds to a particle-tight seal around your nose and mouth.

These masks hardly bother even heavy breathers such as myself. They are also readily available and cheap enough to throw away after one use. If you can abide the sweaty-faced, restricted feeling of one of the more formal, gas-mask–like outfits—which I can't—good for you. If you are going to grind fiberglass on a regular basis, and if it doesn't fog up your goggles and cause you to walk off the staging, one of these just might let you live longer than us risk takers.

Back to the itch—which is caused not by resin particles, but by sharper-than-a-needle glass filaments—this is one side effect about which you will need little cautioning; no doubt you'll do whatever you must to avoid discomfort. The amount of discomfort the dust causes will vary not only among individuals, but for the same individual from one time to the next, according to the condition of one's skin, the nature and material of one's clothing, and even the ambient temperature and humidity. Some say that dark-complected persons tend to be less sensitive than those with light or fair complexions. Speaking as a dark-complected person, I have at times stood comfortably for hours, wearing only shorts and sneakers, while grinding pounds of fiberglass off a boat. At other times I have simply rested my arms on a surface covered with fiberglass dust and begun to itch so intolerably that I couldn't stand to wear a fresh, uncontaminated shirt and had to hold my bare arms akimbo even after washing them with cold water and soap. Glass particles are more irritating when rubbed in by clothing, and when the skin is warm, damp, and open-pored (in other words, when it is sweaty).

The best way I've found to remove fiberglass dust from my skin is to vacuum it away. Next best is to blow it away with an air hose. If neither of these is available, I dust it off lightly with a fluffy brush or cloth. Then, I prefer to wash with cool or cold water and soap.

Give glass-filled clothing a thorough vacuuming and hang it outdoors for several days before wearing it again. Washing helps with some materials, but not with all. *Don't* wash glass-filled clothes in the same load with uncontaminated clothing.

The best method of all, of course, is prevention, which begins by simply avoiding contact with the dust. When working outdoors, stay upwind from the grinder. Indoors or out, stay away from the stream of dust ejected by the grinder; to put it another way, direct the dust away from yourself. When a grinder is tilted to lay one side of the disk against the work surface, the particles will be thrown out in the direction of rotation, tangential to the rim on that side. (See, for example, Figure 4-3). This gives you a 360-degree choice of where to aim the dust, simply by shifting the segment of the rim in firmest contact with the work. After a while, these simple maneuvers will become second nature, drastically reducing the amount of dust coming your way.

The ultimate in dust and itch avoidance is the paper suit, a paper coverall complete with zipper and hood supplied by industrial safety materials suppliers (who are variously dubbed "Osharizers" or "Osharettes," in honor of the Occupational Safety and Health Administration, by more heretical boatbuilders). Denim coveralls or cotton shop coats work pretty well, but paper suits shed the dust better, and are expendable. Add goggles, mask, and gloves to a paper suit and you can be virtually itchless, no matter how thick and fast the dust flies. This is probably overkill for a small grinding job of short duration, but each individual must decide from direct experience what constitutes a short grinding job and what is too long for comfort. If I got into that argument, I would surely invite reproach from sensitive-skinned readers and scoffing from those insensitive to the itch.

The importance of grinding

We grind holes, fractures, or delaminated areas for four basic reasons:

1. To cut away damaged material so that we can replace it with sound new material.

2. To grind out a depression so that the patch can be built up flush with the original surface of the part. This is most important on the exterior of the part; if properly done and refinished, a flush repair will be barely perceptible to the casual eye. Only on the interior of the part, in a location not ordinarily exposed to view, would one want to build up a patch that stood proud of the original laminate.

3. To taper the edges of the depression so that the joint of patch to laminate around the perimeter of the damage will be a tapered or scarf joint, not a butt joint. Long before there was fiberglass it was recognized that the strongest glue joint is one with a large area of glued surface; when two pieces of

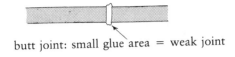

butt joint: small glue area = weak joint

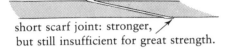

short scarf joint: stronger,
but still insufficient for great strength.

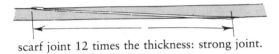

scarf joint 12 times the thickness: strong joint.

Figure 4-1. *The strongest glue joint has the greatest surface area.*

relatively thin material must be strongly joined but kept flush with one another, a tapered or scarf joint is the simplest and most effective approach (Figure 4-1). All fiberglass patches are made this way; the more widespread the glue joint, the longer it will endure.

4. Finally, we grind to remove wax, dirt, grease, paint, gelcoat, and even the shine or polish itself from the damaged area, so that these do not interfere with a strong bond be-

tween our patch and the glass-fiber reinforced layers of the original laminate. The strength of the bond is enhanced by removing materials that inhibit it chemically or physically; by removing the slick surface that may cause the resin of the patch to prefer cohesion to adhesion, the visual symptom of which is "beading up" on the surface; and by exposing the glass reinforcement in the original laminate to the grip of the new resin (Figure 4-2). Indeed, it has been proven in tests that the strongest secondary bond is one where the glass fibers of the original laminate are not only exposed by grinding, but are partially pulled up out of the laminate by laying on a layer of heavy cloth or woven roving in resin, then ripping it off before it cures completely. Few builders or repairers that I know of go to this length.

What grinder to use

For many years, to grind damaged areas, I used heavy, right-angle, high-speed, 6-inch to 8-inch industrial disk grinders with coarse, cloth-backed disks. By coarse I mean from number 36 or number 24 grit down to grits that more closely resemble a scattering of small, sharp rocks on the backing. The coarser the grit, the faster the material is

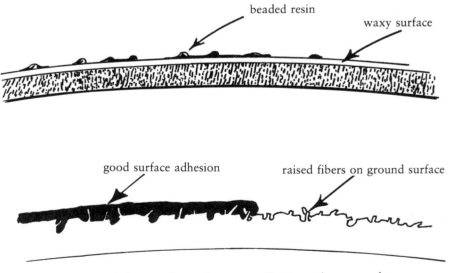

beaded resin

waxy surface

good surface adhesion

raised fibers on ground surface

Figure 4-2. *Judicious use of the grinder will ensure adhesion of new work to old.*

abraded; when there is much material to remove, these big old grinders make short work of it.

If you need to cut a piece right out of a laminate, the grinder can be fitted with a rigid abrasive wheel that will cut through the heaviest laminates with relative ease. Abrasive wheels are somewhat safer to use on a hand-held power circular saw, the guard and platform of which help to contain flying pieces—not only of the work, but of the wheel itself. However, the same wheel in a grinder can attack the work *from* any angle, *at* any angle, making it more versatile. In either case, heed the warnings printed on these abrasive wheels, which, although capable of cutting off solid steel in some compositions, can fly apart at high speeds.

No doubt about it, like any hand-held power cutting tool, grinders are generally dangerous and should be handled with profound respect. The most frequent accidents are caused by winding up a loose shirt or jacket, or sometimes the power cord of the tool itself. Then there was the time one of my men, who was sitting on a staging, tired of holding the grinder up to the boat and dropped the still-turning disk against his thigh. Naturally, a move like that is rarely repeated in the same shop. Indeed, the story spreads far and wide, rendering the surrounding region safe from a sequel.

Not necessarily less dangerous, but certainly handier for grinding and cutting fiberglass, is the recently spawned generation of smaller, lighter, right-angle grinders designed to operate with 4-inch to 6-inch disks. Operating at extremely high speeds, these little rascals can waste away fiberglass like crazy, yet they can be held up to the work using a fraction of the muscle required to wield their heavy-weight predecessors. They are produced in both electric and compressed-air models by a number of domestic and foreign manufacturers. Along with differences in sturdiness, durability, and price between models intended for "home workshop" or "industrial" use, one ought to consider not only the versatility or range of features and accessories offered, but also the availability for it of expendable supplies.

When I was shopping for one of these little machines, I talked with two boatbuilders in cities only 45 miles and a state line apart. One builder was disgusted with his brand X machine because the dealer who sold it to him never stocked more than one or two grits in the disks, and no abrasive wheels or other products at all. He left the machine in its bin and bought several brand Y machines, for which he could get all the supplies right off the dealer's shelf. Meanwhile, the other builder was delighted with his brand X machine, had no trouble getting everything he wanted from his dealer, and pointed out that both the machine and its supplies were cheaper by far than the brand Y package. Both men were sending the same message: Check out the dealer just as carefully as the product.

Cutting

Prior to grinding, irregularly shaped or ragged-edged holes are best cut to a convenient shape with a saber saw or small circular saw. Special fiberglass-cutting blades are available, or an abrasive cut-off wheel can be used in a circular saw or grinder. These wheels tend to throw debris and should always be used with a shield. The outer skins of cored construction are best cut with a circular saw set shallow, or a small (guarded) cutting wheel on a grinder.

Rebuilding

When a damaged area is small and shallow relative to the original laminate's thickness, it is not always necessary to rebuild with glass fiber mat and roving goods. To put that statement another way, when the break or hole does not significantly weaken the surrounding area, it might only need filling with a tough, tenacious material such as polyester body putty, which will protect the spot from water penetration and erase it cosmetically. Naturally, the decision to putty the damage rather than build up a patch similar to the original laminate depends on one's assessment of whether or not a significant amount of strength has been lost.

Assume you've struck some rocks, leaving ugly gashes ¼ to ½ inch deep covering 4 to 6 square inches in the 1¼-inch-thick laminate near the bottom of your 40-foot boat's keel. These would hardly be a serious problem to a laminate not only made thicker than need be to take the abuse of docking and grounding, but also backed up by the ballast keel within.

On the other hand, a ⅛-inch-deep, two-foot-long groove gouged along the single-skin topsides at a boat's bow quarter by a spike sticking out of a piling could be quite serious if the total thickness of the laminate were less than ¼ inch. With nothing backing up the middle of the topside skin, driving hard into sizable seas could split open the skin along the groove. In addition, unless the putty were tough, elastic, and formulated from a base or resin with excellent gluing qualities, flexing of the topsides could cause it to fracture or pop out of the groove.

Thus, in the case of the topside gouge, the wisest repair would be to reinforce the area with alternating layers of mat and unwoven roving; you would need at least one layer of the latter, running across the gouge to "sew" it together. But the gashes in the keel—ugly looking or not—might safely be filled with body putty as long as grinding didn't expose fractures extending farther into the laminate. If deep fractures are found, they ought to be ground open into a very shallow V to provide a suitable gluing surface for glass fiber reinforced laminate.

One obvious clue to whether fractures extend through the laminate is dripping bilge water (or oil). Because ice forming in such holes or fractures is likely to reopen the wound, I would not recommend a shallow, cosmetic covering of the area in freezing climates. A damaged area with water dripping from it often frustrates the would-be repairer. Almost everyone who has worked at all with polyester resin knows that water or dampness will inhibit its cure. Yet many amateurs, and boatyard repairers too, will attempt to get away with slapping a "hot patch" of mat or body putty over a drip coming from a damaged spot. Most of the time it doesn't work, but all too often one will think it has—then soon, perhaps not until the next day, it's: "Damn! There's that drip again."

Even epoxy resin–based products that set up underwater can let a drip through when the boat is hauled. It only takes a high enough head of water, which translates into pressure, to push the uncured resin aside, and the drip will migrate through the thickest patch. Short of a proper repair with fresh laminate, only hydraulic cement is fully effective at stopping a leak through a fracture from the bilge of a boat, especially when applied inside.

Recently, while surveying a fiberglass sloop with its prospective buyers, I pointed out some chewed and battered areas on the bottom, after part of the hollow keel. To see if any of these spots were leaks, I thought we should take another look after the water still dripping from her hauling had dried up. Sure enough, when the rest of the bottom had dried off, one of the gashes was still wet and dripping at the unalarming rate of a drop every 8 to 10 seconds. That afternoon, I received a call from the boatyard's superintendent, who said that because the damage happened on the yard's mooring at low tide the yard felt responsible, and so his men were "repairing the damage with Bondo" before relaunching the boat, which he hoped would save the confusion of listing the damage and recommending its repair in my survey report. I thanked him.

Being in the neighborhood just before the yard's closing time, I drove down alongside the Travelift and hopped out to see the smooth and freshly painted repair. Glistening on the surface under the keel was a gathering drop. Oh no! Oh yes! It was water, not paint. As I climbed back into my car, the superintendent appeared. "It's tricky business," I offered, "stopping a drip with a hot patch, and as you can see on the sloop there, it doesn't always work. Next time there's a drip and no time to dry it up, tell them to try some hydraulic cement, which is often used to stop leaks in masonry. It swells up as the water wets it, and stops a leak in a few minutes. Two brands sold around here are Water Plug and Water Stop."

I am not a swift thinker, so it was some-time later that I began to be bothered by what had transpired. It wasn't the tiny drip itself; it was the true nature of the damage that it indicated. If the hollow part of a boat's keel was crunched deeply enough to have water seeping out, there must be at least one frac-ture extending all the way through. Sure, the glob of body putty might prevent any serious leaking, but in the New England climate, who's to say that water lodging in the frac-ture wouldn't open it up farther during the freeze-thaw cycles of the winters? Probably, I decided, it is always wise to grind back dam-age that is leaking until at or very close to

the interior surface of the laminate around the source of the leak, and to repair the whole thickness of the laminate there (Figure 4-3). That would, of course, require repair with a laid-up patch of laminate, not with a quick filling of the area with putty.

A place for epoxies

Lest readers get the impression that only polyester resin–based laminates or putties are advocated here for patching damaged fi-berglass, it is time again to mention epoxy resin–based materials as a frequently used al-ternative. As a rule, epoxy resin is a decidedly stronger glue than polyester resin. It is also more resistant both to penetration and to

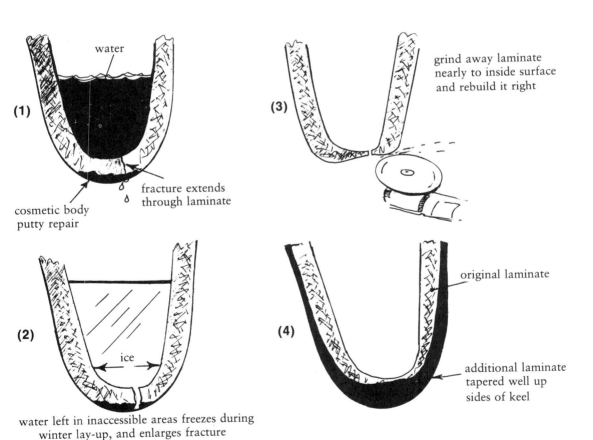

(1) water · cosmetic body putty repair · fracture extends through laminate

(2) ice · water left in inaccessible areas freezes during winter lay-up, and enlarges fracture

(3) grind away laminate nearly to inside surface and rebuild it right

(4) original laminate · additional laminate tapered well up sides of keel

Figure 4-3. *Cosmetic repairs that continue weeping may indicate more exten-sive damage: investigate.*

chemical degradation by water. These are most attractive properties for the base material—the glue, as it is sometimes called in the trade—of a patch, but epoxies do have some unattractive properties, too. They are much more expensive than polyesters, they are more toxic, their cure time cannot be fine-tuned on the job merely by adjusting the amount of catalyst added, and they are hard to use. To explain that last complaint, it is hard to wet out reinforcing materials with epoxy, and also difficult to keep it where you want it—that is, to prevent sagging or draining from a laminate before it cures.

Nevertheless, epoxy products can at times be the best to use, especially in small- to medium-size repairs. In such, the small quantity of material needed makes its cost a minor factor, while its superior glue strength often allows a simpler, less time-consuming approach. Some epoxy body putties are extremely strong and tenacious and will successfully seal damage one might not dare to repair in the same way with polyester body putty. Likewise, a laminate using glass fibers or any number of other reinforcing materials in epoxy is often enough stronger than one made with polyester resin to allow it to be built thinner and lighter, with considerably less labor, yet with undiminished physical properties. Lately, more and more boats are being built with epoxy resins and such high-strength reinforcing materials as the various unwoven rovings, Kevlar, and graphite (carbon) fibers. To date, almost all boats using the latter two have been custom or semicustom built high-performance boats, both sail and power. Nevertheless, all such boats are likely to need repair someday, and when they do, epoxy resins and glues should be used.

Over a decade ago, I carelessly threw an M-80 firecracker in a poorly aimed trajectory that landed it under the forward seat of a grandson's shiny new fiberglass pram. The explosion burst out a small patch of the bottom, which was, I believe, built with two layers of 1-ounce mat and one of 6-ounce cloth, for a total thickness of approximately $\frac{1}{16}$ inch. Not wishing to make a conspicuous patch job of the repair, and being anxious not to endure the joshing of my family any longer than necessary, I pushed the ruptured fibers back flush with the outside of the bottom and patched the inside with one small patch of glass cloth set in a puddle of soupy epoxy body putty (obtained from our General Electric dealer for patching the interior of our 20-year-old dishwasher, and nearly the same color blue as the inside of the pram). That repair, accomplished in about 10 minutes, was cured enough for my grandson to use the boat in an hour or two, has faithfully done its job ever since, and probably will for the indefinite future.

Epoxy body putties are made by innumerable companies nowadays, but one of the well-known earliest products is Marine-Tex, formulated and sold by Travaco Laboratories of Chelsea, Massachusetts. Over the years, repairs with this legendary product have been made to many different types of damage on fiberglass boats, even to such hard-to-repair metal objects as engine parts, exhaust lines, and fuel or water tanks. Everyone long involved in boat repair, amateur or professional, has a Marine-Tex tale to tell, including yours truly.

Some years ago, after repairing and refilling an integral fuel tank that took up the entire after end of a 38-foot fiberglass sloop's hollow keel, we were dismayed to see, just as the tank was topped off, that the fuel had suddenly found a way to drip out around the through bolts of the bronze rudder heel fitting on the after, lower end of the keel (Figure 4-4). It was a discouraging development after several days' work on the only previously evident leak, a crack in the bottom of the keel/tank caused by grounding. That job had required steaming out the tank via a handhole cut in the side of the keel and a drainhole drilled in its bottom, grinding and rebuilding the cracked area, adding more layers on the outside around the bottom of the tank, and filling up a few inches of it inside with a "keel putty"—which comprised a filler of chopped glass fibers in casting resin. Since this filler covered and was presumably sealing off the heel-fitting bolts—I had reached in and molded the putty with my hand into a knee at the after corner—how was the fuel getting to the bolts? Would we now have to start

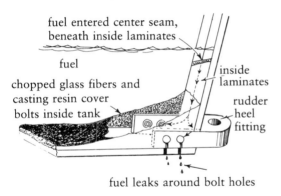

fuel entered center seam,
beneath inside laminates

fuel

inside
laminates

chopped glass fibers and
casting resin cover
bolts inside tank

rudder
heel
fitting

fuel leaks around bolt holes

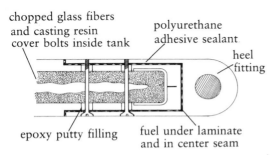

chopped glass fibers
and casting resin
cover bolts inside tank

polyurethane
adhesive sealant

heel
fitting

epoxy putty filling

fuel under laminate
and in center seam

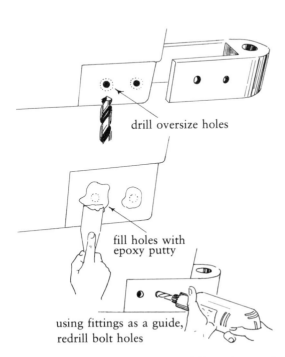

drill oversize holes

fill holes with
epoxy putty

using fittings as a guide,
redrill bolt holes

Figure 4-4. *Repairing an insidious integral fuel tank leak in a two-piece hull joined on the centerline.*

over, emptying, opening up, and steaming out the keel tank again?

It was the best of luck, if not some subconscious instinct, that had us watching closely enough to notice that, after pumping out perhaps ten gallons of fuel, the drip stopped. How could this be?

Somewhere, probably along the after edge of the keel, we reasoned, the fuel must be finding a passage inside the laminate from near the tank top down to the region of the heel fitting. Otherwise, why should it stop leaking out altogether as soon as its fuel was lowered a few inches?

The fact that this hull was one with a centerline joint—one at least partly laid up in the "half shells" of a split mold, then joined with layers of fiberglass bridging the centerline on the inside—gave credibility to our theory. Hoping that the drip really would hold off, we purchased a Marine-Tex kit at a nearby boatstore, quickly removed the heel fitting, overbored the bolt holes across the keel to more than twice the bolt diameter, flushed the fuel oil out through them with acetone, and filled them with Marine-Tex. When that cured, we rebored the holes for the bolts, using the fitting in place as a guide, and refastened it after seeing that everything was well bedded in 3M #5200.

While we had the bolt holes enlarged, we looked into them to see if there was a crack on the centerline where the laminates of each side met. There certainly was, and it was damp with fuel oil. The leak, we knew, would be cured if we did a good job of sealing it off at the bolt holes. Cured it was, and the most satisfying feature of this anticlimax to the main repair was the knowledge that it had the superior adhesion and mechanical strength of Marine-Tex, which would not likely be shaken loose by anything less than another whack against a ledge, and a terrific one at that.

Backing up a hole through the laminate

When damage to fiberglass includes a hole right through the laminate, its repair with limp glass fiber materials and liquid resin requires that one side or the other be backed with a relatively stiff sheet material against which to do the lay-up. The best place to put the backing is against the outside of the boat, provided one has access to do the patching on the inside; if the backing has a smooth waxed surface facing inward, the patch will mirror that surface, and when uncovered will be relatively smooth and fair with the surrounding laminate. Thus, backing a patch on the outside will automatically eliminate most of the fussy hand-finishing labor that is otherwise required to blend a repair with the surrounding surface.

Unfortunately, it is not always practical and sometimes not possible to work on a patch inside the boat. The hole may be located behind interior joinerwork or in a sealed compartment, or even in the overhead, where the repairer would have to defy gravity. When such is the case, one has to console oneself by remembering that it is handier and generally more pleasant to be working outside.

In either case, the following are the steps for patching a hole in the laminate:

1. Grind the edges of the hole on the surface opposite where the backing will be, aiming for a taper width 12 times the thickness of the laminate. The result should resemble a beach around a pond, the edges of the holed laminate tapering upward and outward from the backing, against which they should rest a relatively sharp terminus.

2. Apply the backing, which can be Formica, hardboard, sheet fiberglass, thin aluminum or steel sheet stock, or melamine-coated wallboard. With the exception of melamine-coated board, to which polyester resin will not stick, any of these needs to be well waxed.

What if you can't get at a backing on the interior to remove it once the hole is glassed over? In that event, you could just let the patch stick to it. The backing would then add to the strength of the patch, and if you made it of sheet fiberglass (as described in Chapter 6) and set it in place in wet mat or epoxy glue, the backing would become an even greater asset.

Backing can be held in place over the hole with self-tapping screws applied into the surrounding laminate. When there is too little space to do that on the interior, the backing can be blocked or wedged in place from behind, or, if the interior space is only accessible from the outside, it can be fitted in pieces, the last one held in place with a handle—screwed on or hooked through a hole in it—until it can be fastened.

Fitting the backing over the hole in pieces is also useful to better fit the compound curves that comprise so much of a boat's shape. Reconstructing a compound curve becomes a matter of more acute concern as the hole gets larger, and the subject is therefore dealt with in more detail in Chapter 6; a brief introduction here will suffice. It is impossible to bend any inelastic sheet material in two directions at once. To put it another way, sheet stock can be bent over a cylindrical or conical shape, but never a spherical shape—not unless a number of tapered slices, which dressmakers call "darts," are cut out of it wherever it wants to buckle. One can do that to fit sheet material on gentle compound boat curvature, but a better shape is developed over strong compound curves by cutting the backing material into strips of 6-inch down to as little as 2½-inch width—the more curve, the narrower—and applying them diagonally across the bend. Speaking of bends, one should carry any backing piece that spans a curved area out onto the surrounding laminate—the sharper the bend the farther out—because the depth of overlap is what tends to arch the backing over the hole in a fair curve with the surrounding shape (Figure 4-5). The backing material must be flexible enough to take the local curve as well as to overlap the hole generously, or there will surely be an unfair flatness to it, and thus to the patch.

3. As long as they are reasonably close, seams between pieces of backing should not be a big worry; any resin or gelcoat that works into them will become a ridge on the surface of the patch, which can be ground off when the backing is removed. A strip of Scotch tape over the outside of a seam, a bit of wax or modeling clay worked into it from

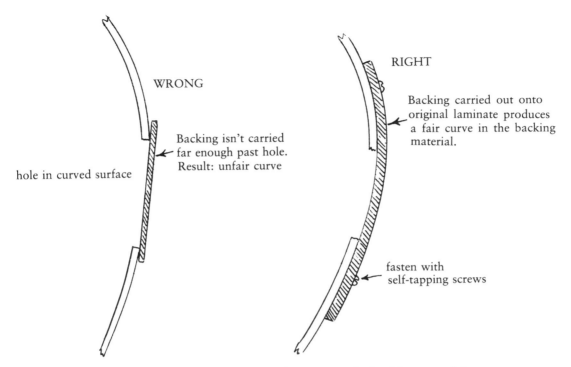

WRONG

hole in curved surface

Backing isn't carried
far enough past hole.
Result: unfair curve

RIGHT

Backing carried out onto
original laminate produces
a fair curve in the backing
material.

fasten with
self-tapping screws

Figure 4-5. *When backing holes in curved surfaces, carry the backing material far enough past the hole so that it will conform to the surrounding surface.*

the inside, or both should suffice to minimize its effect.

Before applying the backing, a wide area of the laminate around the hole, beginning close to its edge, should be waxed to protect it against unwanted bonding with resin or gelcoat that oozes out from under the backing. To protect the area directly below the backing from the almost inevitable runs, newspaper or wrapping paper can be hung with masking tape (Figure 4-6).

4. If the first layer of the patch is contiguous with the gelcoated face of the surrounding laminate, it should, of course, be gelcoat too. Its color should match the original as closely as possible—not always an easy job, even when one can start with the very same product used in building the boat, for staining and fading may have affected its hue since that time. Gelcoat mixing, matching, and application is discussed in Chapter 3.

5. When the gelcoat has cured, two layers of mat should be applied over it and al-

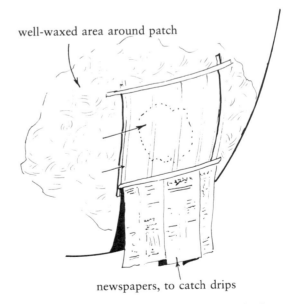

well-waxed area around patch

newspapers, to catch drips

Figure 4-6. *Wax the area to be patched to prevent the backing from adhering to the hull.*

lowed to cure. Under ideal moldroom conditions—65 to 80 degrees Fahrenheit, dry air, and good but not blazing actinic light—one layer of mat next to the gelcoat might be alright. Under any conditions less than ideal, however, two layers are always safer, because their greater mass generates more exothermic heat, helping along the cure. Complete cure is important in these two layers because they will set the shape of the part; pouring on more layers before these two are hard could cause excessive heat and shrinkage, which would distort the part.

6. Once the first layers have cured, the balance of the laminate can be built up over them. Again, it is wise to limit the number of consecutive layers laid up between cures to no more than four, for too many layers at once can overheat the laminate and "cook" the resin. Depending on the size of the patch, the proportion of catalyst in the gelcoat, and the ambient temperature, dampness, sunlight, or other radiant heat/light sources, four layers may be too many. One is better off to pause and let a laminate cool off than to reduce the amount of catalyst below the manufacturer's recommended minimum, since too little catalyst invites a different but most embarrassing problem: undercure. Resin that is so starved for catalyst that it remains partly uncured indefinitely is worthless. Physically soft and weak, it will, when long immersed in water, be washed out of the laminate, returning the fiberglass materials to their limp, cloth-like, prelaminated state. Undercure and cooking are discussed in Chapter 7.

Such limitations aside, building up the patch is a relatively straightforward, quickly completed job. To streamline the process, all or most of the layers of glass fiber materials should be precut before catalyzing any resin. Working from the backing outward, each piece should be cut a little larger than the one under it, so that they spread up the slope that has been ground into the edges of the hole (Figure 4-7). If anything, each piece should be a bit oversize, for it is easier and a stronger job to snip a little off the wet pieces, if necessary, than to fill in the edges with small scraps if they fall short. At the same time, chopped strand mat in particular tends to be

forgiving in that one can compress or stretch its shape considerably once it is thoroughly wet out and the binder holding the strands in position has dissolved.

It is logical but by no means mandatory to employ the same laminate schedule in the patch as that used in the original laminate—the same materials in the same order and number of layers. One can usually see well enough what the schedule is by examining the edges of a laminate, but a precise determination can be made by burning a small sample, which will leave a neat though fragile pile of the glass fiber materials as laid up. If you have the curiosity to burn a sample, be forewarned that fiberglass laminate burns furiously, once it reaches its kindling point of over 800° Fahrenheit, and even a small piece gives off a disproportionately large quantity of foul black smoke. Choose a safe, outdoor place, such as a small fireplace or surround of bricks, and use a propane torch to start the burning. Anyone with access to a small electric pottery kiln that can be moved outdoors will find it an ideal tool for reducing a sample to the glass fiber materials.

The vast majority of existing boats will be found to have laminate schedules based on alternating layers of mat and woven roving. The exteriors of these laminates often have an extra layer or two of mat between the gelcoat and the first layer of roving to keep the roving from printing its pattern through to the exterior finish and to make the first layers more watertight.

Many boats built before 1960 were built exclusively with chopped strand mat rather than alternating mat and roving, while many built in late years have used alternating mat and unwoven continuous strand roving rather than woven roving. Woven roving adds strength and stiffness to a laminate, and unwoven strands make a stronger laminate than woven ones. For convenience in laminating, all types of roving can be obtained with a mat backing, use of which automatically produces an alternating mat and roving laminate.

You need not hesitate to use the unwoven continuous strand materials in place of woven roving, since you can build up more

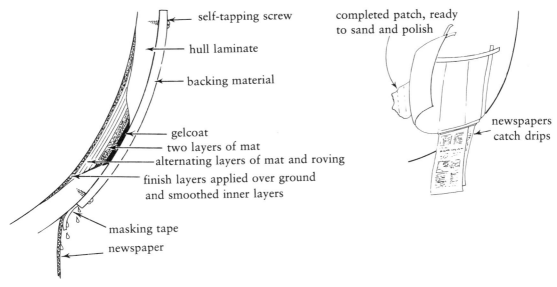

Figure 4-7. *Duplicate the original laminate schedule when patching. For maximum strength, the new layers should overlap the old and be carried up the ground-in slope surrounding the hole.*

strength with them in a patch of the same total thickness. But remember if you use unidirectional roving that a layer of strands running in one direction has almost all its strength in that direction. To get strength in other directions, you must vary the strand orientations of succeeding layers. Biaxial and triaxial rovings fill that need.

7. As the patch approaches the level of the surrounding laminate, looking ahead to how one is going to end it could save some unnecessary work. If the patch is being built toward the outside surface of the part, remember that two layers of mat are best for the final, outer layers before the gelcoat or paint. When building a patch toward the interior, you may want the final layer to be the same material used on the original inner surface, just so that the patch won't be too conspicuous.

In order to bring the repair reasonably fair and flush with the original surface, it is a good idea to stop one or two layers before the last and grind or putty out of existence any pronounced irregularities that have developed in building up the patch (Figure 4-7). Excessive grinding or a great thickness of

putty on the outside of the last layer of glass fibers will thus be avoided, and forethought will be rewarded with a final interior finish that blends well, or an exterior finish that can be more readily polished to perfection.

Patching cored construction

Different core materials yield laminates with widely varying characteristics, including their repairability. From that point of view, the best core at this time is unquestionably PVC foam, the original brand of which is Airex. Along with excellent heat and sound insulation and improved stiffness, this wonderful stuff absorbs no water, bonds chemically with resin, is resilient under impact, and therefore limits damage when clobbered. No other core used at this time—be it wood, plywood, balsa, honeycomb, polyurethane foam, mixed polyurethane and PVC, or fiberglass ribs surrounded by foam is likely to come through an accident with fewer problems than PVC foam.

In general, the presence of a core in a damaged laminate adds two concerns: First, if composed of an absorbent material, the core adjoining the damage may be water saturated; even if nonabsorbent but laid up in small blocks (such as PVC blocks on a scrim backing), the core may have admitted water into the crevices between blocks. The second concern is that there may be unseen delamination of the fiberglass skin from either or both sides of the core, extending outward from the visibly damaged area. Core saturation is dealt with in a separate chapter. Delamination of the skin from the core is treated in the same manner as delamination of layers of skin, as covered in the sections that follow.

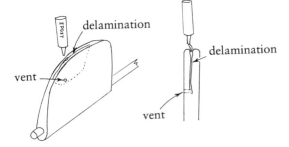

Figure 4-8. *When filling delaminated areas with resin, let gravity work for you; be sure to vent the area to allow air displaced by the resin to escape.*

Delamination

When a laminate is holed or partly broken into, peripheral delamination of the damaged area becomes a crack in the edge of the laminate as one grinds away the separated layers. The sure way to cure such faults is to keep on grinding until they have been eliminated, but one need not cut back the entire thickness of the laminate. Removal of one side, inner or outer, until the laminate has a step or rabbet along the plane of the delamination will do very well.

Sometimes when a damaged area is cleaned up along its edges, a delamination crack will be found enough open—or openable—to allow working polyester or epoxy resin into it. That should take care of it, as long as it is thoroughly sealed and glued, but filling an interstice with resin through a crack in one edge is not an easy thing unless that crack happens to be along the top edge of an inclined or vertical laminate, so that liquid resin can flow in while the air flows out. If practical, it is worthwhile to tilt the part so that gravity will help the regluing (Figure 4-8).

A laminate does not have to be holed, or even showing fractures on the outside surface, to contain delamination. Hard blows or other distorting forces which overbend the laminate can shear internal layers apart—by sliding one past the other—without disrupting the integrity or appearance of the surface layers at all. In a solid fiberglass laminate, such splitting without associated fracture at one surface or the other is rare, and is usually caused by the presence of poorly bonded, resin-starved, or undercured interior layers. Most often, it is the cored constructions that suffer internal delamination without fractures in the exterior layers. The reasons are that the resin bond between fiberglass layers and cores—other than PVC foam—is almost always weaker than that between fiberglass layers, and, again with the exception of PVC foam, the core is usually less flexible. When the laminate is bent, the layers on the outside of the radius of the bend are forced to lengthen relative to the inner layers. A weaker core bond lets the fiberglass skin break away from the surface of the core; when the core material is weaker than the bond between it and the skins, the core will shear internally before the bond lets go.

"Sounding," or tapping with a light hammer or mallet, is the usual method of detecting delamination, regardless of whether it occurs between a core and the fiberglass skins on either side, between layers of the skin, as shearing within the core, or as two or more of the foregoing in combination. Any laminate so affected will sound different when struck than a laminate with no delamination.

If there is no gelcoat or paint on the surface of a laminate, one can often see delamination through the translucent resin. It looks very much like a light-colored sandbar in murky water.

Softness in a laminate, as felt underfoot or noticed as a dent in the hull made by a cradle arm or boat stand, will very often be an owner or surveyor's first clue to internal delamination. Except for such softness, and sometimes a faint puffy look, there is little external evidence: no leaking, and certainly no change in the boat's behavior. True, delamination can usually be found by sounding. But since in my experience the condition has always made itself known in some way on the exterior before it became a menace, I would have better use for my time as owner or surveyor than tapping every inch of the boat on the slim chance of discovering incipient separation, unless there was such probable cause as a recent accident or an alerting symptom.

Repairing delamination

When one does become convinced that an area of a part is delaminated, it will be wise to give the situation some careful study before attempting a repair. In some cases, major surgery may not be at all necessary. In others, it could be a waste of time to do anything but cut the area open. In still others, direct repair is impractical, and the most economical approach is to build up more laminate over the affected area. Prior to formulating a plan of action, one needs to know how extensive the damage is, and whether the interior is wet or dry.

How extensive is the damage?

If you are still unsure how to answer this question after pressing and thumping the delaminated area, you can always bore exploratory holes. Naturally, these should be bored where they will leave the least conspicuous traces, or where cutting for repair may have to be done. You might bore them from the inside of the laminate if the damaged area is accessible there and if the inner surface is unfinished or easier to patch than the exterior surface. The inner skin of a cored laminate is also more appropriate for probing—and repairs too—when accessible, because it is usually significantly thinner and structurally less important than the outer skin. Holes in the exterior of a deck should be located in the smooth areas between nonskid surfaces whenever possible, because it is just about impossible to remove all traces from a nonskid pattern without refinishing an entire section. If you must bore holes in nonskid, at least try to place them in a regular pattern that might somewhat satisfy the orderliness of the beholder's eye. If it helps, mask off a suitably shaped area around the holes while patching them, and fill it in with smoothed and polished gelcoat. Double trouble can be avoided if exploratory holes are kept from breaking through the opposite surface of the laminate.

If studying the edge of a laminate by looking down a hole—or probing its sides with a fine pick whose tip has been heated redhot and bent 90 degrees—is unsatisfactory, you can bore out a sample with a small holesaw, dowel cutter, or even a bung cutter. If there is delamination, the tool will bring up the top layer as soon as it cuts through the plane of separation. Its teeth should be well set on the inside, and it should be fed straight and steady lest it break off the sample prematurely.

Is the delamination dry?

If the interior of the laminate is dry where delaminated, repair will be relatively simple. If it is wet, repair will range from troublesome to nearly impossible. If wetness is confined to a delamination cavity between relatively impervious fiberglass layers within a solid laminate, or to one between a fiberglass layer and a sealed or nonporous core, then it might be dried out by flushing with acetone, or, at worst, by cutting an opening in one side of the laminate down to the delamination.

On the other hand, if there is a saturated core involved in the delamination, you will find that in order to dry it out in a reasonable time one whole skin will have to come off the wet area, and the saturated sections of core may need to be cut out, too. In this instance, covered in Chapter 5, internal delamination requires patching similar to that done on holes and fractures.

In a few still worse cases, one might encounter a hull or deck with an almost entirely saturated core; the core may be a disintegrating wood or a delaminating plywood with one or both fiberglass skins separating from it. This unfortunate state of affairs, too, is covered in Chapter 5.

Regluing by injecting resin

In the late '60s my shop was building the balsa-cored fiberglass hulls and decks of a famous one-design sailboat class for a hot sailor who specialized in fitting them out with "go fast" details for racing customers. Every time he visited our shop he would plead with the men: "Go easy with that resin! That's heavy stuff. The balsa core soaks it up like crazy. The last boat was lighter, but you can get more weight out; just cut back that resin!" A couple of years later, this chap called me to say he was returning a boat whose bottom was delaminated, and that I was to rebuild it or build a new one, free. "The owner is mad as a hornet," he said, "and threatening to sue me. If he does, I'm suing you!"

I was sympathetic but adamant. "Sorry, my friend. You're the one who kept after the men to be sparing with the resin. Now I suggest that you bore some holes in her and feed that starved balsa core some more resin. You're just lucky it's not wet inside or you'd have to cut out both the inner skin *and* the balsa core and replace them. Better use epoxy resin; it's a better glue, and that's what she lacks."

He must have done so, for I heard no more. That's boatbuilding: like walking the high wire. The moral of the incident is that a builder should never never starve the core/fiberglass interface for resin. Doing so is the most common contributor to delamination.

Fortunately, the fault can often be repaired by feeding new glue through one or more relatively small holes, and that's why it is best to study the delamination before committing oneself to the unnecessarily arduous approach of cutting sections of skin off the part. It's another matter when there are fractures of the fiberglass skins, deformation of the shape, water within the laminate, or a crumbling foam core of a kind that resin won't stick to. One cannot expect an injection of resin to cure such problems. But a dry, firm, gluable core from which one or both fiberglass skins have broken loose really only needs regluing. Polyester resin will often do, but epoxy resin is stronger. It is also more forgiving of a wide glue joint or void, does not need to be under pressure between the surfaces to be glued, and is more tolerant of moisture.

Whether internal delamination is in a hull or deck, only a few small holes are needed to reglue it. One for running resin in and one for letting air out are enough if the area is not more than a square foot or two. Additional holes are added as required to spread the resin through larger, irregularly shaped or unconnected sections. To find out whether resin is likely to spread throughout an entire delaminated area, you can bore a hole near the lowest point and another near the highest point, the former for putting the resin in and the latter for letting the displaced air escape. You will know whether resin can make it across the area by whether air blown into the resin hole at low pressure comes out at the vent hole. Whatever you do, *don't* insert an air-compressor hose into the resin hole, for it could easily spread the delamination. If you can't blow easily through the space from one hole to another with a short length of hose and your own lung power, the resin isn't going to make it, either.

Once satisfied that resin will penetrate a given area, you can tap the resin hole and screw a small piece of pipe into it (or, if the surface skin of the laminate is too thin for that, glue the pipe over the hole with hot glue or other fast glue), fit a length of hose and a funnel to the pipe, and pour in the resin (Figure 4-9). The resin should not be too thix-atropic, or viscous, unless the void of delamination is known to be generously wide. The height of the funnel above the area of delamination adds pressure to help the resin penetrate and fill the void. At resin weights of 10 to 11 pounds per gallon, each foot of height adds over half a pound of pressure per square inch, or 72 pounds per square foot. A bit of care is in order not to raise the resin column to such a great height as to put a lump in the part's contour or propagate the separation.

Retaining the shape while regluing

Should the laminate be so flexible as to swell out easily, or should it already be distended, some arrangement to keep it aligned while regluing it will be necessary. If the delamination is in the upper side of a deck, a weight or weights on a waxed piece of plywood should hold the skin in a fair attitude. In vertical or overhead locations, shores, through bolts, or self-tapping screws may be needed to do the same job.

I do not remember a repair in which a fiberglass skin was dished in and tended to

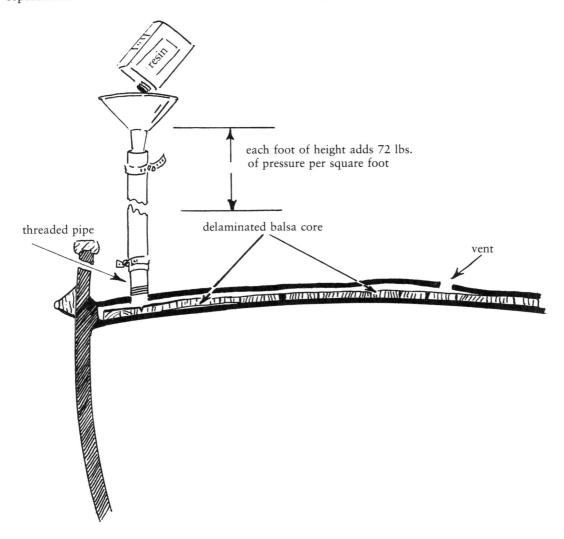

each foot of height adds 72 lbs. of pressure per square foot

threaded pipe

delaminated balsa core

vent

Figure 4-9. *With a little ingenuity, resin can flow under pressure into delaminated areas.*

stay that way without being itself fractured and in need of a patch. If you should encounter such a circumstance, however, the depression can be raised with a method we used for spreading collapsed centerboard trunks. Self-tapping screws are threaded through the dished-in skin, and are used—with their blunted points bearing on the opposite skin—as jackscrews to push it back out to its normal level.

Wax the work area

In this operation, as always when working with resin on a fiberglass part, be sure to wax the surface of the laminate at and around the delaminated area, just in case resin drools over it. Protection of a surface with wax is much easier than cleanup with rags and solvents, not to mention restoring a ruined finish if resin bites it and hardens.

CHAPTER 5

Dealing With Core Problems

Delamination of the interface between a core and one of its fiberglass skins was examined in the previous chapter, but cores sometimes develop degenerative problems that threaten to destroy a part from within. The root of such a problem is inevitably some unsuitable physical property of the core material, and the two properties that most often get cores into big trouble are saturability and crushability. There are two classic examples: balsa core, which is inherently very porous, and the lightweight foams, especially those of 3 pounds per cubic foot or less in density, which are easily crushed. (Any foam, regardless of the material from which it is compounded, can be made excessively light.) Inappropriate use of these cores is one of the leading causes of problems in aging fiberglass boats.

Saturation—an introduction to the problem

Recently, I read a magazine advertisement aimed at eradicating the notion that balsa-cored construction is saturable. Samples sawn out of a laminate cored with end-grain balsa blocks and positioned below the low-water mark for three years were said to have taken no water into their interiors through the raw edges.

Now, despite the fact that you may be reading this because some part of your boat has a saturated balsa core, the demonstration seems to prove that it's possible to construct a balsa-cored laminate through which water does not readily migrate. Admittedly, my experience indicates that a high degree of impermeability can be achieved by piling on resin during the lay-up until the relatively thin balsa blocks are saturated almost from one side through to the other via their end-grain surfaces, and the cracks between adjoining blocks are also filled. The problem is that not every builder wants all the added weight and expense that soaking a balsa core with resin will impart. Thus, in the interests of speed and economy, and out of ignorance or a cavalier attitude as to eventual consequences, we continue to be faced with the repair of balsa-cored decks that spurt water like a clam flat when walked on, and balsa-cored hulls out of which water trickles like a natural spring for days after hauling. If this is your problem, you are not alone. My own experience leads me to believe that most balsa-cored laminates are saturable eventually, once water finds a way in.

Is it always balsa?

By my guess, 80 to 90 percent of all fiberglass decks built between the mid 1960s and mid 1970s were balsa-cored. In the decade before that, natural wood and plywood had a bigger share, first as substructures overlaid with fiberglass, then as cores in sandwich laminates.

Both wood and plywood are still used in both ways (see below), but less often and sometimes only locally, such as beneath deck hardware, where greater compressive strength than that afforded by balsa is needed. Since the mid 1970s there has been a substantial increase in the number of boats built with cores of PVC foam, such as Airex, and foams that are mixtures of PVC and polyurethane. Almost all foam-core materials—as well as several new core products, most notably the honeycomb cores—are "closed-cell" or nonporous and do not pose a saturation problem; some are "crushable," however, as we will discuss a little further on. Saturable foam cores are rare but do exist; I haven't seen any lately, but if you do run up against one, treat it like a balsa core in the matter of whether to dry it out or to replace it if it is too generally soaked.

Balsa is still used in more decks than any other core by a wide margin, and is still being used in a substantial majority of cored hulls, too. It is not surprising, then, that most of the decks and hulls that turn up with saturation are balsa-cored; there are simply so many more of them that their problems greatly outnumber those of laminates cored with other kinds of wood and plywood.

Saturated wood and plywood

If you find that your deck, hull, or other parts contain saturated wood or plywood, the causes and cures are quite similar, except in a few details, to those for balsa, which, after all, is but a very soft wood. Cores of wood or plywood are harder and denser than balsa, and not as easily crushed; they do not readily allow the fiberglass skin to be bent inward until it is fractured by such deck crunchers as lifeline stanchion bases, boat davits, padeyes for turning blocks, or mooring cleats. That is why you may have found wood or plywood blocks substituted for balsa core under such items. You may even have found that your entire main decks are cored with wood or plywood, especially if they consist of narrow side decks and small forward and after decks peppered with heavily loaded

through-bolted hardware, such as on a sailboat with a large cabin trunk and cockpit. Considering the greater strength and toughness of such a core, there is certainly nothing wrong with it, at least as long as water is kept out of it.

Unfortunately, when water gets through the fiberglass, wood or plywood absorbs it just as surely, and eventually just as thoroughly, as would a balsa core. If you are lucky, and the entire deck is not yet saturated, you can locate the causes and repair the leaks. The first thing to do, then, is to figure out and eliminate the causes of saturation; this, of course, applies to any porous core.

How water gets in

In a deck, the many fastenings in hardware and trim—whether self-tapping screws, bolts, or rivets—can leak as they loosen or as the bedding around them loses its "life" (its resilience, or mastic self-healing tendency) over the years. Further, the bases of heavily stressed items such as lifeline stanchions can apply pressures that crush the core enough to crack the fiberglass skin over it.

In hulls, water usually gains access to the core around through-hull fittings and bolts or screws in guardrails or hardware.

The fiberglass skins of both decks and hulls can be cracked by impact, too. Sometimes the fiberglass will split from buckling, twisting, or bending strains, and to make matters worse in cold climates, once water has gotten into the laminate it inexorably enlarges any passage or pocket as it alternately freezes and thaws through the winter. In warm climates the swelling of wood and wood products as they absorb water creates a pressure much like the expansion of water into ice. Thus, once inside a laminate, whether cold or warm, water can propagate damage, making new inroads for itself as it goes. Such damage includes but is not limited to progressive delamination of the fiberglass skins from the core, the splitting open of the skins themselves, and the spread of saturation.

Confined and accessible area of deck saturation

Localized and accessible areas of core saturation are troublesome but certainly feasible to repair. Even if the core must be excavated, the laminate can be rebuilt in place. When the saturation is more widespread—perhaps involving the entire deck—other, more drastic measures are demanded. As discussed later in the chapter, the deck must either be replaced or beefed up with several new layers of laminate to compensate the lost strength. Here we deal with the repair of localized saturation.

Dry out the core if possible

Small saturated areas can sometimes be flushed out with acetone. Water is diluted by the acetone, with which it readily mixes, and is carried away; the residue then evaporates rapidly, leaving the core material dry. Because it is very volatile, one should take care not to ignite acetone with sparks or flame; keep the area well ventilated, and have a fire extinguisher handy.

Heat lamps, hair dryers, and industrial hot air blowers—or just the warm, dry air of a heated building—are helpful in drying wet core materials. But solvents or dry air can only help insofar as they can circulate over the wet surfaces. The more encapsulated the water is, the more difficult or tedious removing it will be. It is almost always necessary to open up either the inner or outer fiberglass skin to expose enough core surface to get at the moisture, and coaxing it out can still be such a frustrating experience that one may become impatient and simply excavate all of the core that is sodden.

When wrestling with the question of how much saturated core to cut out, it might help to remember the words of a boat storage and repair yard owner who said, "I like to build a boat or two every year, even if we don't make a profit on them, because I find that men who have not built a boat recently, or possibly ever, are prone to shrink from cutting away parts that are essentially destroyed. They'll go to ridiculous extremes to preserve the shape and form by patching up what's there, when they ought to cut it out and replace it with new work. A patch that doesn't make the area as good as new is bad for business in the long run."

Try for repair from the interior first

Because of the nonskid pattern and the high polish that would have to be replaced on outer deck surfaces, one should first study the possibility of removing the less difficult-to-replace inner skin to get at a saturated core. Should total saturation be confined to a cabin top, a modest section of the main deck, or a cockpit sole, there is often hope of reaching it from below without disturbing the boat's interior too drastically. Of course, the overhead is nobody's favorite place to laminate fiberglass. Even with advice from those who've been there, it can be a tricky business. If you decide to do it anyway, here are a few tips to ease the learning process:

- Cover the surfaces below the work areas with resinproof dropcloths, paper, or plastic.
- Use a fluffy paint roller to apply resin to the surface. It will drip less than a brush if rolled carefully.
- Wait until the wetted-out surface is sticky before trying to lay up fiberglass materials against it.
- Rather than plastering wet mat on the overhead before offering the core up to it, wet the mat down on the core, then shore the pieces of core up against the overhead. (Note that one may also use a filled epoxy or a polyester core-bonding adhesive such as Mor-Bond, available from the Airex distributor, to offer core material up against a vertical or overhead fiberglass skin.)
- Another way to save labor and trouble— provided the deck is not too curved—is to

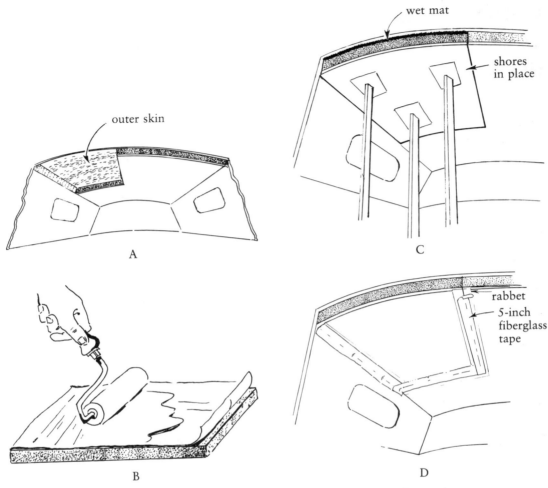

Figure 5-1. *The easy way to repair a section of saturated core from the inside. A. Remove section of saturated core, leaving the outer skin. B. Add laminate to the underside of the fitted core material. C. When the laminate on the replacement core has cured to the consistency of leather, add a layer of wet mat to the mating surface of the core, then shore and wedge it in place until cured. D. The new joints are then bonded to the surrounding laminate with fiberglass tape, no less than 4 to 5 inches wide. Grind a rabbet into both parts to receive the tape, then use enough layers of tape to fill flush.*

surface the *underside* of the pieces of core with one or more layers of the fiberglass inner skin, and allow this to cure to the "leather-hard" stage before shoring the core up against the overhead (Figure 5-1). Thus, only a tape of fiberglass around the edges will be needed to extend the layers onto the adjacent original laminate, sealing in the new core.

How about installing a new core and outer skin from the exterior?

When a section of deck outer skin is cut out, it creates the problem of matching your new surface to the gelcoat and nonskid pattern of the original deck. A close match is not necessary if the repaired part is separated from the rest of the deck, as are house tops or cockpit soles, but when new and old areas are adjacent, they need to look alike. Should the original nonskid pattern be dulled, faded, crazed, or cracked, the easiest way out of the matching problem is to grind and repaint the deteriorated surface with nonskid paint or gelcoat, and finish the new laminate the same way. Should the original nonskid pattern be in good shape and nicely finished, you *can* make your new nonskid areas match it. To do that, you would take a mold off some of the original nonskid (Figure 5-2), then lay up a thin piece (or pieces) of gelcoated nonskid fiberglass to cut, fit, and glue down on your repaired work.

If the two steps of making a mold and then making a piece of nonskid seem too much, it is possible instead to make a relatively thin and reasonably flexible mold off the original gelcoat, cut it to the size and shape needed, wax it well, weight it down in wet gelcoat on the repaired and smoothed deck, and leave it there until the gelcoat cures. A serious objection to this shortcut is the possibility of trapping air bubbles, which will ruin the look of the imparted pattern and leave you with the onerous job of grinding a spoiled attempt off the deck. In contrast, a piece made in a mold can easily be disposed of if spoiled, and it is much less likely to be spoiled, because one can see and eliminate bubbles during the lay-up.

Because it is virtually impossible to match the tiny bumps and grooves of nonskid, you should always leave smooth margins around new sections applied over a deck patch, either making your cuts in the deck in the middle of existing margins or making new margins

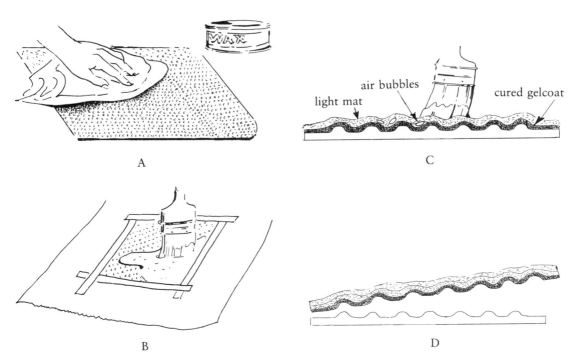

A   C

B   D

Figure 5-2. *To replace damaged deck areas that have molded-in nonskid, make a mold from a similar, undamaged area. A. After cleaning, thoroughly wax the nonskid area with parting wax. B. Tape and mask off the desired size and shape, and spray or brush on gelcoat. C. Add one layer of lightweight mat to the cured gelcoat. Be sure to work out all air bubbles. D. When enough layers have been added and cured to make the mold retain its shape, the mold is removed, the entire process repeated, and there's your new section of deck.*

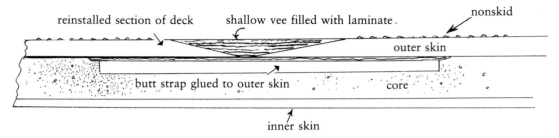

Figure 5-3. *When a cut-out section of deck is to be reinstalled over a core, the joint should be ground to a shallow vee and filled with laminate, leaving a smooth, 2-inch-wide margin around the repair. If you can work a butt strap of laminate under the edge of the work area as shown, letting it flush into the core and gluing it across the joint, you will make the repair even stronger.*

if necessary. If your new margins create a problem with symmetry, tape off and fill in matching margins in the original nonskid.

It is all but inconceivable to me that you could find a totally saturated and physically endangered deck under an adequately strong outer skin with a crisp, well-preserved non-skid pattern, but if you do, and need to cut it open from on deck, then you ought to try to save the piece cut out. Later you can re-place it, making smooth margins spanning any edges that had to be cut across the non-skid pattern. A margin in which the upper skin is butted ought to be at least 2 inches wide to allow a tapered V-shaped joint with its apex in the center of the margin (Figure 5-3).

Getting rid of the causes

When a deck flexes and squishes underfoot—especially if it has cracks and splits through which water oozes—you know that the upper skin was built too thin. It will not do merely to patch the lesions; the entire deck must be made thicker and stronger with ad-ditional laminate (see below). On the other hand, if you find that the fastenings of hard-ware or trim are admitting the moisture, aided perhaps by localized fractures at the bases of highly stressed items of hardware, you should rebed all suspect fittings, trim, and through fastenings. To prevent the re-currence of fractures, you may want to re-move the core under the hardware causing

the problem, then fill the pocket—which should extend as far as is practicable past the perimeter of the base—with solid fiberglass laminate, a filled polyester or epoxy resin, or at least with a piece of hardwood to prevent further crushing of the core. Most effective in spreading out such cruel stresses as those imposed by stanchions are backing plates, preferably of stainless steel, bronze, or—when weight is critical—aluminum (see Fig-ure 9-2). These should be larger in area than the hardware base (unless the base is very large), installed below deck, and in severe cases complemented by a matching plate above deck.

Total deck saturation—mushy balsa, rotten wood, delaminated plywood

I wish nobody needed the following discus-sion, but I have seen enough decks destroyed by saturation to know that as long as thou-sands of decks are built yearly with porous cores, there will be unfortunate owners won-dering what can be done about total satu-ration with associated mushiness, rot, or delamination. If your boat is in such a condition, don't despair. The nature of fiberglass is such that a boat can be resurrected from almost any disastrous state short of complete fragmentation. Before we discuss cures, let's review the ways in which these conditions develop.

What causes it?

It would be blunt but quite accurate to ask "who" causes it rather than "what," for proper actions by builders, storage and repair yards, and owners could have prevented every deck saturation disaster I have seen. Neither natural occurrences nor acts of God, they stem from the following:

1. Builders cause initial saturation by making the deck's fiberglass skins too thin. This is especially true of the outer skin, which becomes fractured and, being exposed to the weather, lets water into the core. But, of course, a too thin inner skin tends to make the laminate more limber and causes the outer skin to bend more, initiating and propagating more fractures.

2. Builders are also responsible for the grabrails, lifeline stanchions, bow and stern rails, and sundry other items of deck hardware and trim whose fastenings, if not properly bored for, installed, and sealed off with bedding, feed water into a porous core. In truth, it is almost inevitable that the best such installations must develop leaks someday.

3. After the builder, the responsibility for preventing saturation rests with the owner in conjunction with his repair and storage yard. It is, one would think, the owner's concern and the yard's job to head off saturation through preventive maintenance, but owners are often uninformed, sometimes penurious, and sometimes cavalier. At the same time, many storage yards today are so loaded with captive customers that their operators do not need to care about proper storage, know much about repair, or have anything to do with monitoring or improving a boat's condition. A deck that has leaks has a fair chance of becoming totally saturated through a series of mistreatments: The boat may be

stored outdoors without a cover, or with one that is inadequate, inviting water to penetrate every deck weep for the entire storage period. Every fracture may then be split open by swelling of a wood core, and every leak enlarged by ice in cold weather. To make matters worse, the boat may not be leveled in storage so that its deck and cockpit sole will drain; she will acquire a pond in each unscuppered low point, thus guaranteeing a supply of water to hasten the destructive process. Worst of all, even though it usually takes six to fifteen years for saturation to creep throughout the deck laminate, nobody notices until the process is well advanced. That total saturation is ever reached is incredible; one would think that somebody along the way would become aware of squishiness underfoot or of water weeping out of the laminate, and warn the owner of impending trouble. But until the deck is grievously soft, or water drips onto the accommodations, the slow deterioration is often unnoticed or ignored.

Why a mushy core is a disaster

Saturation, aside from adding more weight to a deck than you might think—which is certainly a detriment to stability—is not itself the ruination of the laminate, but the destructive events it engenders are. First, there's mechanical damage. When you stomp around on a saturated deck, the water your foot hammers down, being incompressible, tries to hammer the laminate apart with about equal force, eventually delaminating the skins from the core. Moreover, the swelling of a wooden core and the freezing of water inside any laminate both tend to blast the laminate apart with expansion.

Another saturation byproduct is core disintegration. This is not the place to take up the long-standing argument about whether or not balsa core rots; nevertheless, anyone who has cut into many balsa cores knows that—call it what you will—balsa can get very mushy. From a practical standpoint there is usually so much delamination of a badly saturated core from the fiberglass and dissociation among the core fibers—not to

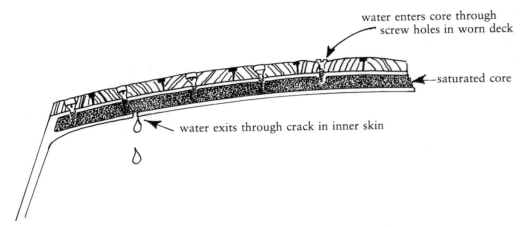

water enters core through
screw holes in worn deck

saturated core

water exits through crack in inner skin

Figure 5-4. *A saturated core's cause can be far removed from its symptom,
and can remain undetected until the core is near complete saturation.*

mention the difficulty of drying the core
out—that the question of whether it would
return to its original stiffness when dry would
seem academic.

There is no question that, in the presence
of fresh water and oxygen, natural wood
cores can and do become infected with rot,
which causes them literally to disintegrate.
Rot begins as a local condition around each
split or other access passage of the saturating
water, but over a long period of time it will
continue to spread as far as moisture and oxygen permit.

A saturated plywood core can also be attacked by rot, but if it was made with non-
waterproof glue it can be destroyed much
more quickly by delamination of its plies. Interior-grade plywood is manufactured with
non-waterproof glues, while the exterior and
marine grades use waterproof varieties.
Either of the latter grades, if free from voids,
is acceptable for use in cored fiberglass construction. I cannot remember having seen any
U.S.-built boats in which interior-grade plywood was used for a laminate core. Not so
with foreign-built boats, which, at the time
of this writing, regularly turn up with delaminated plywood deck cores. Two examples I
saw in 1985 and 1986 were in boats manufactured in 1975 and 1978, respectively.
Both had teak decking applied over the fiberglass outer skin, which had developed
myriad leaks through the holes of the fastenings for the teak staves. Even if this obvious

engineering failure was caught and the use of
interior-grade plywood core was subse-
quently discontinued in conjunction with a
teak-deck overlay, one may still wonder
when sisterships built at the same time without teak overlays (the teak being optional)
will develop the same problems. In another
5, 10, or 20 years? Could it be that the other
shoe will never drop because the core will
never get wet, except perhaps locally? In the
normal course of events it would seem that
some of these cores, too, must eventually become delaminated.

The nature of a boat's construction con-
tributes heavily to the disastrous nature of
total saturation. The deck is often completely
inaccessible from below without cutting out
overhead liners, removing lockers and other
joinerwork, or both. Even if one can get at
a deck quite handily from below, he is still
faced with the awesome job—which we will
discuss a little further on—of working from
beneath to repair it.

Cutting away either the inner or outer
skin of a deck in order to remove mushy core
leaves but one fiberglass skin to retain the
shape of the deck, without the supporting ri-
gidity of the core and the second skin. If the
deck supports a cabin trunk, cockpit tub, and
possibly a pilothouse, connecting these to the
hull as well as fixing the plan and profile
curves of the sheer or deck edge, these structures will be left literally resting their not in-
significant weight upon the remaining single

skin and an occasional bulkhead or bit of joinerwork. Careful shoring up would be crucial to prevent distortion of hull and deck and sagging of the deck structures.

Taking the above factors into consideration, it is indeed a disaster when a deck's core is destroyed—or at the very least a big and expensive repair job.

The alternatives open to you as the owner are to buy a new part or to add more laminate to the outer fiberglass skin, making it strong enough to stand alone.

Replacing the deck with a new one

It may be possible to obtain a new deck or section of deck from the manufacturer, if the mold is still available. This is a neat, clean way to put a boat back into like-new condition as far as her deck is concerned. The main obstacle is the frequently very realistic doubt that the rest of the boat is worthy of such drastic action. There can be no doubt that it will be expensive to replace the entire deck molding, which usually includes the main deck, its cabin trunk(s), and its cockpit tub in a cruising sailboat. In a powerboat the molding will probably not include a cockpit tub, but may include some part of a pilothouse as well as a cabin trunk. Only on a small, half-decked, open or cuddy-cabin craft can the replacement of the deck with a new one be considered a relatively simple, inexpensive job.

The only way to ascertain the viability of installing a new part is to find out the cost of the part and get—or make up—the best estimate possible for the job of taking out the old part and installing the new one. Add to the subtotal what the boat would sell for in its present state, then compare the total with the likely fair market value of the same model with a new deck. All yacht brokers have the BUC Book of yacht prices, plus experience in what boats like yours are selling for locally, but you would be wise to seek more than one estimate; assessments of a given boat can vary substantially.

A new deck is a good option in a relatively new boat, but a boat with a ruined deck core is likely to be in her teens, by which time her fair market value may be considerably diminished relative to the cost of a new part and labor.

Procedures involved in whole deck replacement

When replacing an entire deck molding, the most convenient place to join the new deck to the hull is at the original deck joint, for that is the established faying surface to which the new deck's edge fits as molded (See Figures 1-12 through 1-16.) With most deck joints you have but to remove the metal fastenings from the joint, then cut away the old deck and any mastic, filled resin, or glue between the deck and hull. You will often find, especially in the better-built craft, that the joint was sealed with a layer or two of fiberglass; you will have either to cut the glass along the line of the join or perhaps grind it away.

There will sometimes be a great number of connections that must be parted. Fiberglass tabbing and mechanical fasteners between the deck molding and bulkheads, lockers, and other joinerwork must be cut or removed. The rudderport, if it is a tube from the hull to the cockpit sole or aft deck in a tiller-steered boat, must be cut loose at its upper end. Wheel steerers with cable drive to a quadrant need only have the wire removed to break their connection to the hull, unless the rudder stock continues up past the quadrant to an upper bearing fast in the deck molding. A hydraulic steerer's tubing must merely be disconnected, but almost all mechanical steerers have to be disassembled before the deck can be lifted off. Any electrical wiring that crosses from hull to deck must be disconnected. All hoses, pipes, deck drains, tank fills, and vent lines leading to deck fittings must come off, as must ventilation ducts and hoses, smoke pipes, engine exhaust line hangers, centerboard pendants, chainplates, and hawsepipes.

The above list may sound too obvious to mention, but enumerating the connection points serves not only to point out how many systems may need to be disconnected before the deck can be lifted off, but also to remind you that these systems plus myriad items of deck hardware, joinerwork, and trim must be removed from the old deck and reinstalled in the new one. My aim is not to discourage you from the task, for it involves fairly straightforward mechanical boatbuilding work in almost all facets, and I believe that any handy person can manage it.

Are you sure you can handle installing the new deck?

An entirely different set of logistics, however, is involved in actually lifting off the old deck, lifting on the new one, and fastening it in place. This is a move for which any manufacturer worthy of the name is particularly well set up, and for which you are likely not to be prepared in any way except will and savvy. Given the will there is certainly a way, but it could be more economical to ship the hull to the manufacturer to have the new deck fitted when it is pulled from the mold. There is another reason for having the hull nearby when the deck comes out of its mold: Not all deck-to-hull joints were created exactly equal. The two parts sometimes need a bit of force to make them match, and having at least one of the parts "green" or recently molded makes the slight necessary distortion easier. Then, too, if there is a head liner involved that the manufacturer normally pops into the deck before joining the deck to the hull, you may face another tricky business best accomplished with green parts by workers who do it regularly.

Even if you have the manufacturer fit the new deck, you will have plenty of work loosing connections and removing trim and hardware from the old deck and reinstalling it all in the new one. From cockpit scuppers to liferails, lifelines, grabrails, hatches, and deck hardware, there may be as much or more work than you want.

If you *do* want to take on the whole job yourself, you can enlist the lifting power of a boatyard's mobile sling lift or a contractor's crane. Your decision boils down to your particular circumstances, your location, and above all the economics of each alternative.

In any event, keep in mind the weaknesses or flaws in the original deck's construction, installation, or fitting out—especially those which caused the total saturation—and see that they are not repeated. Foremost consideration should be given to elimination of the porous core. Unless the manufacturer has already upgraded his laminate schedule, you might have to pay extra for a nonporous core, but the gain is worth the expense. Should the manufacturer refuse to alter the core, you might prevail upon him to add a number of layers to the fiberglass skins—the outer one particularly. If he won't even do that, you might have the part made without gelcoat and add some layers yourself, or you might eschew a manufactured deck and rejuvenate the one you have as described below. After all, at this point, you're not to be blamed if you're a bit squeamish about what's in your deck laminate.

Even if you get a proper new deck schedule with a nonporous core, it is important that every fastening through or into your new deck be well bedded, that there be generous backing plates, and, if I may leap ahead to the time when your boat is back in action, that she be covered or stored under cover if in a cold climate. It's difficult to take seriously, because you can't watch it happening, but wet, freezing, and thawing weather needs only time to work its way into an exposed deck.

If replacement of the deck turns out to be unfeasible, don't be discouraged; read on.

Leaving the deck in place and adding laminate

A wonderful attribute of fiberglass is that if it isn't doing its job, you can often bring it up to full performance by adding more layers. When total core saturation has ruined a large portion of your deck, and all other repair methods are too complicated, disruptive, or costly, you still have the option of adding laminate onto the exterior until the outer skin can, in effect, stand alone as a single-skin structure. This simple, direct avenue of repair requires little preparation other than removal of any hardware or trim from the area needing reinforcement and grinding away the gelcoat so that the new layers of fiberglass can get a good grip on the original laminate. With the surface thus readied, you will find it relatively easy to lay up enough fiberglass layers to restore full physical strength and watertight integrity to the structure.

This repair has but one possible disadvantage: The added fiberglass will add some weight to the deck, about 1 pound per square foot per 1/8 inch of thickness. (On the other hand, it can be argued that letting the saturated core dry out will remove the very substantial weight of water the deck has been carrying around.) Only in a high-performance racing boat will the added weight affect performance noticeably, which is why I consider this method of repair best suited for cruising boats.

Fortunately, the core in most decks is confined to the horizontal walking surfaces: to the trunk top, but not its sides; to seats, hatch tops, and cockpit soles, but not coamings or seat fronts; and to the center of the main deck, but not where it turns up into coamings, trunk and house sides, and bulwarks or toerails, or where it fits into a deck joint. In these non-walking areas, builders usually bring the skins of the sandwich together into a single skin (Figure 5-5) for a number of reasons: The extra stiffness of the sandwich is mostly needed for the intense local pressure of walking. It is less expensive and troublesome to fasten hardware through a single skin, be it portlights, fairleads, genoa tracks, or hinges. It would be quite impractical to fasten the edge of a sandwich to the hull at the deck joint, and unnecessarily difficult to carry it around bends onto trunk or coaming sides or bulwarks. It is troublesome to install core against the vertical surfaces of the deck mold, but relatively easy to put it down against the horizontal surfaces, which, with the mold upside down when the part is being laid up, are actually the undersides of the overhead surfaces. Even if none of the above mattered, sandwich construction would still be left out where possible simply because it is more expensive to produce.

The frequent reversion of a sandwich to a single-skin state as you trace it across a deck is good for your repair efforts, because it limits the span of the cored area you have to reinforce and at the same time offers an abutment of solid single skin on which to anchor additional layers.

Let's examine the repair procedure in a bit more detail, applying it first to a cockpit sole.

Beefing up a sole that's ruined by saturation

If sodden, or perhaps sopped, are the best words you can think of for the condition of the core in the cockpit sole of your boat, then she has something in common with a 12-year-old, fast 22-foot bass boat that I saw recently. Underfoot, the balsa-cored laminate felt more like thin saltwater ice than a deck. Stepping near a 2-inch hole for wiring, normally covered by the steering console, caused water to squish out as from a sponge, and I could pluck chunks of balsa out of the raw edge of the hole with my fingers. Just from walking around on a sole like that, one can tell that almost every square foot of it is saturated. What should one do?

As outlined for other parts of the deck, you can, if the boat is worthy of the expense, cut out the entire sole and either rebuild it or, if possible, consider having the manufacturer make a new one for you.

Dry it out and repair it? Not likely! It took years for this sole to be attacked through its too-thin outer fiberglass skin—around hardware fastenings or through stress cracks that developed into fractures. It took more years for these leaks to be enlarged and extended, and for saturation to spread by gravity, capillary action, the pumping effect of crewmembers tramping on the sole, the destructive action of freezing, the separation of the fiberglass skins from the core, and finally the collapse into mush of the bloated end-grain fibers. To undo this long process of saturation would also be a long process. It would call for nothing less than complete perforation with holes followed by a long bake in a hot, dry atmosphere. Even if dried out, the original structural stiffness, which depended upon the I-beam effect of the two fiberglass skins (in effect, the flanges) held apart and anchored by the core (analogous to the web of the beam) would be destroyed.

No, in a sole this badly damaged, simple repairs won't do. In the case of the 22-foot bass boat it was decided that an entirely new sole would add too much expense. In addi-

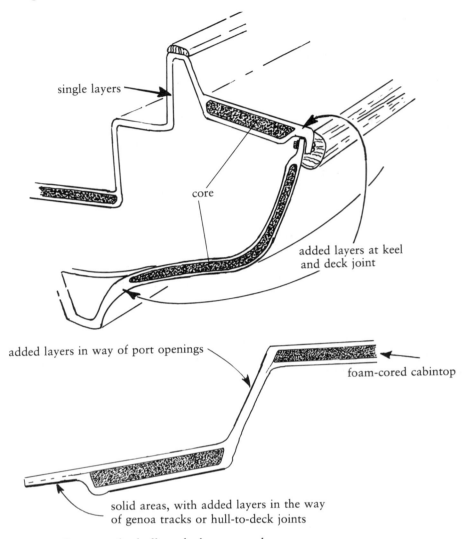

single layers

core

added layers at keel
and deck joint

added layers in way of port openings

foam-cored cabintop

solid areas, with added layers in the way
of genoa tracks or hull-to-deck joints

Figure 5-5. *Not all areas of a hull or deck are cored.*

tion to the sole's problem, this boat's single-skin bottom had become hand-push flexible due to stress fractures caused by pounding at high speed, and it would be unreasonable for the cost of repairs to exceed the limit posed by the cost of a new hull and deck parts with the small parts, hardware, and engine transferred to them. To stay well below the $12,000 cost of that alternative while leaving several thousand dollars for the more crucial hull work, I outlined the following procedures for the sole repair:

1. Bore regularly spaced 3-inch holes through the fiberglass skin with a hole saw, letting only the lead drill make its 1/4 inch

hole in the lower skin. Space the holes no less than 6 inches nor more than 12 inches away from each other and from all solid edges, the exact spacing depending on the flexibility of the particular area underfoot. Stagger the holes in each row halfway between the holes of adjacent parallel rows, so that you create diamond patterns, not squares. Clean the balsa core from the holes.

2. Let the water in the core drain through the hole saw's lead drill holes, a process you can encourage by walking around the sole. Hasten drying with a blast of hot air, by letting the boat sit in a dry, heated environment, or by using radiant heat such as a heat lamp or sunlight. Finally, plug the 1/4 inch lead

holes and flood the 3-inch holes with acetone.

3. Once the holes are reasonably dry—or you are ready to give up—fill them flush with the top surface of the sole using wafers of PVC foam core. If any moisture remains, use underwater epoxy rather than polyester resin to glue in the wafers, or seal the weeping balsa core with hydraulic cement, then follow with epoxy glue for the wafers. If the holes are thoroughly dry, you can use polyester resin.

4. Grind the deck to clean it, rough it up, and remove the gelcoat. Do not grind across the PVC-filled holes, or the grinder may scoop out deep recesses in the soft foam.

5. Shim up the removable hatches until they project above the present deck level the thickness of the proposed added laminate—in this case 1/8 inch—and pad out their edges with sheet patternmaker's wax, thin wood, or aluminum strips (Figure 5-6). The strips should be well waxed with bowling alley or mold release wax. When the additional sole laminate is brought up against the hatch, these strips will ensure clearance around the hatch perimeter to raise and lower it freely. That clearance should be no less than it was in the original rabbet. By the way, you should wax the hatch rabbet so that any resin running into it will not stick. Later, you will want to build up the bottom of the rabbet so the hatch will come to rest flush with the top surface of the added laminate. Depending upon the hatch construction, it might be easier to build up the bottom of the hatch instead, but usually, building up the rabbet is easiest.

It is not necessary to raise a caulked-in tank hatch. You can simply grind its top and cover it with the added laminate. To help prevent gluing it fast with resin, its rim should be plugged with wax if not already caulked. To provide for the day when the hatch must be opened to service the tank, make a shallow groove over the rim in the still-translucent added laminate that will print through subsequent paint or gelcoat. Cutting around the rim with a saw or cutting wheel, using the groove as a guide, will release the hatch.

6. The lay-up schedule for the additional laminate should include a number of layers of a nonwoven roving alternated or backed with chopped strand mat, followed by two layers of mat on top for watertightness. The total thickness of the added laminate ought to be no less than 1/8 inch.

7. Finish with paint or gelcoat, imparting a nonskid pattern.

Preparing a deck for its added outer skin

Turning our attention to the main deck, the following steps will get it ready for the addition of more laminate:

1. If the deck has a teak overlay, remove the teak.

2. Remove all deck hardware installed over the sandwich part of the deck or in the immediately adjacent single-skin laminate of house sides, deck joint, or bulwarks where you want to terminate the new layers.

3. Cut away the outer skin wherever the base of a stanchion or some other item has compressed the core and perhaps fractured it. Make an opening extending a few inches beyond the sides of the base that are over sandwich laminate. (Stanchions especially are likely to straddle the transition from sandwich to single skin.)

4. After scooping the core from those areas and drying the exposed edges of the excavations as much as is practicable, refill the openings with a harder, less compressible core, such as polyester autobody putty, aluminum, wood, or plywood—whatever the situation and your circumstances seem to require. You can even build up a solid block of fiberglass laminate for all or part of the thickness, using scraps of glass fiber materials to make a good, stiff filler. That takes a bit of patience, but it gives you an excellent solid footing for hardware.

5. This is the hardest step on which to advise you. You should provide some way for the saturated core to dry out. I do not mean that you must eliminate all saturation before you can proceed with the additional upper skin lamination. Far from it; after all, the core may take a very long time to dry. I favor laying up the extra layers while the core is still saturated, simply by sealing off any lesions in the original outer skin with hydraulic cement, underwater epoxy, water-

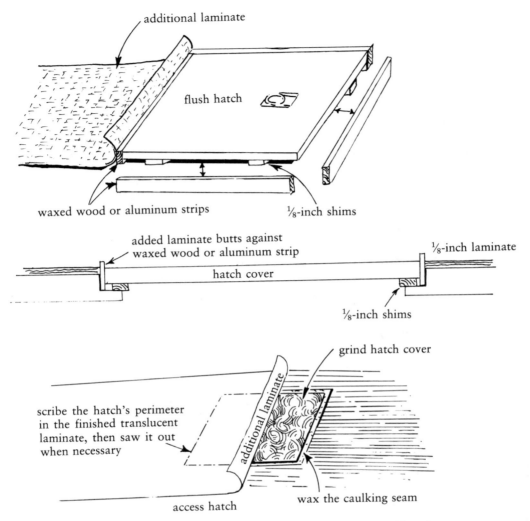

additional laminate

flush hatch

waxed wood or aluminum strips   ⅛-inch shims

added laminate butts against
waxed wood or aluminum strip   ⅛-inch laminate

hatch cover

⅛-inch shims

grind hatch cover

scribe the hatch's perimeter
in the finished translucent
laminate, then saw it out
when necessary

additional laminate

access hatch   wax the caulking seam

Figure 5-6. *In sole areas that will receive additional laminate, most hatches can be shimmed flush with the new surface. Caulked-in-place access hatches can just be laminated over (bottom).*

proof tape, or "hot patches" of presaturated polyester: whatever will ensure that the water within does not penetrate the new fiberglass before it cures. First, however, perforate the inner skin with small holes to provide a way for the water to escape, however slowly.

Should it not be possible or desirable to perforate the inner skin—perhaps because intervening joinerwork and headliners would be expensive to remove and reinstall—you will have no choice but to work patiently at drying out the saturation from above. One

choice, short of ripping the outer skin open and rebuilding the core and outer skin as previously discussed, is to perforate the outer skin with small holes and apply heat or hot, dry air. Alternatively, using a hole saw, bore holes or "wells" through the outer skin and core only—without lead holes extending through the inner skin—into which acetone can be poured to dilute the moisture and help it to evaporate. (*Remember when using acetone that it is volatile and flammable. Be careful.*) These holes should be refilled with disks of PVC foam and capped with a few disks of mat and resin flush with the surrounding surface before laying up the additional outer skin.

In some boats a loose headliner, not bedded to the deck laminate, offers a solution to drying the core from below as well as on deck without disturbing the liner or joinerwork. Bore many small holes through the whole sandwich from on deck, being careful not to penetrate the headliner. Whatever water drips out of or off the edge of the liner can be caught in pails, plastic dropcloths, or toweling. You might even happen to own one of those boats whose headliner is deliberately terminated outboard of the freestanding top edge of a hull liner to funnel drips behind it. That arrangement is sometimes used to keep the occupants of a boat comfortably unaware of deck leaks, and it might be the reason your deck got so saturated before you realized it.

Perforating the sandwich through and through is about the best way you can dry it out without opening it up, for gravity and air can both then extract moisture from it. Even so, you might be surprised how long it takes to get the moisture out. Give it as much time as you can spare, using whatever hot, dry air you can provide. When it's time to get on with the repair, seal each hole at the top only with a dab of polyester or epoxy body putty. Time will extract any residue of moisture from the core, as long as your added layers remain watertight.

6. You should grind off the original deck's gelcoat over the entire area that will receive new fiberglass. You can be doing this while you wait for the core to dry. Grinding will give the additional layers a much better grip than gelcoat can provide.

7. Wax, tape off, and paper the areas surrounding the new work as described in Chapters 3 and 4. Now you're ready to lay up the additional laminate.

Adding the layers

Once the deck has been prepared, you should establish a laminate schedule for the added layers; then you can cut the pieces for each layer and stack them in order, so that you won't have to paw through them with sticky hands as you proceed. For laminating on deck it is most convenient to use the 38-inch-wide fiberglass materials, always cutting your pieces so that the 38-inch width runs fore and aft. As you work along, putting down pieces in wet resin, wetting them out, and rolling them flat, 38 inches is far enough to have to reach back into the work while standing or kneeling on the dry deck ahead of it (Figure 5-7). Actually the reach is 42 to 44 inches, for it is customary to bring two layers down the deck at a time, and the pieces of the second layer overlap those of the first by 4 to 6 inches. You must therefore lean that much farther over the wet area to butt the edges of the second-layer pieces. Working up and down the deck with but one layer at a time would not only be inefficient, it would put down a thin layer of resin which, with no second layer as a backup in the event of an uneven dispersion of catalyst and with perhaps insufficient exothermic heat to kick the curing process along, would be susceptible to incomplete cure. Conversely, one can rarely get away with putting on more than four layers at a time. Too many layers curing at once can build up so much heat that the resin "cooks," and the laminate becomes brittle and worthless.

A recommended laminate schedule The choice of materials yielding the best mix of moderate weight, moderate cost, watertight integrity, adhesion to the original deck, and adhesion between the added layers is alternating mat and roving, always with at least one layer of mat against the original deck and two at the end. The first mat layer provides the best adhesion to the original deck. Mat between layers of roving is needed to prevent the peeling or separation to which layers of roving are prone. Two layers of mat at the outside of the laminate help make it watertight, because mat resists water penetration better than roving. Its randomly oriented chopped strands tend to prevent fractures from propagating through to the next layer, and each strand in the mat leads nowhere if water follows it by capillary attraction—which is far from what happens if water gets into a resin-starved bundle of the continuous strands of roving.

Why should there be *two* layers of mat

at the outside of any laminate? Because to get a smooth job that is not filled with faint ridges where they overlap, *all* layers ought to be butted. Adding layers on the deck's exterior is not like laying them up in a mold. On the exterior, every lump you make, while it may get partially buried by subsequent layers, continues to leave unfairness in the surface of the laminate. To save fairing work at the end, every effort should be made as you go along to keep the work rolled flat, and overlaps or wide gaps between layers should be avoided. Because the layers are butted, there have to be two of them, with the butts staggered to make the surface watertight.

How many layers should you add? The minimum number would be two layers of mat. If you want to incorporate roving for its greater strength, you are committing yourself to three layers of mat, one under the roving and two over it.

If you are using 1½-ounce mat, a very commonly used medium weight, and if the boat is not more than 20 feet long and its original deck not especially weak, two layers of mat (or possibly three) might be enough, added as they would be to an underlying structure that was itself once considered, if wrongly, to be strong enough. To gain added strength without much added weight, you could use one layer of biaxial or triaxial unwoven roving (stronger for their weight), or woven roving (the old, satisfactory standby, probably present in your original deck), but cut the weight of the mat back to 1 ounce or even ¾ ounce. Then the laminate schedule

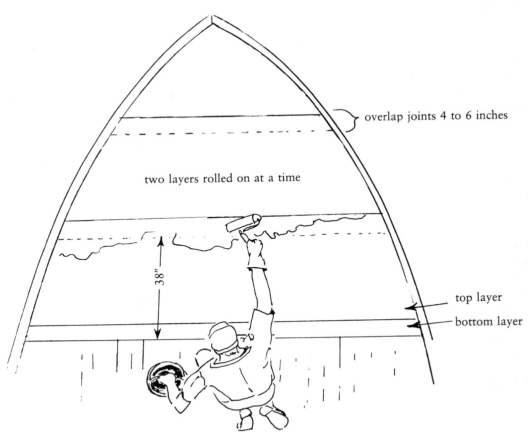

overlap joints 4 to 6 inches

two layers rolled on at a time

38"

top layer

bottom layer

Figure 5-7. *Adding layers of laminate to a weak or saturated deck. Forty-four inches is about as far as one can reach while standing or kneeling ahead of the work.*

would read: 1-ounce (or ¾-ounce) mat; 18-ounce (or 24-ounce) roving; mat; mat. The last two layers would be whatever weight you choose or feel is wise.

The larger the boat, and the weaker the deck, the more layers you should add to the outer skin. In all cases, however, you simply extend the basic laminate schedule given above with more alternating layers of mat and roving. Except on high-performance sail or power boats and very light little boats there is no reason to deviate from the standard or average material weights: 1½-ounce mat and 24-ounce roving, either woven or unwoven. That much I can tell you. Unfortunately, there is no way I can chart for you the total number of layers you ought to add. There are too many variables involved in the structure and condition of any given boat versus another, similar boat. But fear not. On every boat with a saturated deck, the laminate thickness that didn't quite suffice is right there in front of you. That reduces the problem to your best assessment of the deck's condition and of what amount of additional laminate ought to bring it back to a greater strength than it had when it was new.

Say, for example, you are catching saturation of the core at an early stage, with but scattered patches of squishiness, and find that the rest of the core and inner skin are in reasonably sound condition. The problem is the tendency of the outer skin to fail, so half again the thickness of the outer skin in an added laminate ought to be a good starting point. To that you might add an extra mat and roving pair, or more, over any areas that are noticeably weaker than the rest underfoot. Such layers would of course be put into the laminate first and tapered by carrying each one 6 inches past the one beneath, thus keeping their edges from showing up as a gross unfairness on the final surface.

If, on the other hand, the core is in generally bad condition, with extensive weakened, delaminated, or squishy areas, I would want to start with double the amount of glass used in the original outer layer, and I might still add an extra mat and roving pair or two over any areas in which the outer layer is extensively fractured.

Terminating the added layers Except at a place like the side edge of a deck, where you might want to end all your added layers in the same vertical plane, they should be tapered out onto the single-skin areas surrounding the sandwich part of the deck (Figure 5-8). The idea is to anchor the added layers to the single, solid layer in which inner and outer layers of sandwich construction always combine sooner or later, as a bridge is anchored in the shore. In tapering a laminate, the innermost layer is the shortest, and each succeeding layer is carried past the one before. Each layer thus makes a new bond to the original deck, and the top layer's edge is the only one exposed. With careful tapering and rolling a relatively fair and even transition from full thickness to the last-rolled mat layer can be made.

Reconnecting delamination

Where there is a lot of delamination or mushy core, you might want to reconnect the outer skin to the inner skin with PVC foam disks in holes cut with a hole saw. It depends on whether the inner skin seems stiff enough to be worth connecting to. If it is very thin and flexible, and if weight is not a great problem in this particular deck, then the simpler and quicker repair is simply to add all the layers you think necessary to make a good stout outer skin that can stand on its own. Don't forget, the weight of a solid laminate is about 1 pound per square foot for each ⅛ inch (approximately four layers) of thickness. To find out how much weight you would be adding, measure the deck for square footage and multiply the total area by the pounds per square feet of the thickness you contemplate. The equation will be altered by the different weights of material you might use and by your own ability to laminate, which will affect the resin-to-glass ratio of the lay-up. You can get the most accurate figure by laying up a sample laminate, cutting a square foot from it and weighing it. I do not think on most boats you will find the added laminate's weight alarming.

If you decide to use PVC connectors, the holes for them should be drilled through the outer skin and core only. Whether or not you

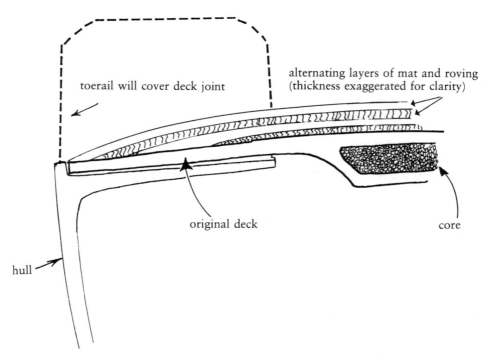

toerail will cover deck joint

alternating layers of mat and roving
(thickness exaggerated for clarity)

original deck

core

hull

Figure 5-8. *Carry the added layers of laminate out onto the single-skin areas surrounding the core. Taper the edges of the laminate by carrying each succeeding layer past the previous one, ending at the deck's edge.*

can afford to allow the lead drill of the hole saw to punch through the inner skin depends on whether or not you can stand to have water dripping into the boat. The holes should be dried out and the PVC foam glued to the inner skin with underwater epoxy if the moisture persists, and with polyester resin if not. The foam can be brought up flush with the top of the original outer skin if the laminate to be added over it is heavy. If not, it can be left flush with the bottom of the original skin, the edge of the hole tapered down to it, and a cap of fiberglass applied over it before the additional layers are laid up.

Reapplying a teak overlay

If my own experience with saturated decks is any indication, a number of those that show up are caused by leaks around the fastenings of a teak deck laid over the fiberglass sandwich. If yours was such a deck, you may well have enjoyed the teak surface so

much that you are determined to have it again, despite the problems caused by the original overlay, but you will no doubt be anxious to see that the installation is done right this time.

In this instance it will not be necessary to put a finish coating of gelcoat or paint on the added laminate. Sand it after it is cured to remove wax and to provide "tooth" for the bedding under the teak, and it will be ready for the overlay. Every step in a teak overlay is important:

1. Prepare the laminate surface as above.
2. Cut, fit, and temporarily screw down the staves with spacers between them to set the seam width, using the screws that will be the final fasteners. For a durable, troublefree deck, do not use staves more than three times as wide as they are thick. Narrow is always better. Use stainless steel flathead self-tapping screws, being careful that the holes you drill in the fiberglass fit them tightly. Their

heads should be sunk just as deep as the staves allow, from not less than half and up to three-quarters of the stave thickness.

3. The wooden bungs, or plugs, that hide the screwheads, if made as deep as practicable and glued in with thickened epoxy, will not wear out soon. They should be made from scraps from the same batch of teak as the staves, lest they differ too much in moisture content and never fit right, and they should need smart but light mallet knocking—not hammer smashing—into the countersunk hole.

4. When all of the staves have been fitted, they should be marked with serial numbers or letters that orient forward and aft ends, identify sections, and differentiate port pieces from starboard, etc. Then they are taken up.

5. Just before the staves are put back down, their undersides should be washed with acetone to remove the natural teak oil, which inhibits bonding, from near the surface. There is a solvent available from the Sika Corporation (manufacturers of the Sikaflex polyurethane adhesive sealants) that can be used in lieu of acetone and also serves as a primer for the teak. The deck should be wiped down, too.

6. As the staves are reinstalled, the deck should be smeared ahead the width of several strakes with a generous bedding of polysulfide or polyurethane adhesive sealant. Polyurethane adhesive sealants are acceptable, though not preferred, for bedding a teak deck, but should not be used for seam sealing due to their low chemical- and solvent-resistance. They can be permanently softened by fuel spills and some teak cleaners and treatments. An even coat can be assured by using a saw-toothed spreader made of metal or any other thin, hard material. You can adjust the thickness of the coat by adjusting the size or depth of the spaces between the teeth to suit.

7. After the staves are installed, their seams should be primed and filled with a two-part polysulfide adhesive sealant. When that is set and trimmed, the teak deck is finished with a floor sander. Any added layers of fiberglass extending beyond the overlay can be finished with gelcoat or marine paint as described in Chapter 2. Nonskid should

not be necessary, assuming the teak will cover the walking surface of the deck.

Other deck overlays

Of course, teak is not the only material with which you can overlay an added laminate to add protection, good looks, and a nonskid surface. There are many proprietary deck coverings available from marine chandlers and discount houses, ranging from a film of wood-grained plastic to slabs of rugged stuff with a cork or rubber base. The choice depends in part on the type and size of boat.

You can also cover your deck with patches or sections of nonskid pattern molded into the gelcoat on thin sheets of fiberglass, as described earlier in this chapter. Lay out a pattern of borders and dividing strips, make these strips smooth, then cut out each piece of molded nonskid fiberglass sheet to fit with its edges slightly overlapping the smoothed margins and glue it down. Do *not* mold the smooth areas as part of the applied sheets, then butt the sheets; if you do, the butts will all crack open when the deck is walked on.

My shop once got a job to repair the fiberglass-over-plywood deck of a 70-foot aluminum luxury yacht whose owner wanted a "deck like a molded fiberglass deck." I went to the shipyard, picked up the shape and measurements off the deck, laid it out on our loft floor, and got ready to build a throwaway mold for the forward deck just overlapping the cabin trunk, and one for each of the long, narrow side decks aft to the enclosed pilothouse wings. Then along came the owner of the company we were working for, who asked, "Why can't we make patches of fiberglass with nonskid patterns out of one small mold and glue them down?"

"Because the owner said he wants it all molded and seamless."

"That's ridiculous. We'll make up the deck in individual rectangular sections as wide as the roll of embossed vinyl we're using for nonskid in the mold, with a little extra for smooth margins. Then we can take all the pieces out of one small mold and join them on the boat in the middles of the smooth sections. That will cost a lot less, and it'll be easy to fill the joints with gelcoat putty after the pieces are fitted and glued down."

He was the boss, and he didn't think much of our objections, so that's the way we did it (Figure 5-9). But fixing all those joints took a lot of puttying, sanding, and polishing. He was losing money by the time the job was finished, but that was only the beginning; the joints began to crack almost before the men could pack their tools. Of course, the boat owner was disgusted to see more cracks than his failing original deck had had, and his yacht captain was furious that he had recommended us. Our boss billed them for double the estimate, but he was lucky if he got the estimated amount plus 10%. As for the joints, they were still cracking the last I heard. Now you know why I suggest you glue each piece of nonskid fiberglass down on an already smoothed deck, leaving margins around it, and do not butt any sheets.

Finishing the added laminate

Unless your deck gets an overlay of some sort, its added layers will need a finish that is cosmetic, protective, and at the same time nonskid wherever it will be walked on. The quickest and easiest way to fullfill those requirements is to accept the texture of the last two layers of mat as your nonskid surface. When rolled with knubbly rollers and not filled with resin, gelcoat, or putty, this surface has plenty of traction—enough so that a couple of coats of good marine paint won't fill it too much, and that's all it needs for protection and a cosmetic finish.

If an entire deck of rolled mat pattern is too drab for you, you can divide it up with strips of masking tape and create smooth

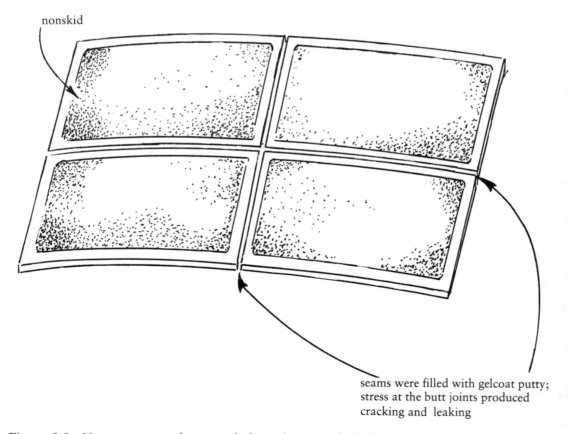

nonskid

seams were filled with gelcoat putty; stress at the butt joints produced cracking and leaking

Figure 5-9. *How* not *to apply a nonskid overlay to a deck. See text for an explanation.*

margins between and around nonskid sections by filling up the pattern with polyester body putty, sanded and polished smooth before painting. Such slick margins make good waterways and easily cleaned corners along rails and deck structures and around hardware.

Another way to turn your added laminate into a nonskid deck is to smooth it and then paint it with nonskid paint, either uniformly or in patchwork. Patches of nonskid in any deck can always be a different color from the margins.

Reinstalling the deck hardware

Now that you have rescued your deck from core saturation and self-destruction, don't put it back into long-term jeopardy with inadequate fastening, reinforcement, or sealing of reinstalled hardware. As discussed earlier in this chapter, be sure that the areas on which hardware is installed are solid enough to take any likely heavy compression, and that hardware is well through-bolted with backing plates below deck where possible, and on deck, too, if needed. If heavily loaded hardware cannot be through-bolted, the next best bet is a metal replacement of the deck core, such as a piece of thick aluminum plate, into which machine screws can be tapped. Such a plate should be bedded against the inner skin with epoxy glue or polyurethane adhesive sealant; if its thickness is less than that of the core, the difference can be made up with solid laminate. Needless to say, the larger the area of the plate and solid laminate, the more ruggedly they will secure the hardware. Stainless steel machine screws should be used both for their enormous strength and their ability to get along with the aluminum backing plate and whatever metal is in the hardware. There is certainly no more durable combination than a backing plate, hardware, and fastenings all of bronze. It's just more expensive.

Just one more reminder: Bed the hardware *very well*. There are many good bedding compounds around, but I am so pleased with the results of using 3M #5200 and Sikaflex #241 that I am afraid I have ignored all others. I should warn you of one problem

with these: You'll have a tussle getting the hardware off the deck, if you ever want to move it. It often takes a thin, sharp blade slicing the stuff while you pry the hardware up.

Core saturation in hulls

It is just as possible for the part with a saturated core to be the hull as the deck. About ten years ago, my former boatshop was involved in the repair of a 42-foot fishing boat that had broken her mooring line and gone ashore in a storm. The builder already had a huge share of the fishing boat market, with three beautiful models by a famous designer, yet there were rumbles in the industry to the effect that the workmanship in these boats was not all that it ought to be. As we cut away her outer skin preparatory to patching holes in her side near the waterline and the corner of her transom, we found large areas of balsa core thoroughly saturated—not merely adjacent to the holes, but well removed from them in several directions. Most of the transom's core was saturated. We knew that she had gone ashore at high tide, and thinking that saturation could hardly spread so far during the hour or so that she had lain on the rocks, we searched the hull for other sources. It soon became obvious that water had been leaking into the balsa core around the through hulls and the guardrail bolts, for now it was weeping back out around some of each. We found that these had been installed in raw holes; nothing had been done to seal the core around the walls of the holes. Whatever bedding compound had been used under or around the fittings and fastenings had, within five years, let the water in, and the balsa core was saturated as much as a few feet away from each access point. Much of the soaked balsa was by now quite mushy.

A few years later I was involved in the refitting of a 55-footer by the same company.

She was only four years old, and her balsa core was already widely saturated from the same sources. In a few more years, that company was out of business. I'm not saying that all or even most companies using balsa or other porous core materials are going to have such problems showing up in a large percentage of their boats. Some, indeed, have had no problems that I have heard of. But saturation of porous cores will be a possibility for the foreseeable future, so don't be shocked if you find it in your boat.

Hull desaturation tactics

Let me tell you what we did to repair the two fishing boats whose hull cores were saturated. Since most fishermen don't have much money to spare, we didn't try any involved, expensive schemes on the 42-footer. We first cut away all damaged areas and took out the wet core, scooping it from between the fiberglass skins for an inch or two past the edge of the hole cut in the outer skin. Then we used every reasonably quick and economical means available to dry out the core around the edges, including some of those described earlier in this chapter, plus some perforation of the inner skin with small holes wherever it could be reached with a drill and fiberglassed over later.

In places where the core adjacent to the damage didn't dry out within a reasonable time, we sealed it with hydraulic cement and went ahead replacing the sections of core that had been removed, and rebuilding the outer fiberglass skin. Those areas of the inner skin that we had perforated were sealed over with additional layers of fiberglass, but only in the last day or two before relaunching the boat, so that drying could continue as long as possible.

Concurrently, all of the through hulls and fastenings that had been leaking water into the core were removed. The inner skin around these was perforated where feasible in the hope of aiding the drying of the nearby core, and any drying tactics we thought appropriate were applied. One soon realizes, however, that one is limited in what one can do to dry core water in widely scattered pockets around a 40- or 50-foot boat. Only time can really be depended upon, for what worked its way into the labyrinthian core over several years is not likely to be drawn or driven out quickly.

A summary of hull desaturation tactics

It is very difficult and time-consuming to dry out a saturated core. A saturated hull is tackled in the same manner as a saturated deck. The following are the usual drying procedures in the order of their efficacy:

1. Remove the wet core and replace it.

2. Strip the inner or outer skin of the laminate and apply heat, hot air, or acetone.

3. Perforate one skin—preferably the inner, because it is structurally and cosmetically less critical—with many small holes, and subject the area or the whole boat to heat or hot air. When the core is dry—or when you get tired of waiting, whichever comes first—plug the holes in the skin and reseal with two layers of mat. Be patient; drying might take a long, long time. If it's too long, consider (4).

4. Ignore the saturation except where one or both skins are cut open to repair damage and where it is sensible to drill drainholes, leaving them open as long as is reasonably possible. If saturation has made the core mushy, and the outer skin is untenably flexible, add more layers to the outside of the laminate. In large, widely unsupported areas—especially flat ones—you can install tabs or connectors between the skins using PVC foam disks or a body putty made from fiberglass chopped strands and resin. If the area has a lot of shape, however, just building up a thicker outer skin will be good enough. It will make the outer laminate essentially a single skin, one that is independent of the core and inner skin for strength.

5. If through hulls or fastenings through the hull were a cause of saturation, take them out. Remove an inch or more of the core around the edges of the through-hull holes, dry the surrounding core as best you can, use hydraulic cement if necessary to stop any weeps, and fill the space around the edges of the hole with a strong body putty such as an

epoxy or polyester resin filled with chopped or ground glass fibers.

To seal the fastening holes, overbore them with a drill to at least three times their desired size, fill them with strong putty, and, when the putty is cured, rebore for the fastening size. When reinstalling the through hulls and fastenings use plenty of good bedding, such as 3M #5200 or Sikaflex #241.

Crushable cores

If your craft is bashed in, caved in, trampolining, or just oil canning a bit, you may find that its core has been crushed. Not all cores are readily crushed. Wood and plywood, for example, have good strength under compression relative to other popular cores, although saturated, rotted, and very soft woods and balsa, unless the latter are petrified with resin saturation, have lower limits and will succumb to such cruel pressures as the bases of lifeline stanchions and boat davits can apply.

By their nature, it is the lightweight, rigid foams used as cores and fillers that are most often found to be crushed. These include polyurethane foam, polyurethane/PVC foam, and (though rarely seen) polystyrene foam. In general, the lighter their weight the more easily they are crushed.

The word "filler" is used here to designate a special kind of foam core wherein the foam fills a space in the boat—often a very large one—to exclude water and to provide flotation or insulation. A filler stiffens the structure only as a secondary mission, if at all. To that list of tasks for foam cores, we can add one more in which I was very much involved from the mid 1960s to the mid 1970s: building cored laminates with integral fiberglass ribs or stringers formed around or against planks of foam, the whole thing being installed between and connected to fiberglass inner and outer skins (Figure 5-10). The types of boats whose foam cores can be crushed include:

1. The Boston Whaler–type developed by Dick Fisher, in which an inner and outer hull are fastened together around the sheer, and the large void between them is filled with foam that is usually poured in place (Figure 5-11). In such craft, the foam supports the double hull against impact and compression and at the same time provides flotation.

2. Boats, pontoons, surfboards, and sailboards in which the entire decked-over hull is foam filled (Figure 5-12). These may be built by laying up the fiberglass shell around a preformed foam core or by foaming the hull and deck after assembly. They are effectively quite similar to the Whaler type.

3. Small sail and motor boats whose hulls contain sealed, foam-filled sections, mostly for flotation.

4. Boats or parts built with a sandwich laminate that is cored with foam (Figure 5-13).

5. Boats or parts built with ribs or stringers between two skins that were either formed against foam or filled with it.

Repairing foam-filled craft

Is your Whaler or board-type craft's foam core crushed locally where the fiberglass skin was punched in? Is the fiberglass skin loose and trampolining over a large area where

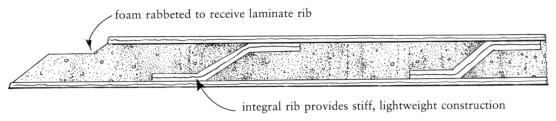

foam rabbeted to receive laminate rib

integral rib provides stiff, lightweight construction

Figure 5-10. *Foam-core construction reinforced with integral ribs.*

pounding or heavy pressure has pushed deeply into the foam, mashed it, and destroyed the bond between skin and filler? If so, you will want to build the foam core back up to its full shape and reattach the fiberglass skin.

Before you begin building it back to the surface level, you'll have to find out what kind of foam was used to fill this craft, for the foam in some boats reacts with the materials you might use to repair them.

Styrofoam meltdown

Polystyrene foam (Styrofoam is the common trade name) is dissolved rather quickly and completely by polyester resin and other petroleum derivatives such as paint thinner. Yet this foam, which is relatively cheap but fairly stiff in densities as low as 2 pounds per cubic foot, was poured in place to fill the interior of most of the early Whalers and board-type boats, and still is used in many of them. If you want to glue new pieces into a craft that is filled with Styrofoam, be sure

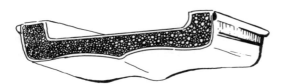

Figure 5-11. *The foamed-in-place core of Boston Whalers and their imitators provides flotation.*

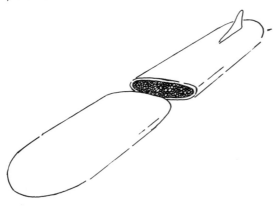

Figure 5-12. *Similar to "Whaler-type" hulls are foam-cored surfboards or sailboards.*

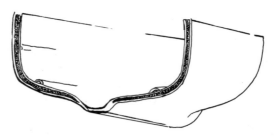

Figure 5-13. *Foam sandwich construction.*

to try the glue on a small piece first to see whether it's compatible. Then, before you rebuild the fiberglass skin over the foam, use a material not affected by resin to insulate the foam from the new laminate. One of the resin-compatible foams such as PVC, polyurethane, or a polyurethane/PVC combination will do nicely. For that matter, you can use chunks of these foams to replace any crushed Styrofoam that was cut out. Your only concern should be to use a glue against the Styrofoam that won't attack it. You will find that water-base or water-soluble glues and mastics are, as a class, unlikely to affect Styrofoam.

More generally, almost any resin-resistant material can be used to insulate the Styrofoam filler from attack by resin while the fiberglass skin is patched. If the patch is large, a gluable material such as cardboard, thin hardboard or wood, or, best of all, a thin sheet of cured fiberglass can be glued on one side to the Styrofoam with a compatible glue while the resin glues the fiberglass skin to its other side. For patching small holes, where a glue bond is not important, a piece of cardboard, sheet polyethylene, or ordinary waxed paper placed over the Styrofoam will keep the resin at bay until it cures. This will work best if you wax the margin of the exposed foam right up to the edge of the fiberglass skin before you cover it, then employ the good fiberglassing technique of putting on two layers of presaturated mat and letting them get hard and cold before adding more layers.

Once a nearby layer of fiberglass has fully cured, it will no longer affect the Styrofoam.

CHAPTER 6

Rebuilding Large Holes and Shattered Areas

It never ceases to amaze those of us who once struggled to rebuild wooden boats how easy it is to restore a badly damaged fiberglass one to robust health. Naturally, there is a point beyond which it becomes uneconomical to attempt to put all the pieces together again, but unlike the aftermath of Humpty Dumpty's great fall, this is less a case of "couldn't" than "it isn't worth it." By buying and rebuilding a wreck from an insurance company, impecunious but resourceful people manage to sail around in nice yachts. That's been done with wooden wrecks as well, but because the labor needed to repair a fiberglass boat is only a tiny fraction of what is involved in repairing the same damage in wood, it becomes feasible to rescue boats that otherwise would be relegated to the breaker's yard.

The absence of age-related infirmities is another factor that more readily encourages one to undertake a fiberglass boat's repair. With increasing age, but sometimes all too early in its life, a wooden boat may develop fastening problems, broken ribs, leaky seams, incipient rot, or any number of other ailments that detract from the undamaged portion's viability and may continue to present problems after the damage is repaired. This is not to say that older fiberglass boats are without problems, but there are few signs of properly built fiberglass boat parts weakening or deteriorating as rapidly and drastically as do the best-built wooden ones. This happens not only with the least slackening of maintenance efforts, but often with just a decade or two of normal use.

Is she worth repairing?

When a fiberglass boat is badly holed, the first question to ask is whether the sum of the labor and expenses required for the repair adds up to less than the boat's worth when restored.

Answering this crucial question will require a hard look at not only the physical damage to the hull itself, but also immersion damage (particularly salt water) to interior joinerwork and fittings. In addition, physical damage to the interior may include invasion by oil, sludge, debris, beach sand, gravel, and even rocks. Topside damage could include a ruined rig, sails, electronics, and deck hardware. All of these must be factored into the equation. When you arrive at your best estimate, perhaps with the help of a surveyor, comparing it with the current fair market value of a boat similar to the one in question will quickly indicate whether the project is worth undertaking. Don't go by the asking prices of used boats alone; check them against the BUC Book of used boat prices and use the lower of the two.

Salvaging the boat

The action needed to save a badly damaged boat can be divided into two parts: salvage and repair. The manner in which salvaging is handled, while tangential to this book's theme, is so crucial to determining the feasibility of repair that we should at least list some important do's and don'ts.

Let's assume the subject boat has been driven ashore in a storm or has been rammed and sunk by another boat. If you are involved, or have any influence over the salvage operation:

1. Try to prevent further damage caused by heedless rough handling. Many sunken or beached boats have had struts, propellers, shafts, rudders, and even large portions of the bottom and transom ripped off while being dragged along the bottom. Float, lift, cradle, or roll your boat on rollers, but don't drag her.

When lifting the boat, use longitudinally placed timbers to support a broken keel or deck, just as you would use a stretcher to lift a person with a broken back. Strong spreaders can be used to keep lifting slings from crushing the hull in the way of damage, or, if she is deemed too delicate to withstand the pressures, a cradle can be constructed.

Although few boats today are built with lifting eyebolts through the keel, the eyebolts or staples used to lower the ballast casting into the hull during production are often left in place. Because the ballast is usually well fiberglassed across the top and onto the deadrise to both keep it in place and tie the hull together, a wire or line led to such an eyebolt will at least take the weight of the lead off the straps around the hull. How much more weight than that the cast-in eye could carry only the builder can say, but lifting separately the 30 to 50 percent of the displacement that the ballast usually represents would be a big relief to a badly wounded hull.

If your wreck has no eyes left in place, but does have a one-piece ballast fiberglassed over or bolted to the outside of the hull, you should ensure that at least one lifting strap is directly under the ballast, as near its center as possible. If the hull or deck in the way of the keel is too badly weakened to withstand the pressure of lifting straps, even with spreaders to keep the topsides from squeezing in, you can make your own lifting eyes

by installing tangs under the keelbolt nuts or by inserting bolts into or through the ballast, depending on its shape. You could even bore two horizontal bolt holes athwartships through a lead fin keel and reeve wire straps down through vertical holes in the bilge, and through holes in the deck if no hatches are handy, to tangs on these bolts. Repairing holes made in the keel, hull, or deck to accommodate such boot straps is easier than dealing with the extension of serious damage to the structure that could result from lifting the boat with unsupported ballast.

2. Engines and all other electrical or mechanical gear should be flushed with fresh water and dried as soon as possible.

3. Ensure that all sails, cushions, and other fabric or foam products are washed and dried.

4. After cleaning out the boat, get her under cover or otherwise protected against the weather, so that water does not continue to collect in exposed cracks, separated layers, porous core materials, or wooden joinerwork. Weather is the great destroyer, and it very often takes longer than expected before the rebuilding project gets underway.

5. Do not leave her sitting in a distorted or stressed position. Straighten her up as true to her shape and as level as possible, and add extra support under any hanging, leaning, or broken parts.

6. Store all loose and disassembled parts in a clean, dry place, lest you find them damaged, lost, or borrowed when you need them again.

Working out a repair schedule

Only after you have done everything you can to salvage and preserve the boat should you begin to plan the repairs. A well thought-out list of projected operations will make the repair process better in every way, and can easily save you from painting yourself into a corner from which it will be expensive and time-consuming to escape. There are a few questions that you will have to answer as you work out a schedule suitable to the particular nature of your boat's damage.

1. Will you be able to work on the inside of the boat, only on the outside, or both? There are trade-offs. For example, working on the inside of the boat against an outside backing lets you mold a more or less finished surface, gelcoat and all, that when done will need a minimum of smoothing and polishing. Climbing in and out of the boat, however, wastes time and energy and is a menace to the joinerwork, which must be protected against scars and spills. The cramped working space slows the job and makes the fumes a lot worse.

2. Should you remove joinerwork in the way of the damage, or work around it? If the joinerwork is badly smashed, you might as well clear it away; but I would not be too quick to remove parts whose shape and location could help shape the backing against which the new laminate will be laid up—at least not until the backing is in place. Bulkheads, floor timbers, stringers, berth and sole edges, engine beds, and other parts that meet the hull or deck and are not too badly displaced or misshapen can become forms over which to bend your outside backing materials. If the original laminate was torn away from these parts, pad them out with temporary blocking to compensate the lost thickness, so that the inner face of the backing material will be flush with the outer face of the part.

If you're working outside the boat you can fit pieces of the backing material between these same members, flush with their outer faces, so that the inner surface of the new laminate will contact them just as did the original.

Still another way to get started when working from the inside out is to lay up sheets of fiberglass on a waxed table and, before they harden completely (while they are still "green," as the builders say), glue or fasten them against the outer faces of these same internal members. In this system of backing a hole, worked out by the John Col-

limores (father and son founders of Hulls Unlimited East, Deltaville, Virginia) and myself for building fiberglass boats, the inboard face of the semiflexible fiberglass backing is flush with the inboard face of the original laminate. This feat is accomplished by hot-gluing pieces of wood to the inner face of the laminate in the undamaged area around the hole; each piece of wood overlaps the edge of the hole, forming a rabbet to receive the backing. Since the fiberglass backing will be incorporated in the patch, it can be permanently glued or fastened to any convenient interior members that are also permanent. Further details of the method are discussed later in this chapter, and illustrated in Figure 8-1.

3. Can replacement parts be obtained from the boat's manufacturer? The difficulties of reestablishing the shape of large missing sections and of fitting backing materials to compound curvatures make it worthwhile to try to obtain replacement parts from the manufacturer, molded to the original shape and laminate schedule. These can be fitted into the hole in the boat and "welded" there by filling in a tapered V that is ground back from the hole's edge and either ground back or molded into the edge of the new piece. Molding this taper requires that you step back the laminate layers as they are laid up, or glue temporary wedges into the mold, defining the edges of the piece.

Methods discussed in previous chapters for repairing surface finishes, punctures, fractures, delaminations, and core problems are essentially the same as those used for larger jobs. But as bigger and bigger portions of the part are destroyed, special problems with retaining or restoring the shape of the part call for different methods and materials.

All these procedures will be discussed in greater detail later in this chapter. It is difficult to plan, however, without having at least an idea of available options. And the importance of planning cannot be overemphasized. As the old circular-stair builder said to the homeowner, who was restlessly watching him measure and sketch: "Cal'cation's half, y'know." Time you spend "cal'clatin" will pay dividends as the repair proceeds.

Backing damage with sheet stock

If all parts of fiberglass boats were made up of flat planes or planes curved in only one direction, as so many steel and some wooden boats are, there would be a lot less to discuss in this chapter. All you would need to reform the missing shape and back up the most extensive holes or distorted areas would be sheets of such materials as plywood, hardboard, or Formica. With a damaged flat, V-bottom, radiused-chine, or multichine hull, for instance, it is a relatively simple matter, after cutting away shattered materials and grinding back the edges of the holes, to fit sheet stock backing over them, as described in Chapter 4, and then rebuild the missing section of laminate.

If the hull is broken open at the deck edge, chine, keel, stem, or transom, you may have to use a relatively stiff sheet material, fastened in place with screws or bolts, to hold the gaping original laminate in place while you fill in and patch across the gaps with new fiberglass. Should the shape be lost for some distance, badly distorted, or the original laminate stubborn about returning to a fair curve, you can pick up the shape from the other side of the boat, using a wooden template to guide you in pulling or pushing everything into place (Figure 6-1). If the sheet stock itself isn't stiff enough to hold the shape, you can reinforce it with laminated stringers built up from narrow staves. Alternatively, you could transfer the curve to wide boards or planks and cut them to shape, so that when set on edge against the outside of the sheet stock they serve as a combination template and strongback. Theoretically, a template cut to fit against the skin of the undamaged side of the boat will not pull the skin of the damaged side to *precisely* the same shape when placed outboard of an ex-

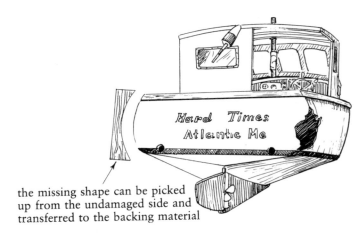

the missing shape can be picked up from the undamaged side and transferred to the backing material

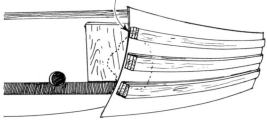

stiffen insufficiently strong backing stock with laminated stringers

Figure 6-1. *Even seemingly traumatic injuries can be repaired.*

ternal backing material. A perfect match would require deducting the thickness of the backing material from the template. In practice, however, the longitudinal curves of a boat are usually so easy that there is little noticeable difference.

Working the boat back into shape

All is fair in pushing or pulling a boat back into shape. To hold backing materials and bent or sawn stringers in place, you can use shores (or boat stands) from the ground or shores from a building's sides, or overhead. Inside the boat, shores from the opposite side can push an area out. Long bar clamps, especially those made from fittings applied to standard ¾-inch steel pipe, are good for both pulling and pushing if the cranking end is reversible.

The "Spanish windlass" is an ancient, simple, cheap, but wonderfully effective device for pulling the surfaces of the part inward. The movable part and an immovable

anchoring point are connected with a closed loop of line, which is then tightened by twisting the two sides of the loop around one another with a stick or bar. Using today's enormously strong synthetic line and a stout bar, you can generate tremendous pull. More important, the Spanish windlass is so cheap and quickly set up that you can use an unlimited number of them to exert pull in many places at once. The easiest way to attach them to the damaged side of the boat is to bore two holes, reeving the line out one and back in the other (Figure 6-2). If the line passes through a sheet of the backing material, so much the better. Passing around a stringer outboard of the backing or the original laminate will also help to distribute the pressure more evenly. Lacking a stringer to pull on, a wooden club slipped between the line and the outside surface will deter the formation of a local depression. The wood can be sawn to the area's curve, or its ends can be wedged to spread the pressure over three points rather than one.

Attachment points for the stationary ends of pulling clamps or Spanish windlasses are as easily found. Given no better way, two holes could be bored in the undamaged side,

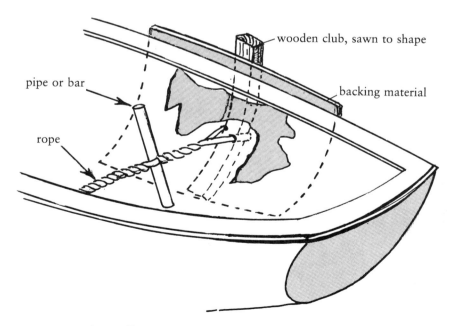

Figure 6-2. *The Spanish windlass in action.*

too. With so much repair work to do anyway, what do a couple of additional holes matter? On the other hand, you probably can hook onto a bulkhead or a locker that is well fiberglassed to the hull. Clamping a block or padded bar to the structure will save it from scratches, and more than one clamp will help to spread the strain over a wider area.

If you're worried you will rip out tabbed-in joinerwork or fiberglass liners, you can fiberglass your own padeye to the inside of the hull or underside of the deck, perhaps inside a locker or behind a removable panel. A padeye can be built by hot-gluing a short piece of cardboard, plastic, or metal tubing or pipe to a well-sanded surface, and bonding the member across its axis with several strips of alternating mat and roving (Figure 6-3). When a glassed-on padeye's job is done, it can be peeled off with a chisel, ground off, or, if not a nuisance or an eyesore, even left in place. Once you have faired up any misaligned surfaces, you can fasten your backing

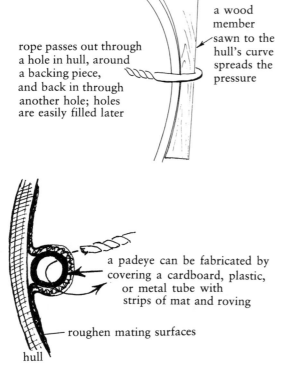

rope passes out through a hole in hull, around a backing piece, and back in through another hole; holes are easily filled later

a wood member sawn to the hull's curve spreads the pressure

a padeye can be fabricated by covering a cardboard, plastic, or metal tube with strips of mat and roving

roughen mating surfaces

hull

Figure 6-3. *Attachment points for a Spanish windlass are readily fabricated.*

material tightly to the original laminate all around the damaged edges.

Backing compound curves

When the hole is very long, or in an area with strong compound curves, large or long pieces of sheet stock will not fit over it without buckling. If there is only a slight tendency to buckle, you can cut darts—V-shaped slots in the edges—just as garment makers do. These will allow the sheet to assume a slightly spheroidal or ellipsoidal shape. But as the damaged area's curves become more compound, it will become necessary to cut the backing stock into ever shorter sheets, then finally into planks or strips as in a diagonally planked or cold-molded boat. These narrower planks, which can be quite thin, as they must only support a few layers of laminate until they harden, fit best when laid in diagonally. If lapped over the original laminate well past the edges of the hole, they will take a lengthwise bend that duplicates the missing part's shape, provided there are no reverse curves in the way of the hole (Figure 4-6). Because the boat's curves at each end of the plank may differ, these diagonal planks must reconstruct the curve longitudinally by lying flat against and being fastened to the original laminate at each end.

You should check the backing material's shape with patterns taken from the undamaged side of the boat. If the curves are such that a single layer of pieces doesn't form a fair and decent backing surface, you can bend some light stringers across their back sides, fastened with small screws from either direction, small straps of fiberglass mat, or both.

You can, of course, double plank the backing, although that should rarely be necessary. I have single planked some large—up to 55-foot—and intricately shaped temporary molds with planks of such diverse materials as thin wood, plywood, Formica, melamine-coated wallboard, and sheet fiberglass. It can be done using any material with the right stiffness and homogeneity to bend in fair curves over a large hole in an area of compound curvature. Of course, you cannot use a material that is attacked by or disturbs the curing of polyester resin, and, unless melamine-coated, it must be waxed to prevent the resin from welding it to the laminate.

If you can't seem to make the pieces or planks behave, it may be because you are forcing them edgewise. You should lay each plank alongside its neighbor, not bending it to the left or right, then mark and cut its contiguous edge so that the two planks are fitted together without one being bent against the other, a process called spiling by boatbuilders (Figure 6-4). "Edge setting a plank," they say, "makes it want to curl up along one edge."

If you use for your backing material thin sheet fiberglass made by laying up one layer of woven roving on a waxed table, as mentioned under "Working Out a Repair Schedule" earlier in this chapter, you may intend the backing to become the first layer of the patch's laminate. To encourage good adhesion, be sure to sand the fiberglass well on the side over which the laminate will be built. With this method you can actually overlap the planks' edges rather than worrying about spiling them for a close edge-set joint. This works best for backing that will become the inside surface of the skin; as the laminate is built outward the small ridges of the overlap will be obscured by rolling down the final few layers. Because the overlap would form unsightly ridges, you would not want to back the exterior of the skin this way. For exterior backing, butted pieces yield the smoothest surface. If you are planning to refinish the whole side, which may have been badly chewed up, Scotch taping the seams of butted pieces will leave only shallow grooves to be filled. But if you want the smoothest surface possible, it's better to fill the seams as best you can with polyester putty, wax, or modeling clay, then sand down any remaining ridges.

Framing in a missing shape

If there is too little support for your backing in the way of a large hole, patterns taken from the boat's other side can be used as guides to framing in the open space. Although we have previously mentioned doing this in several different contexts, there are so many possible ways and degrees of framing that we should probably summarize them.

Ribs or stringers?

The decision whether to use vertical framing, similar to ribs, or more-or-less horizontal longitudinal stringers depends entirely on the location and shape of the damage. You will generally find that crossing the damaged area in the direction that requires the shortest members works best. Thus, a relatively narrow gash along the boat will probably be best framed in with ribs; a hole that extends from deadrise up into the topsides, but not too far fore and aft, would do better with stringers running more or less horizontally along the hull.

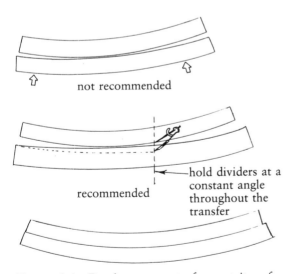

not recommended

recommended

hold dividers at a constant angle throughout the transfer

Figure 6-4. *Don't attempt to force strips of backing material edgewise into place. Edge setting will cause one side of the plank to curl. Instead, scribe the shape into the new plank edge, and saw it to fit.*

If you are faced with an enormous hole, you may find you need framing in both directions. This can be done by installing a few deep vertical or athwartships frames—what boatbuilders call moulds—and notching a number of stringers into them, just as would be done when building some wooden or one-off fiberglass boats (Figure 6-5).

Whether set up on the inside of the boat for building the patch outward, or on the outside for building it inward, the framing must be notched or spaced away from the surface of the original laminate sufficiently to allow the pieces of backing material to fit between the framing and the surrounding surface, where the backing will be overlapped and fastened. Again, some exceptions to that rule are: (1) If the framing is only needed to perfect the shape of the backing, apply the lightly fastened backing first, and add the framing over it. (2) If you are using prelaminated pieces of sheet fiberglass as both the backing and the first layer of the patch's laminate, then install the framing against the surface

of the original laminate and fill in the hole with the sheet fiberglass.

Taking a pattern off the good side

For vertical sections of framing, or ribs, study the hole, decide where you need to install temporary ribs, and mark the location of each on the surface of the hull at what will be its top and bottom ends. The rib should overlap the edge of the hole onto the sound part of the original laminate far enough past any taper you have ground or will be grinding into the edge to allow it to be securely fastened. Where the frame crosses an unsupported area or a flexible flap of the original laminate, extend the overlap as far as necessary to ensure continuity of shape between the relatively rigid areas well back from the hole.

Lay out longitudinal stringers in the same way, marking the locations of their ends past the hole on the original laminate.

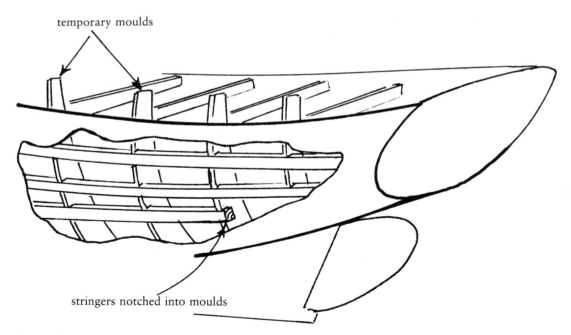

temporary moulds

stringers notched into moulds

Figure 6-5. *Large damaged areas can be framed with temporary moulds and let-in stringers that are spaced a sufficient distance back from the original laminate to permit the backing to overlap the hole on the inside. The new laminate is then built up over the backing, and finishes flush with the original.*

Locate the ends of each member on the good side of the boat by measuring from the bow or stern and from the rail or keel. Mark these locations. Hold or prop edgewise against the hull a wide board, or several boards nailed together to roughly follow the hull's shape, and, using a pencil compass, dividers, or block of wood and pencil, scribe onto it the shape of the hull between marks (Figure 6-6). You can use the piece that will become the member, or, for a pattern, thin stock such as ¼-inch plywood.

Time out, while we discuss at what angle to the boat's skin you should set the pattern or the member to be made from it. There could be some confusion here, because in building boats, the frames and bulkheads are always set up plumb: at 90 degrees both to the waterline and to the boat's centerline. All this leveling and squaring follows from the fact that naval architects find it convenient to slice a hull into sections (planes) and lines when drawing plans on paper, and builders find it best to follow the same convention when drawing plans full-size and setting up the frames or parts around which the boat is built. But, *except when replacing joinerwork or bulkheads*, setting members plumb is of little importance in repairing the skin. It is much easier to take what navigators call the

great circle route—the shortest distance between two points on a spherical surface. A member set edgewise along a "great circle" will tend to be everywhere perpendicular to the surface it helps describe, and this largely eliminates bevels from your pattern and from the member (Figure 6-7). I say "tend to be," and "largely" because the surface of the roundest boat bottom is seldom truly spherical, and some beveling will probably be necessary.

At any rate, if your only concern is to set up a framework for backing on which to lay up a patch that fairs into the laminate, keeping your patterns and members as close as possible to 90 degrees to the surface makes life much easier than trying to set them all up plumb or level.

Once you scribe and cut your pattern to fit the hull on the good side, it should fit fairly well against the surface. It need not fit perfectly, but if it bridges a section or rocks grossly on the surface, rescribing it might make you feel better. If you have difficulties fitting a very hard curve, whether convex or concave, you may be tilting the dividers; if using a block, you may be creating two concentric curves, one larger than the other by the width of the block, that will never be identical. Curing this type of misfit is quite

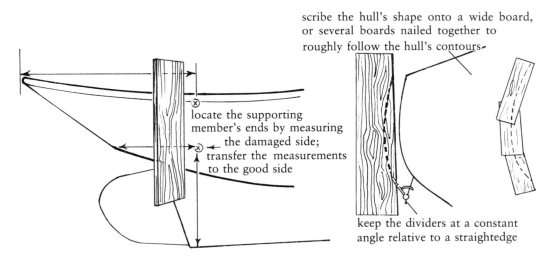

scribe the hull's shape onto a wide board, or several boards nailed together to roughly follow the hull's contours

locate the supporting member's ends by measuring the damaged side; transfer the measurements to the good side

keep the dividers at a constant angle relative to a straightedge

Figure 6-6. *Using simple "navigation" and scribing techniques, the damaged area's shape can be readily taken from the undamaged side of the boat.*

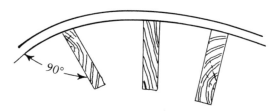

Figure 6-7. *Patterns and temporary moulds should be set 90 degrees to the surface plane to avoid an onerous job of beveling.*

simple: The second time around, just use the smallest block you can and geometry will smile on you.

Curing tilted dividers is almost as easy: if you don't tilt them, you will get a nearly perfect fit the first try. Not tilting the dividers (most of us actually use a pencil compass) means holding them at 90 degrees to a straight line more or less tangent to the curve at an arbitrary point along the curve's length. You see, a pair of dividers held perpendicular to a straight line, such as the edge of the pattern board, produces an identical line on the pattern board (Figure 6-8). When the wood between the hull and the scribed line on the pattern is cut away, the pattern can be moved against the hull along the line at which the

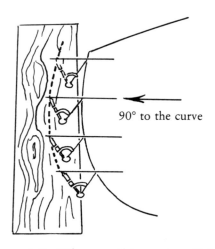

90° to the curve

Figure 6-8. *When scribing, the dividers should be held at a constant angle. Here they are perpendicular to a straight line (the edge of the board) that is more or less tangent to the curve.*

dividers were held, and it will fit the hull perfectly.

If there is no nearby straight line to serve as a guide you can use an imaginary line, such as a plumb or level line or even the centerline of the boat. That isn't as difficult as it sounds, for if we couldn't estimate plumb and level we'd fall down as soon as we tried to stand up; we align a crossroad's direction at a glance lest we head off over the curb instead of turning onto it. He or she who doesn't trust dividers can always use the block; its only disadvantages are that it requires two hands, and on hard curves, a second try with a smaller block.

Sawing the member to shape

The easiest way to make a rib or vertical frame is to saw it to shape after either taking a pattern from the good side of the boat or scribing the shape directly onto the member. It is not, however, necessarily the easiest way to produce stringer-type members. These can be awkward to make up and install if they are very long. With enough bulkheads, frames, or both in the holed area to support them, stringers can be laminated in place, using several relatively flexible layers glued and screwed together and set in notches in the vertical members. When forming them this way it is not necessary to take a pattern off the good side except as an extra check on the shape, because the vertical members will index a stringer to the surface at each crossing, and your eye should tell you whether it forms a fair curve between them.

Taking a mold off another boat of the same model

If the damaged boat is a stock or production model, there may well be one or more sister vessels in the locality. Assuming you have a complicated portion of your boat to replace—as when a sizable section of the stern or bow has been knocked completely off—and you cannot acquire a replacement part from the manufacturer, it would be eminently worth your while to approach a sistership's owner about taking a mold for the part from his boat. Properly done, there would be no harm, but *should the mold stick, it is possible to make a terrible mess of the donor boat.* This could happen from improper mold release techniques or one of many other potential disasters. While a great way to acquire a shapely part, taking a mold from another person's boat is *not* a project to be undertaken cavalierly.

Building the mold

In essence, building a mold over part of an existing boat amounts to laying up on it a fiberglass shell. The boat or part from which the mold is taken is called the plug. Following are the steps and precautions involved:

1. Make sure there is sufficient draft—the molder's expression for the ability to remove the mold from the boat when done. To put it simply, there is draft when every section of the mold is bigger than the parts of the plug over which the mold must pass as it is withdrawn, and when there are no lumps, offsets, undercuts, or sharp curves on which it will hang up as it is pulled away (Figure 6-9).

After marking off the area of the boat that you wish to use for a plug, examine it for features that might hinder removing the mold, and remove any applied parts such as hardware or trim. If a projection or change in size or direction is molded into the boat, it may be necessary to use a two-part or even multipart mold, each section of which can be pulled off in a different direction, allowing convoluted shapes to be fitted.

Should you find it necessary to make the mold in two (or more) parts, you must build a fence along the line where the parts will meet. Plywood cut to fit along the parting line and held against the plug with hot glue—or any glue that can be removed without damaging the boat/plug's surface—would work well for this. Wax the fence; lay up the first part with a flange turned up against the fence; remove the fence; wax the face of the first half's flange; and lay up the other half with a matching flange turned up against the first one (Figure 6-10). The two flanges are bored and bolted together before taking the parts off the plug.

I might mention that in making two-part production molds, projections called "keys" are built onto one flange to engage matching recesses in the second flange, thus indexing or keying the two parts together when reassembled—a job done admirably by the bolts on a mold intended for one-time use.

2. Before use, the surface of the plug must be well covered—not less than five

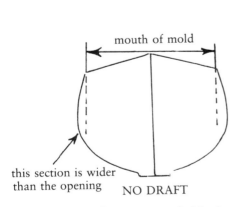

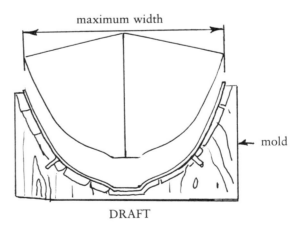

Figure 6-9. *Make sure your finished part has sufficient "draft," so that it will come out of the mold.*

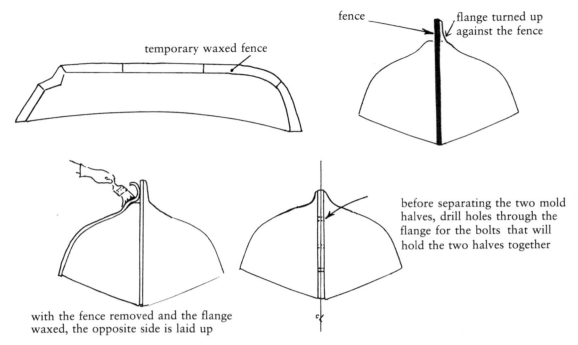

Figure 6-10. *Two-part molds are needed to accommodate complex shapes.*

coats—with mold release wax. Each coat must be allowed to dry completely—at least an hour—if they are to provide the maximum protection from the laminating resin. Extra care must be taken when *any* plug or mold is used for the first time. Each time a mold or plug is waxed and used to build a part, its surfaces become more saturated with wax and the danger of the laminate sticking is diminished.

Since this plug is not a throwaway item, but another person's boat, adding another layer of protection over the wax is in order. Polyvinyl alcohol, or PVA, is commonly used on plugs and molds to facilitate releasing a part in potentially difficult situations. Sprayed over the waxed surface, PVA produces a resin-resistant yet water-soluble film that is easy to clean off later.

3. Once the boat/plug has been well waxed and PVA-coated, laying up your mold is a relatively simple operation.

Gelcoat is optional for the mold's surface, its advantage being that it can be brought to a tough, high polish against which to lay up your repair. The softer surface of a laminating resin is often marred with tiny bubbles which, when the surface is abraded by sanding and polishing, will become unsightly tiny pits.

For one piece, on the other hand, omitting gelcoat saves both time and money. Although any scratches or pits in the mold's surface will become corresponding bumps in the gelcoat of the repair (if indeed you use gelcoat on the repair), these are easily sanded and polished off. Further, it is likely that the boat's surface adjacent to the repair will be so badly scratched that, after the new piece has been fitted and fiberglassed in place, the entire area will have to be refinished anyway. In this case a gelcoated finish on both your mold and molded piece would be largely wasted.

Gelcoat was discussed at some length in Chapter 3, but if you intend to use gelcoat for the surface of both the mold and the new piece, it will be helpful to fix in your mind these imperatives:

• Catalyze the gelcoat well.
• Stir the catalyst into it thoroughly.
• Allow the gelcoat to cure completely before you apply any laminate layers. It

should be firm and dry, not soft and sticky to the touch. On the other hand, you ought not to leave it uncovered longer than a few hours, or it might fall away from the waxed surface of the plug or mold.

- Stay within the manufacturer's recommendations for the amount of catalyst to use and the thickness of gelcoat to apply.
- Apply no more than two layers of mat (one layer is alright in a warm, dry place where you are certain the cure will not be inhibited), and allow them to cure thoroughly before applying any more. Overnight is best.

If you follow these guidelines, your gelcoat should be as smooth as the surface to which it was applied.

4. The size of the mold and the piece you are building will determine the laminate schedule you should follow. Because the mold will only be used to make one piece of the boat, only enough layers are needed to give it the stiffness to hold its shape, and to transfer that shape to the molded piece. However, struggling with an ill-fitting piece produced on a mold distorted by your material parsimony is false economy. As a general rule of thumb, the smallest and shapeliest mold taken off a boat should have no fewer than two layers of 1- or 1½-ounce mat and one layer of 90- or 45-degree biaxial 18-ounce continuous-strand roving, either backed with mat or set in light mat. Unless the piece is very long and lacking in shape, this schedule should work well for molds as large as 30 to 50 square feet.

Shape adds much to a fiberglass laminate's stiffness, and flat panels always need more layers, or stiffening reinforcement, than do curved ones; compound-curved panels are the stiffest of all. For instance, a section of the hull that includes the hard turn of the bilge aft, the reverse curve onto a molded-in skeg, and an aft corner and part of the transom would produce a very stiff mold. But a section of the topsides or deadrise away from the turn of the bilge and including little flare, tumblehome, or reverse curve would be quite limber.

Nevertheless, using the above-mentioned laminate schedule as a point of departure, few sections of any boat will need more than six total layers for a single-skin mold. These are best laid up in the order: mat, mat, mat with roving, and mat with roving. If the mold still isn't stiff enough not to distort from its own weight or the weight and shrinkage pressures of the piece laid up in it, applying external reinforcement against warping and bending to the mold's back works much better than piling on more and more layers of fiberglass.

Stringers and stands are the most appropriate external reinforcements for a temporary mold. Many production molds are stiffened with external core materials, but these are too expensive for a temporary mold. Firm materials such as balsa core or wood blocks can "print" a pattern into the mold; in addition, these insulate the mold and inhibit the dissipation of heat. Thus, for a one-time mold, shape-retaining stringers, ribs, or exterior bulkheads work best.

The quickest and cheapest reinforcing members are made by laying up fiberglass over a form, such as cardboard tubes split lengthwise or such easily shaped, resin-compatible foams as polyurethane or PVC—*not* Sytrofoam, which resin dissolves. Wooden members can either be cut to fit, or, if the curve is gentle, laminated. A word of caution is in order when using wood or any other hard, rigid material: You *must* install it over a soft pad, such as corrugated cardboard or foam, before tabbing it to the back of the mold, or the tabbing will squeeze it into the skin of the mold, imprinting a ridge in the surface.

Very often, overall shape retention is combined with a "stand" of bulkhead-like pieces arranged both to support the mold on a level surface and keep it from warping. After all, the two purposes are mutually effective, since nothing will distort a mold more quickly than uneven support. A shape-retaining stand is easily made from two or more plywood cutouts fiberglassed to the back of the mold and configured so that at least two of them present feet in the same plane as the floor or table on which the mold sits. Parallel plywood rockers may also accomplish this. Again, padding should be placed between the plywood and the back of the mold. Very large molds may need boxing or bracing—possibly interspersed with ribs or stringers—added to their stand pieces. All reinforcements should be tabbed to the mold *before* it is removed from the plug, but *not* until after the mold's laminate is well-cured.

Making the piece

In building the new piece you will, of course, have to replicate the damaged area's laminate. Nevertheless, a stronger splice could be made between the new part and the surrounding area by leaving off several inside layers when molding the part, and adding them in place, carrying the new layers past the taper ground into the edges of the adjacent laminate. Similarly, if the core or some inner layers of the laminate have suffered delamination over a larger area than have the exterior layers, laying up only an outer skin in your mold and building up the rest of the laminate after the piece has been fitted in place would result in the join being spread over a wider area and provide a more flexible piece with which to work, entailing less tugging and pushing to fairly align the all-important outer surfaces.

Another way to increase the strength of the patched area is to add extra layers to the inside after the whole piece is fiberglassed in place. Provided the joinerwork is not interfered with, these layers could extend well past the join, with each succeeding layer carried a little farther out than the last.

What about the deck joint?

If a deck joint is included in the repair, you don't have to try to duplicate it. As long as you make sure there are no mold-trapping notches, such as a projection on the topsides and another on deck, which would prevent your removing the mold from the plug/boat, there is no reason not to mold a piece that extends right over the rail onto the deck, and even up onto any coaming or deckhouse. The resulting one-piece section of the boat will have what the builder would have liked, were it possible, for the whole boat: no deck joint.

Faced with a configuration that won't allow easy release, as discussed, you can still make a two-part mold, placing its bolted-together flanges where the joint's flash line is easily concealed, such as under the rub rail or at one edge of the toerail, and in it lay up a single piece for the boat.

Unless you luck out and have a boat of only one color, you will probably have either to mask off the deck or hull in the mold, spraying one pigmented gelcoat and then spraying the other color, or else fix the color after the repair is in place. More than likely the deck, hull, or both were scratched so badly the area around the patch will need repainting or regelcoating anyway.

I hope this description of molding a new piece for your boat doesn't sound too complicated. It really isn't terribly difficult when planned ahead step by step, and it's possible to remake what seems a hopelessly smashed section of boat—not *like* new, but *new*.

CHAPTER 7

Undercured, Resin-Rich, and Cooked Laminates

Undercure is really quite rare. My own knowledge of it is imperfect, as is the dearth of published literature. This is not really surprising: To builders it is their worst dream come true—one on which they'd rather not dwell. When resin fails to cure, what was to have been fiberglass does not in fact exist; it is but a number of layers of glass fiber materials saturated with a water-permeable substance. There are of course different degrees of undercure, from a still soft and sticky state to an apparently hard, firm, but incompletely cured laminate. It can occur in differing amounts in a given part, affecting very small local spots or the entire piece.

Another fault that occurs in laminates often is called undercure but really should be called overcure. It is the result of adding too much catalyst, causing resin to gel before it has saturated the glass material. Resin in that state will neither penetrate nor stick to the glass materials, yet it prevents their being wet out by the resin applied to succeeding layers. Thus, glass materials that were to have been saturated remain dry, crumbly, relatively soft, and vulnerable to the passage of water. Another name for this condition is resin starved; because there is really no undercured resin present, one can readily tell the difference. The ways in which the two faults cause a laminate to fail are very similar, but while there is some hope of completing the cure of undercured resin, there can be no hope at all of curing the nonexistent resin in a resin-starved laminate.

At least one case has been published in which the undercured hull of a cruising sailboat fresh from the factory began to crumble during a shakedown sail in preparation for a transpacific cruise. I myself have seen half the deck of a new boat go soft before the boat was launched; another time the resin washed out of most of one side of a two-month-old motorboat as she sat on her mooring. In yet another case in which I was involved, one side of the after end of a sailboat's hollow keel leaked for the first half of the summer. The owner had the dealer haul her out, and they found about two square feet of the laminate to be soft and porous, and so sent her back to the factory.

Fortunately, such cases are rare, and even small areas that "go soft" are not everyday occurrences. Of course that may be little comfort to you if you are reading this because some part of your boat is leaking water through the laminate, getting suspiciously flexible under pressure, or turning out to more closely resemble cookie filling than flint-hard fiberglass.

Go back to the manufacturer—if possible

By definition, undercure is the weak, vulnerable condition of a laminate in which the resin has not completely cured. There are a number of possible causes: Perhaps the catalyst wasn't well mixed throughout the resin; perhaps not enough was used, or it was weaker than it should have been, or the resin itself was improperly formulated or applied under adverse conditions. Whatever the cause, undercure owes its existence to the boat's manufacture, as does resin starvation. Therefore, if you find either, the manufacturer should be contacted immediately. If a dealer was involved, and nowadays one usually is, he will probably help you, and because he buys more boats, his leverage with the manufacturer may be greater than yours. Because they have reputations to protect, it is in the best interests of both the dealer and the manufacturer to clear up your problem as expeditiously as possible.

It is possible that the manufacturer received faulty materials, and the problem was therefore not directly his fault. I have been involved in similar cases myself, and have known the material vendors to fund the replacement or rebuilding of the part. It is most logical for you, the customer, to start with the one who sold you the boat, then work back if you must.

Unfortunately, I must admit I have been right in the middle of cases where no one would do anything for the owner until he went to court and let the judge decide who, if anyone, should pay. I do hope you don't have to go that route: It's a long, enervating process, suited only to masochists.

Since this book is about repair, it is probably too late to warn you to examine carefully the guarantee against defective materials and workmanship in the sales contract *before* you buy a new boat. It is equally important to subject the reputations of both the dealer and the builder to the same scrutiny. Here's why:

I once consulted on needed repairs to a newly built diesel trawler yacht with three integral fiberglass fuel tanks between her stringers, under the hand-laid teak parquetry of her large after-stateroom sole. The tanks were undercured, and had begun to dissolve, and the owner had not been able to leave harbor for two seasons without having glass fibers clog the fuel filters and stop the engines. When the cause was determined, and it was realized that the tanks extended not only under the entire sole, but under built-in teak berths and dressers on three sides as well, a boatbuilder was hired, who, in an attempt to harden up the undercured gelcoat and resin, painted the interior of the tanks through inspection plates with a "hot mix" of resin. But the undercure was not just skin deep, and despite steam cleaning, traces of fuel oil probably inhibited the work as well. Flakes of the new resin coat soon began to appear in the filters along with the ubiquitous glass fibers, leaving no alternative but to remove the sole and cut off the tops of the three tanks. Only then could the undercure be treated and new tanks built within the same spaces. It would have been cheaper to abandon those tanks and install new ones elsewhere, but, without spoiling the boat's arrangement or performance, there were no other suitable spaces for such large capacity tanks, and that fuel capacity was one of the owner's main considerations in her purchase. The repairs finally cost around twenty thousand dollars; the foreign builder refused to pay, and was beyond the reach of this country's law. Fortunately for the owner the dealer was found liable, and the owner eventually received full compensation.

How to repair undercure—if you must

Investigate the condition

Determine the perimeter of the affected area, starting with such nondestructive tactics as examining, pressing, and tapping both the exterior and interior surfaces. A Barcol Impressor, if you can find one to borrow, is a simple spring-loaded device with a sharp pin which, when held against the surface, might tell you a bit more accurately where there is undercure than will tapping with a hard object. To use it, you need to know what numbers at the low end of the Barcol scale indicate a bad laminate, and what high numbers indicate a fully cured laminate for the type of resin and fillers or reinforcements used in your boat. A reading down around 25 is said to indicate a very bad laminate, while one in the 45 to 50 range is characteristic of a good one. Of course, an impressor held against the gelcoat cannot tell you what's going on in the middle of a thick or cored laminate. Tapping is still a valuable technique.

Probe the undercured area at some spot that will not be too difficult to refinish, attacking it from the interior or an inconspicuous spot on the exterior, to determine the depth of the undercured portion of the laminate. A small hole saw can bring out a nice sample for this.

It goes without saying that if water has been leaking through the laminate it is undercured all the way through, or so nearly so that the surface has cracked, letting water pass through the thin crust that did cure. Because radiant heat and the actinic rays (violet and ultraviolet) of light, especially sunlight, tend to cure resin, undercured areas often have a crust that is slightly more cured than the interior.

Another factor that tends to hide undercure is that gelcoat, being separately catalyzed and applied, is usually well cured whether the underlying fiberglass layers are or not. Careful boatbuilders, to prevent rovings and cores from "printing" their patterns through the gelcoat, also allow the first "veiling" layers of mat or chop laid up over gelcoat to cure hard before continuing with the laminate. The ensuing stiff crust effectively conceals any undercure beneath it, but is barely strong enough to support the boat's weight before launching or the weight of workmen stepping on it (if it is part of the deck laminate), never mind withstand the rigors of the marine environment.

Any given layer or layers of the laminate can evidence some degree of undercure; different areas may have received different batches of catalyst or resin during lamination, or been locally deprived of catalyst. Make your best judgment of what fraction of the part's area and thickness are affected.

Plan the repair

General undercure is usually uncurable with catalyst or catalyzed resin. There's just no way you can get these into the laminate's interior, and even if you *can* reach the affected area, the catalyst's reaction will travel only a short way into the undercured resin. If you can cut out the layers overlying or underlying the affected region and still leave enough cured laminate to retain the part's shape, you can rebuild the laminate from there back to the surface. If most of the laminate is undercured, however, you may need a new part.

There is, nevertheless, some hope of completing the cure if you have the time and patience. Hope lies in the following:

- Resin will eventually cure by itself—even when sealed and stored in a container.
- Heat causes resin to cure. Check with the manufacturer. I've found 150° to 180° F a safe range for this.
- As mentioned, the actinic rays of light, and especially sunlight, have a powerful curing effect on resin.

Thus, the presence of catalyst is not essential to complete the cure. Rather, the catalyst's role is to encourage and speed up the cure under normal conditions of temperature and light. Given time, your undercured boat part will tend to harden, but are you willing to wait? It's a relatively sure thing, but no one can predict the time required in a particular case without knowing a number of variables, some of which will almost certainly remain unknown.

The fact that cold curing could take years may turn off many owners. But if the affected area can be kept heated, exposed to strong sunlight, or both, the process can, depending on the undercure's extent, severity, and location, be reduced to months, weeks, or even days. When working to complete the cure, remember:

- The part must be kept dry. Nothing inhibits the cure of resin more than moisture. No way should the boat be in the water or exposed to mist, dew, or rain.
- The part must be kept warm. Cold temperatures inhibit the cure, which is why

resin's shelf life is extended by refrigeration. Thus, to accelerate the cure, the warmer the better—but don't exceed the boiling point of water without the benefit of expert advice.

- Plenty of light will help—especially sunlight, but also artificial light or heat lamps directed at local spots of undercure.
- Support the part with care and watch for signs of sagging or warping. Years ago, when we were finishing off a line of catboats at my shop, the molder used to unload the hulls and decks outside, where they would sit for weeks—an empty resin barrel under each side of the deadrise—until we were ready to take them in. One day the men brought in one with a large hollow in each side of her bottom, where she'd been sitting on the barrels. Obviously, she had come in undercured, but she was cured now. We had to build out those barrel hollows with more laminate, an example of an undercure that got cured too well too soon.

If you decide to cut out the undercured area, follow the guidelines for repairing holes, using tapered edges and placing backing on one side or the other on which to build up the patch. If the surface is smooth and fair, and shapely enough to require it, you can lay up over it a backing piece or temporary mold before you cut the hole. When the hole is cut and its edges tapered, put the mold back in place, well waxed, and lay up a perfectly shaped patch against it. *Do* make sure the surface over which you lay up the mold is well cured and well protected with wax and PVA, for the mold's freshly catalyzed resin would sure like to find an undercured surface with which to bond forever.

Resin-rich and cooked laminates

These problem laminates both appear hard and strong, but are actually brittle. Each may evidence itself by an area of developing cracks, or by suffering extensive damage from seemingly minor injuries.

Recognizing resin richness

A resin-rich laminate is normal in most respects, but, as the name implies, it contains much more resin than reinforcing glass fibers. During manufacture, resin-rich sections of laminate are most likely to occur in low spots, where resin accumulates and puddles, although a degree of resin richness can be achieved anywhere during lay-up by flooding the laminate with resin and not rolling out the excess. Burning a sample is the standard test to determine the percentage of resin and glass fibers in a given laminate. The resin will burn away, leaving the glass fibers intact, so that you can actually identify and count the layers used in the lay-up. By weighing the sample before and after burning, you can readily calculate the percentage of resin to glass. *CAUTION: Once it gets going, fiberglass resin burns hot and fast, with a foul, toxic, smoke, so do it in a fireproof, well-ventilated, and preferably outdoor location.*

Fifty-fifty is an ideal rarely reached, but percentages all the way down to 70 percent resin and 30 percent glass are considered acceptable in the trade. The reason for such a wide tolerance is that more resin increases the total thickness of the laminate; because the materials are spread out more, given equal quantities of glass reinforcement, a thicker laminate is stronger than a thin one.

Repairing resin-rich areas

Unfortunately, the only way to repair resin richness is to add more layers of laminate containing a proper percentage of glass reinforcement; if that is for some reason impractical, then you are faced with cutting the area away and replacing it. Nonwoven types of roving, such as biaxial (which comprises two unidirectional layers stitched together), would add the most strength with the least bulk; adding layers to both sides would be stronger than adding to only one, but, as always, there should be more layers on the outside than on the inside.

The photographs on the following pages depict fiberglass boat repairs in a Connecticut boatyard. They show more eloquently than words that virtually any damage is repairable, and the repair can be made at least as strong and handsome as the surrounding undamaged area. All the techniques and procedures mentioned in the captions are discussed in detail in this book. (Photos by James M. Curry, Killingworth, CT)

Following seven photographs: *Repairs to delamination in the balsa-cored deck of a stock 40-foot cruising sailboat, as discussed in Chapter 5. Leakage around traveler bolts saturated and rotted the core and caused extensive delamination. The size of the area was determined by sounding with a hammer, and the outline marked on the deck.*

2. *The outer skin removed, showing discoloration from the rotted core. The dark splotches are a polyester filler used to fill the bolt holes so that the new core and outer skin can be vacuum bagged. (Vacuum bagging can help achieve an even bond of core to fiberglass and an optimum ratio of glass fiber to resin, but it is by no means necessary and is not discussed in this book.)*

1. *The outer skin is cut out using a circular saw with a carbide blade.*

3. *The new core is bedded in resin putty for a good bond to the inner skin.*

4. Holes have been bored in the core for the traveler and hardware bolt compression points, which will prevent crushing of the core when the bolts are tightened. These holes are now being filled with a resin putty/chopped fiberglass strand mix.

5. Wetting out the new core preparatory to laying up the outer skin.

6. Precut pieces of fiberglass are set in place. . .

7. . . . and wet out. Proper laminate schedules and techniques for deck repairs are discussed in Chapter 5.

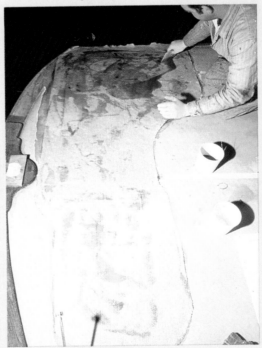

Top: *Grinding back the fairing compound and outer skin of a holed 48-foot racing sloop. The Klegecell core (pink areas) has been removed. The glass is usually beveled 10 to 1—that is, 5 inches wide for a 1/2-inch thickness—but 12 to 1 builds in an added margin of durability.*

Middle: *Fairing the repair of the boat in the previous photo with epoxy microballoon fairing compound. As mentioned in several places in this book, polyester fairing putty is acceptable for this purpose. Epoxy putty is more durable, more water-resistant, and bonds more tenaciously.*

Bottom: *Chopping back the fairing compound on a foam-cored ocean racer. The Klegecell core has been removed, exposing the carbon fiber inner skin, which will be repaired after the core and unidirectional S glass outer skin are in place. As Chapter 1 discusses, S glass and carbon fiber are expensive, and their use is mainly restricted to high-performance sail and power boats.*

On this page: *Repairs to a balsa-cored Tiara 36 powerboat. The topsides above the knuckle are solid fiberglass.* **1.** Starboard side: *Standard layup of biaxial roving in the solid section above the knuckle and in areas of minor damage to the outer skin in the cored areas. The balsa core has been cut back for replacement where the damage was more extensive.* **2.** Port side aft: *Repairs have been made to the inner skin below the knuckle, prior to installation of the replacement core. A new solid glass section has been laid up on a bench to fill in the topsides above the knuckle, and is now being glassed in place.* **3.** *The new topside section is being faired prior to closing in the inner skin at the corner.* **4.** *The inner skin repairs are complete and ready for fairing and installation of the core and outer skin.* **5.** Starboard side aft: *The core and outer skin in place and being faired. The excess glass in the overlap is being planed off with a carbide-blade hand power plane, which is faster for rough fairing than using a grinder, but not markedly so for small repairs. This workman should be wearing goggles and a toxic-dust mask.* **6.** *The finished Tiara after final recoating (in this case with Awlgrip), as discussed in Chapter 2.*

Cooked resin

Cooked resin is resin that became overheated during cure, making it darker in color, very brittle, and prone to crumble. Surprisingly, once resin has fully cured it can withstand very high temperatures: it won't ignite until heated to between 800° and 900° F. Where resin puddles in a deep, confined recess, or is cast in large volume, or when a very thick laminate is laid up at one time without either adjusting the catalyst to compensate or using a special, low-exotherm casting resin, the resin may build up too much exothermic heat, begin to smoke, become cooked, and consequently have little or no strength. Unfortunately, there is nothing you can do about it, except cut it out and replace it, or encapsulate it in a sufficiently strong laminate. Again, the burn test can determine for sure whether this is a cooked or resin-rich laminate: it would help to know.

To recap, resin-rich or cooked-resin conditions are created by the manufacturer, and if possible that's the first place to turn for help. If you have to repair either condition yourself, the procedures are much the same. The only difference will be in the extent of the repair or the amount of reinforcing material needed.

CHAPTER 8

Repairing Keels and Other Underwater Parts

Damage to hollow fiberglass keels

One of my pet peeves is that the hollow fiberglass keels on motorboats and sailboats of traditional design are as hollow as they are. For many years I have been comparing the thin skins most manufacturers use in their keels, deadwoods, and skegs with the solid oak or yellow pine counterparts traditionally used in most wooden boats. It's as if these builders have never heard of rocks or coral and think that all bodies of water have ooze bottoms. They schedule their keels' skins to withstand being lifted in slings, or sitting on blocks ashore, as if these are the worst forces their boats will ever encounter. If, however, you have a cracked or holed hollow fiberglass keel, you at least know better. Even if you only have an annoying weep around the rudder hardware or a shaft log that is fastened through relatively thin fiberglass, you may be wondering why these regions of the hollow keel couldn't have been built up or filled in solidly enough to prevent leaks around the hardware. They certainly could have been— and should have been. If you learn nothing else from this chapter it will have been worthwhile if you are encouraged to build up a thicker laminate while making your repairs, or to fill in these vulnerable areas with solid reinforced keel putty, or both.

Cracks and fractures

If you have examined a spot where water is dripping from your keel and have found a crack in its bottom face, it is likely that the keel came down hard on a ledge or very hard bottom. If the crack is fore and aft down the centerline of the boat, then she might be one whose two sides were at least partly laid up in the two halves of a split mold, then joined with layers crossing the centerline after assembling the mold. You can determine this by cleaning off the bottom paint, for no builder that I know of grinds and fills the "flash" or line perfectly where the two halves of the mold meet along the bottom of the keel. Why bother where it is not seen? At the same time, an athwartships crack does not necessarily mean that the boat does not have a centerline join. I've seen at least one boat with a crack at 90 degrees to the join, which simply indicated to me that the bottom of the keel was struck evenly and folded upward to the breaking point along the line of contact.

If you have been unlucky, and your boat has sustained one or more chewy fractures from a more lingering contact with rocky bottom, the repair needed will be about the same as is needed for a single, relatively clean crack. In either case, the existence of a break that extends all the way through the laminate demands a patch that also extends all the way through at the point of the break. The patch should taper out to the surface all around it at the recommended scarf width of approximately 12 times the thickness of the laminate.

In most cases, the best approach is to build the patch from the outside of the boat, because the inside is too confined and inaccessible. Indeed, you may be physically excluded from the interior in the damaged area by encapsulated lead ballast or integral tanks in a sailboat; also, there may be an on-center engine, propeller shaft, or related gear that would be too expensive to move out of the way in any craft. Not to worry, almost everything you have to do to effect a sound repair can be done from the outside.

There are, however, two operations on the interior that you should seriously consider: (1) If the bilge is oil-saturated, or if the damage is in the way of an integral fuel tank, these should be steamed out before you patch the keel. (2) If the laminate is weaker than it ought to be (perhaps it broke too easily in your opinion), yet it is not feasible or aesthetically practical to add to it on the exterior, then you should reinforce it on the inside.

If you decide that additional laminate must be added from the inside, steam cleaning will be necessary or there will be no adhesion. In any event, damage that breaches the watertight integrity of the keel provides an excellent excuse for cleaning the keel sump and bilges. A great tool for this job is a Steam Jenny or steam cleaner rented from a tool rental shop or possibly from an auto repair garage. A steam cleaner is a portable machine that pumps out a stream of steam, which literally melts grease and oily sludge away. For a badly fouled bilge, you can add detergents; then you can make a final, drying wipe-down with an acetone-soaked rag. *Caution: Take care not to develop an explosive mixture of air and acetone fumes! Always provide good ventilation when working with volatile solvents in enclosed spaces.*

Holes in the keel

Holes in the hollow keel need essentially the same kind of treatment as cracks and fractures. The only difference is that they will need a backing on which to get the lay-up started, or if there is a huge missing area, a hole will require a form or mold-like structure on which to lay up the new piece. With extensive damage, it is likely that a part of the interior will be demolished, giving you better access to the interior than if there is only local damage to the keel itself. That opens up two courses of action: Either you can fit some backing on the outside and build up the new laminate from inside the boat, or you may be able to fit some backing in flush with the interior surface of the hollow keel, build up the new laminate from the outside, and then remove the backing from the bilge.

The exact thickness of the laminate is unimportant in the hollow keel or bilge area, except where tanks or other items fit within its walls without much clearance. As a result, an excellent way to start in replacing a big piece of keel with a lot of shape would be to fit pieces of sheet fiberglass to the inside of the hollow keel. Sheets of fiberglass can be made of a single layer of woven roving laid up on a waxed table. This method (Figure 8-1) was described in Chapter 6. The sheets of fiberglass are cut into strips or other shaped pieces as necessary and bent to any curves while still "green" or semicured. Hard curves, those that cannot be bent in the green laminate, can be laid up over appropriately shaped waxed objects. Temporary members of wood can be fitted within the keel as needed to serve as a form for the sheet fiberglass, and then removed after the laminate has been built on it. Copper or brass nails or bronze staples are used to fasten the sheets of fiberglass pieces to the wood, then clipped or ground off after the laminate has been built and the wood pulled out.

It should be mentioned that when sheets of fiberglass are used as the starting material for a laminate, it is customary to overlap the various strips or pieces. This is because the single thickness of woven roving used to make the sheet is so thin that by the time a few layers are built up over the ridges caused by the overlap, the ridges have just about disappeared.

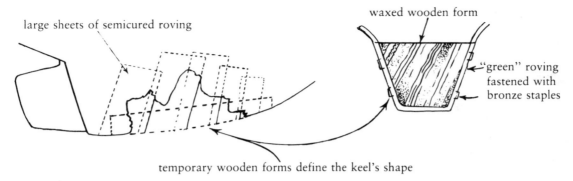

Figure 8-1. *Large, shapely, heavily damaged areas are most easily repaired with sheets of "green" fiberglass.*

Weeps around metal hardware

Fiberglass is not inclined to stick to metal or to stay stuck to it for long, so a watertight fit around hardware or fastenings is ultimately dependent either upon the tightness of the fit or upon a bedding material between the metal and the fiberglass. When a laminate laid up around metal shrinks tightly against it, or an object with tapered threads is screwed into a hole in the glass, the pressure of one material against the other excludes water fairly well. Such a joint will remain watertight until some force such as differential contraction and expansion, penetration by corrosion, a slow wedging apart by freezing moisture, or a constant vibration or bending works the metal loose. Knowing that the watertight integrity of metal passing through a fiberglass skin is not particularly trustworthy, most builders use a secondary seal of bedding compound or filled resin glue, or they use a preformed gasket under the metal hardware or around its fastenings. Many such sealants work long enough to free the manufacturer of blame when they fail, but, as you may have learned (to your intense annoyance), all fail sooner or later. A further sad commentary is that the longest-lasting sealants tend to be the most expensive and the most messy and time-consuming to apply. As a result, only builders who are dedicated to building a durable product use them.

The above paragraph may seem to be too much of an explanation for the weeping of such fittings as metal shaft logs, rudderports, pintles, gudgeons, heel fittings, skegs, and other metal fittings in or about the keel. My purpose, however, is to lay out the causes in detail so that we may dismiss any notion that the weeping or eventual leaking of underwater fittings is something you have to live with.

You can, of course, replace the bedding compound under any piece of hardware. Take it off, clean it and the underlying fiberglass, and reinstall it over fresh bedding. Use a high-quality bedding that is as tenacious and immune to penetration by water as possible.

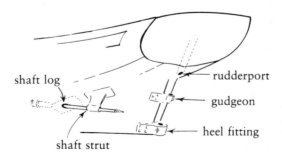

Figure 8-2. *Every hull penetration is a potential source of leaks.*

Through hulls

Actually, rebedding is all you can do to fittings of the through-hull type, which are made with an exterior flange and an interior nut on a threaded body. These fittings are intended to be clamped against both sides of a single skin with bedding under the flange, under the nut, and lining the hole (Figure 8-3). Usually, they don't give much trouble for many years, unless something is wrong with their installation or they are wasted by corrosion.

Incidentally, it has never been a good idea to switch to molded plastic through hulls for underwater use. As you may have noticed, builders dearly like to substitute these much less expensive items for metal, but so far they have confined the use of plastic through hulls to above the waterline. The reason is simple: they are more easily broken. There is always a chance that a heavy object, such as a spare anchor, might be thrown against them, suddenly opening a bad leak.

There is usually no core in the laminate of a hollow keel, but as discussed in the chapter on core problems, the area around the hole for any through hull installed through sandwich construction should be of solid fi-

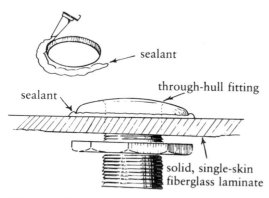

berglass. The edge of the core should not be exposed by the hole. This can be accomplished by cutting out a patch of the inner skin and core and then building up the inner face of the outside skin with layers of fiberglass. This will make the outer skin thicker and also seal off the core if some of the layers are turned up and out to overlap the inner skin of the sandwich (Figure 8-4).

If you suspect that the single skin in which a through hull is installed is too thin and flexible to have a through-hull fitting in it, by all means build up a pad of extra laminate, or cut a block of fiberglass from a thick sheet and install it by bedding it in resin and wet mat, to stiffen the area around the fitting. Despite the fact that it was common practice in wooden boats, I would not use wood for this, especially in the dank recesses of the bilge or hollow keel. It will not last as long as the fiberglass and no one will remember to poke it for softness every year or two; to use wood is just asking for trouble someday.

Replacement with fiberglass through hulls

There is another way to treat through hulls, particularly those that are directly connected with hose and do not have seacocks or valves on them. You can replace them with a through hull of fiberglass tubing that is fiberglassed to the hull. Fiberglass through hulls are frequently used for cockpit scuppers, deck drains, exhaust lines, bilge pumps, and occasionally for sink or toilet outlets. Fiberglass through hulls are best where a seacock is not required to shut off the flow into a piece of equipment, and where they can be carried above the waterline as a one-piece

Figure 8-3. Weeping through hulls can be eliminated by judicious applications of sealant between the hull and fitting. Silicone sealants work well underwater; polysulfide adhesive sealant is an excellent choice; polyurethanes, such as 3M 5200, provide a permanent bond. For maximum insurance, bed under the nut as well.

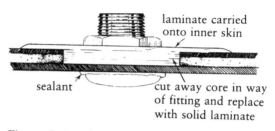

Figure 8-4. Through hulls installed through cored hulls require extra attention to avoid core saturation.

tube fiberglassed to the hull, with no joints below the waterline.

What could happen to a stout piece of fiberglass tubing that is "welded" to the hull and carried above the waterline? While we can't say positively how long it will last— any more than we can say how long a boat will last—I have surveyed a number of boats up to 30 years old with fiberglass through hulls that appeared to be no less viable than when they were built. I was once startled to find that the hose on a cockpit scupper through hull in a 25-year-old sloop had a hole just above the waterline that I could put my finger through. Perhaps the hose was as old as the boat. Who knows how many seasons it had been leaking. Fortunately, because the fiberglass through-hull tube extended above the waterline, she had not yet settled quietly to the bottom when left unattended on her mooring.

Yes, integral fiberglass through hulls are probably the most durable and trouble-free in the long run, especially when they can be carried above the waterline. Nor can there be any doubt that they save both installation and maintenance expense when they eliminate seacocks or valves. Seacocks are often forgotten by the owner, and are sometimes so frozen with corrosion after awhile that they can break if you try to use them in an emergency. Fiberglass tubing for various sizes of through hulls can be purchased ready-made, or you can make up tubes yourself if you want to bother (see below).

At the same time, if you want a valve in the line, it is best to install a seacock right at the hull on a threaded bronze through hull, for there is no reliable way to connect a seacock's metal body to a fiberglass through hull. Despite my appreciation for the simplicity of the fiberglass through hull, do not underrate the ruggedness of a bronze through hull flange and the nut that clamps it to the hull. In the past, when bronze underwater fittings were regularly used, if they were well maintained and not undermined by electrolysis or corrosion, they sometimes lasted so well that they were taken from a worn-out wooden hull to be used in the construction of a new vessel.

Shaft logs and rudderports

Shaft logs and rudderports are two other pieces of through-hull hardware that are more trouble-free when they consist of a fiberglass tube glassed into the hull. If you have a bolted-on bronze stern bearing/stuffing box unit that has been knocked loose from its location, or if your rudder has been knocked around and torn the bronze stuffing box/bearing off its boss on the interior of your hull's laminate, then you know how easily disrupted these installations are.

Unfortunately, the use of these bronze castings is but a carryover from wooden boatbuilding methods to fiberglass boatbuilding. Few events have caused more floodings of fiberglass powerboats than those in which bronze stuffing box/bearing units were torn loose. To make matters worse, they are much more expensive to buy and to install than a fiberglass shaft log or rudderport. A fiberglass rudderport or shaft log needs but a rubber bearing in a bronze sleeve at its outboard end and a "rubber neck" (a short length of rubber hose) with a bronze stuffing box attached at the inboard end. One can marry this type of rig to the laminate and surround it with fiberglass reinforcement until nothing short of total destruction of the surrounding hull could open it up.

A fiberglass shaft log through a hollow keel is very easily and cheaply buried in a solid section of the keel, rivaling the solid oak keel timbers of yore. This can be done by setting up a dam immediately aft of the rubber neck of the stuffing box and pouring in reinforced resin. In confined or low-volume situations, regular general-purpose polyester resin and chopped or milled glass fibers can be used. In large-volume areas (wide or deep hollow keels), polyester casting resin will eliminate the danger of overheating when the mass cures. In addition to milled glass fibers, there are a number of other reinforcing materials that can be used to cut the cost and weight of the compound. You need not mix up your own compound if you don't want to, for suppliers to boatbuilders carry a number of reinforced resin compounds suitable for filling hollow keels.

Once a shaft log is buried in keel putty, I like to cover it with a laminate of alternating biaxial roving and mat that extends well onto the hull laminate on each side.

It is not difficult to incorporate a rudderport of fiberglass tubing solidly into a reinforcing buildup of the laminate where it enters the hull. The upper portion of the tube can be braced with knees or other glassed-in supports. In addition, a rudder stock should have a strong upper bearing placed as high as feasible to keep it from prying a chunk out of the hull if the rudder is badly battered. Like the fiberglass shaft log, the fiberglass rudderport is better, cheaper, and has an indefinite life expectancy. Of course, a rubber-necked stuffing box or other sealing cap around the rudder stock should be fitted atop the fiberglass rudderport, unless the tube extends so high above the waterline that it is not needed.

In tiller-steered sailboats, where the rudderport is often carried into the cockpit or above the after deck, the fiberglass tube is a natural, for it can be easily fiberglassed to the hull and to the cockpit sole or to the deck.

Thus there are two ways to repair a metal rudderport tube which has been loosened or knocked out of place where it was glassed or mechanically fastened to the hull: First, as long as the metal port is still usable (perhaps it is only loose and leaking where it is attached to the hull), you can refiberglass it. This time, however, wrap the metal port with fiberglass all the way up to the underside of the sole or deck, and fiberglass it well to the underside of that laminate, too (Figure 8-5). In effect, this gives you a fiberglass rudderport lined with a metal one, which cannot leak anywhere between the hull and sole or deck. If you use this method, you should make sure that the ends of the metal port are sealed where they project through the hull at the bottom and the sole or deck at the top, by cleaning out the crack between the metal and the laminate and working some bedding into it, or by rebedding any nut, block, or metal collar around it on the exterior surface. This is needed to keep water from penetrating the laminate, especially in cold climates where freezing can enlarge any tiny pool.

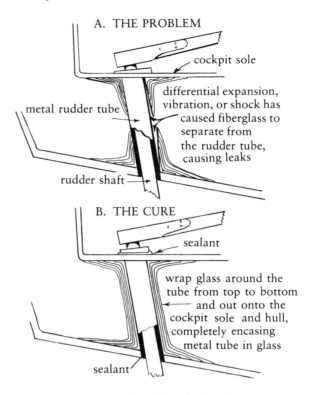

Figure 8-5. *A metal rudder-shaft tube can be an irritating source of leaks. Eliminate them by encasing the tube in fiberglass for its entire length.*

If, however, the metal port is destroyed, you can replace the whole unit with a fiberglass rudderport, stoutly glassed in place at each juncture with the hull and deck laminates (Figure 8-6). There should be a bearing fitted in the bottom of the tube, extending from the outer surface of the hull upward. This can be a rubber-lined bronze insert of the type used on propeller shafts (a cutlass bearing), as long as it is at or below the waterline so it gets the water lubrication that these rubber bearings must have. The bearing can also be an insert made of one of the nylon-like plastics, or it can simply be a bronze bearing made from a piece of fairly close-fitting "red brass" pipe.

Making fiberglass tube fittings

Because manufactured fiberglass tubing is now easy to buy, it is rarely worthwhile to

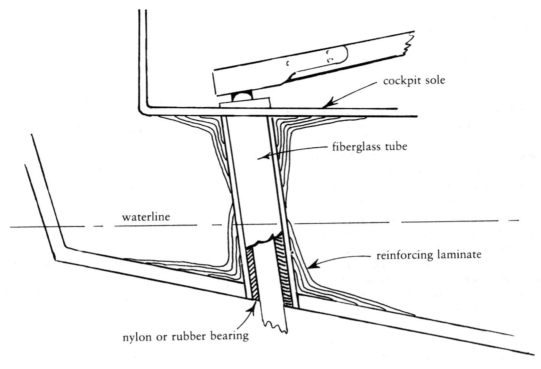

Figure 8-6. *If the metal rudderport is destroyed, replace it with a fiberglass tube.*

make it up yourself. Still, when you are in more of a hurry than the supplier is, or when you are faced with a situation in which an odd size or shape of tubing would be better than anything readily available, you can certainly make the tubing yourself.

To make your own fiberglass tubing, the first step is to find a form or mandrel on which to lay it up. Almost any cylindrical object will do, if its outside diameter matches the inside diameter of the tube you want to make. This can be anything from a cardboard tube to a metal pipe or piece of shafting, as long as the material is unaffected by resin and is not too unwieldy to rotate easily while you lay up fiberglass around it.

The ideal mandrel would be one turned out of wood on a lathe. If the tube to be laid up on it is a shaft log or rudderport, the mandrel can be turned to the same diameter at the outboard end as the bearing that will be pressed in (Figure 8-7). Regardless of the tube's purpose, the inboard end of the man-

drel can be turned to the proper diameter so that a tube laid up to a given skin thickness will have the right outside diameter to accept the hose that will be clamped onto it. Finally, with the lathe bed and other parts protected from dripping resin, you could even lay up the tube with the mandrel mounted on the

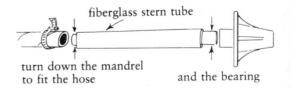

turn down the mandrel
to fit the hose   and the bearing

or build up by wrapping

Figure 8-7. *Fiberglass stern tubes can be laid up over a wooden mandrel turned on a lathe to the correct size.*

lathe. The lathe would have to turn very slowly, maybe 10 to 20 turns a minute, while the tube is laid up, and then be left turning while the resin cures.

Nice as a lathe is, it is not at all necessary. I have made all kinds of tubes without that luxury, including a recent patch and a new heel piece on a sailboard mast. It really is only important to set up some sort of bearings, if only a V-notched block beyond each end of the work area, in which the mandrel can be rotated by hand. A spindle, such as a nail in each end of the mandrel, can also be used to rotate the work between a pair of boards. As long as you can put together a mandrel out of a cylindrical "found" object and rig it up to be turned, you're in business.

There are two pitfalls to watch out for when laminating a fiberglass tube. First, don't let the tube stick to the mandrel; wax the mandrel heavily. Also, don't let the tube shrink so tightly around a solid, unyielding form that you must destroy the tube to get it off. One way to avoid this is to make the mandrel from a destructible material such as cardboard. Another alternative is to slice the mandrel lengthwise to make a removable wedge of its center portion. If the mandrel is made of metal, then you should lay up a thin laminate, make a lengthwise cut in it with a sharp knife while it is still green, then pry it off and finish laminating it on a looser fitting mandrel.

If you are building a fiberglass shaft log or rudderport, you can set up the mandrel with the cutlass bearing on its outboard end. Then, after waxing the bearing to facilitate pressing it out someday when it needs replacement, let the laminated tube shrink tightly around it. As a precaution against its working loose, you should lay up a threaded nut or small piece of bronze that can be bored and threaded for a set screw on each side of the bearing near the outboard end of the tube.

You can wind a tube with any of the fiberglass fabrics, but the simplest method is to use a strip of fiberglass cloth as wide as the tube is long and at least as long as several tube circumferences. As you wind it on by rotating the mandrel, the fabric wets out easily and can be pulled tight enough to squeeze out the excess resin without fear of pulling the tube apart. The reason why cloth is preferred over woven roving is that it is soft enough to conform to the shape easily, thereby helping to prevent voids in the laminate. For the safest possible arrangement, I like to use a layer or two of mat both at the beginning and the end of the laminate. Cloth peels easily; without a layer of mat over it, there's a slight possibility that a loose strand could wind up on the shaft if it is exposed to wear on the inside of a shaft log. On the outside of any through-hull tube, mat will improve the adhesion of the fiberglass which bonds it to the hull. Mat is by far the most waterproof of all fiberglass fabrics, a virtue never more important than in an underwater through-hull fitting.

Sealing through-bolted hardware

While you have the choice of replacing some metal through-hull fittings with fiberglass ones, there are other, bolted-on metal parts for which there are no substitutes. These are the most likely fittings to be seen leaking in any collection of hauled-out boats. These through-bolted fittings include rudder heel fittings and intermediate pintles or gudgeons on sailboats, and metal skegs on single-screw powerboats. Regardless of how these fittings are bolted or riveted to the hull, if the bolts or rivets terminate inside a hollow fiberglass keel, sooner or later the fittings will work loose and begin to leak. Worse, such a fitting can be knocked loose, perhaps taking some of the hollow keel with it. As you may have learned from experience, a small leak from bedding that lost its grip and washed away does not always require immediate attention, but few boats can survive the inundation that breaking out a piece of the hollow keel can cause. Over the years, many floodings have been traced to hardware broken out of hollow keels. Most of these could have been avoided if the region through which the hardware was bolted had been sealed off from the rest of the bilge.

Whether you are simply repairing a weep from such a fitting, installing a replacement for a damaged part, or rebuilding a keel from which one or more fittings have disappeared, I recommend that you fill the region solid with keel putty, lay up fiberglass over the bolts and nuts on the inside of the keel, or better yet, do both.

Fixing fin keels and separate skegs

Perhaps it was the ease of laying up a canoe-bodied hull in fiberglass and bolting on a fin keel, versus the difficulty of laying up deep hulls with hollow keels. Perhaps it was the improved performance of short-keel designs combined with the readily adaptable fiberglass construction techniques. Even the switch to mobile sling lifts and cranes in boatyards may have had something to do with it (fin-keelers were always a nuisance to haul on a railway). Whatever the factors, boatyards and marinas today are filled with millions of fin-keeled, shallow-hulled sailboats with separate rudders. With the switch from the long, traditional keel to the short, fin keel have come new problems and different kinds of damage.

With a fin-keeled boat, the force of a collision with a rock or a hard bottom, transmitted to a small area of the hull, is quite likely to damage the hull in the attachment area. The force of a similar collision is almost always dissipated in the longer attachment area of the traditional keel. With either type of keel, a collision with a hard bottom is likely to cause damage at the point of contact. With a fin keel, however, you should also look closely for damage to the hull in the area of the keel's attachment.

Looking for damage

When a fin keel collides with the bottom, whether the boat is underway or driven ashore in a storm, the keel bashes the hull like a battering ram when it is struck from below, or it tries to break a section out of the hull when struck from forward, aft, or from either side. After a hard grounding, always

look at the surface of the laminate around the top of the keel and on the adjacent hull surfaces for cracks that will often indicate more serious fractures.

Blows to the side of the keel, whether from the keel striking the bottom or from the hull pounding as she lies on her side, can result in cracks along the curve or angle where the hull joins the keel. Fortunately, these cracks are rare because builders tend to beef up the laminate along either side of the keel to absorb the strains of heeling under sail. Many builders also install athwartships members similar to the floor timbers in wooden boats for added strength in that direction. Don't let cracks in the gelcoat fool you into thinking that there are fractures in the laminate. Hairline cracks in the gelcoat alongside the keel-to-hull joint are often due to the fact that the gelcoat is more brittle than the laminate, and cracks as the hull flexes slightly when the boat is heeled over under sail. Stress cracks in the gelcoat tend to be fine, shallow, and more or less parallel to the top of the keel. A fracture, on the other hand, will be coarse, deep, and will often have broken strands of glass protruding from it. Naturally, if the crack is leaking, it is surely a fracture.

On the inside of the hull, the laminate in the area of the crack may show broken glass fibers, or a white line may be visible in the dark laminate if it is unpainted or "raw" fiberglass. A fracture may appear as a dark line when the laminate is back-lighted, provided that the gelcoat is thin enough for light to penetrate the area from outside. Another way to differentiate between gelcoat cracks and fractures is by sound. Fractured fiberglass has a different sound than solid fiberglass when struck with a hard object, even when the solid laminate has gelcoat cracks. Should the gelcoat actually be flaking, it can sound a bit crunchy, but that, too, is a different sound from the unmistakable reverberation or "cracked" sound of a fractured laminate.

Unfortunately, it may not be possible to view much of the interior of the hull in the keel attachment area without exploratory surgery. Builders seem to be providing fewer access hatches in the cabin sole, and they have tended recently to make them smaller. As a result, I have been involved in many repairs to hull fractures where the cost of cutting open the interior and then closing it up again was far greater than the cost of the repair. Should you suspect a fracture in the hull-to-keel joint area, don't be hasty about cutting open the sole. First, examine the exterior carefully.

In my experience, the most frequent damage to the hull caused by a fin keel is an athwartships break in the laminate just forward or just aft of the keel, and occasionally in both areas (Figure 8-8). This type of damage is caused when the boat is in forward motion and the fin's lower end is stopped dead by a collision. The fin tries to rotate, stretching the laminate down at the forward end of the keel and folding the laminate up into the hull at the after end. So powerful is this concentration of pressure at the ends of the keel's attachment that even an extra-thick laminate often breaks all the way through and begins to weep. Apparently because fiberglass is stronger in tension than in compression, it is less likely that the laminate will be broken forward of the keel, where it is pulled down, than aft where it is pushed or buckled upward. Nevertheless, I have seen a number of boats in which it was broken at both ends.

Making the repair

The preferred method of repair for breaks in the hull around the keel is to grind them out

in a very shallow V-shaped notch on the inside and build them back up with alternating layers of mat and unwoven roving. A majority of the strands of roving (never less than half) should run across the break. There are good reasons for making the patch on the inside. First, making the repair on the inside of the hull helps to avoid having to fair, regelcoat, and smooth a large area of the outside surface. Applying the patch from the inside also allows extra layers to be added, reaching far out onto the surrounding laminate. Thus, a stronger laminate can be built up in the keel attachment area than existed before, again without the need for a lot of refinishing of the exterior surface.

Despite the good reasons for working on the inside, you should study the boat carefully before ripping into the interior arrangement to repair a simple fracture or a clean break. It's embarrassing to pull up a glued-down rug and cut a piece out of a hatchless sole (despicable as these features are), only to find one's path to the damage blocked by a tank, a mast step, or a fiberglass table support. If much destruction and refurbishing of the interior will be required, it might be cheaper, faster, and less trouble to bite the bullet and make the repair on the outside of the hull.

Working on the outside, of course, you simply reverse the procedure for patching on the inside. Grind out the break in a wide V that penetrates to the interior only along the actual break line. Then, fill the V back up with ever-widening pieces of alternating mat and biaxial roving. When the patch within the V is built up flush with or a bit above the surface, you must decide whether to fair the patch and finish it off flush, or to continue on with some additional layers. If you decide to apply additional reinforcement, each layer should extend farther out past the patch by a good distance, so that they taper into the shape of the bottom without making an unsightly bump. Whether you continue past the damaged area with additional layers depends upon whether you are satisfied that the patch laid up within the V is strong enough. If you made the V at least 12 times as wide as the thickness of the laminate, preferably wider,

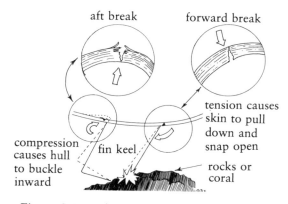

aft break   forward break

tension causes skin to pull down and snap open

rocks or coral

compression causes hull to buckle inward   fin keel

Figure 8-8. *A hard grounding with a fin keel warrants a thorough examination.*

then your patch should be as strong as the original laminate. Laying up your patch thicker and wider will make the area stronger than it was when it broke, and will strengthen and waterproof any fractures or extensions of the break that may have gone undetected. A patch like this is good insurance, with the only significant added cost being the fairing and refinishing work. Fortunately, this type of finishing work is not as fussy and time-consuming to do below the waterline, where it will be covered with bottom paint, as it would be in the glossy topsides.

Damage to interior reinforcing members

To reinforce the hull where a fin keel is bolted on, builders often increase the hull laminate thickness in the way of the fin enough to support the weight of the keel without installing special reinforcing members. In other boats, they supplement the hull laminate's stiffness with fiberglass "floors" similar to the floor timbers in wooden boats. These may be single floors, glassed in as needed, or a number of floors may be combined with fore-and-aft stringers in one large molding similar to a giant waffle. This molding is laid up separately and is later installed in the hull with wet mat or keel putty. The design of the grid includes recesses for the keelbolts' nuts and washers, and the cabin sole is usually fastened to the leveled tops of its integral members. (See Figure 1-17.)

Glassed-in floors and fiberglass floor grids should be checked for damage if your keel has sustained a collision or a hard pounding. In a collision, the members over the after end of the keel are most likely to be damaged, with those over the forward end next. This order of likely damage locations, similar to the hull laminate's, is important to note if you are confronted with probable damage under a sealed cabin sole and must decide where to cut it open for inspection.

Other signs of broken reinforcements you can watch for are cracks or bumps in the cabin sole, and tabbing that is delaminated from the hull around the edges of the sole. On the exterior, aside from cracks in the laminate, watch for distortion of the hull shape in the area around the keel and for some distance out from it. A canoe-bodied boat that is relatively flat bottomed, without much deadrise or "reverse turn" onto the keel, will sag noticeably around the fin when its weight is brought to bear on the top of the keel. This can be tested by loosening the stands or poppets supporting the hull as she sits on her blocking ashore. The same test of the stiffness of the hull in the region of the fin can be made quickly in a Travelift by relaxing the tension on the straps and watching for any tendency of the bottom to flatten or cave in as the weight of the hull is brought down on top of the grounded fin. Significant bending of the hull laminate indicates damage to reinforcing members or delamination of the members from the hull skin.

Repairing reinforcing members

Broken reinforcing members must be ground back in a shallow V and spliced together across the breaks, like all patched single-skin laminates. When delaminated from the hull, the tabbing should be refiberglassed or reglued, as the case requires. If the damage is in the way of the keelbolts, the nuts and washers must be removed at least. In other cases, the whole keel must be dropped away (see below) while the breaks are repaired. If the breakage does involve keelbolts and you take off the nuts and washers, be sure to wax the bolts and wrap them with paper to avoid clogging their threads with resin and glass fibers.

It is an excellent idea to add more layers than those needed to fill the usual shallow V flush with the original laminate's surface. In those boats whose cabin sole rests directly on the tops of the reinforcing members, however, increasing the thickness can cause an unacceptable disruption of the sole's height. The simplest solution is to cut off the top of the member in the way of the break at a

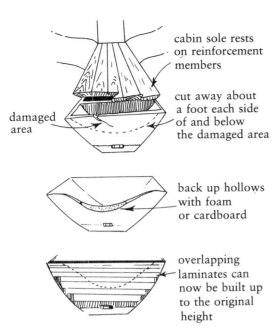

cabin sole rests on reinforcement members

cut away about a foot each side of and below the damaged area

damaged area

back up hollows with foam or cardboard

overlapping laminates can now be built up to the original height

Figure 8-9. *Repairing reinforcement members that directly support the cabin sole.*

height that will allow the extra thickness. Make a tapered cut from the surface at a point a foot or so to one side of the break, curving down below the break and back up to the surface at a similar distance on the opposite side (Figure 8-9). If this opens up a hollow member, use hot glue to install a backing piece of foam or cardboard roughly flush with the top of the cut. Now lay up the new piece, lapping it well down over the sides of the members before tapering it. Finally, build up the top of the repair until it is flush with the original top surface.

Lead-ballasted fin keels

A bent or dented fin

Since fin keels are made in many different ways, I should start by stating that I've never seen a bent cast-iron keel. Further, I believe that most fiberglass hulls would be demolished before most iron keels I've seen would

bend. That's one of the best things about an iron keel. In any event, you should consult someone who works with cast iron if faced with such a problem. Or you could try to buy a new one, assuming that there is enough left of the boat to make it worthwhile.

Lead and fiberglass are another matter. Lead can be bent back and forth many times if it is thin and relatively pure, fewer times and not as far if it is thick and impure. I confess that once we cast a great, deep fin of lead at my shop, only to have it slip out of control while standing upright and fall to the floor. Of course, it had to fall athwart a timber, which put a neat bend in it at about the middle of its height. Not wishing to recast it without at least trying to straighten it, I told the errant employee to hoist it back up and let it fall on its other side, with the timber placed as exactly as possible in the same location. Would you believe that the keel was almost straight after the first drop? By dropping it a few more times from a lesser height, followed by pressure from timbers clamped over cross timbers and much pounding on the latter with a sledge hammer, we succeeded in returning it to its original cast shape.

With a little ingenuity, some rented tools including hydraulic jacks, timbers, or I-beams, and some bolts made from threaded rod for clamps, I think you would be surprised at what you can do to straighten a lead keel.

I also think you might succeed in straightening a fiberglass-covered lead keel that has been bent. If the fiberglass has been broken and parts of it need to be removed, I suggest that the fiberglass be removed first to make it easier both to straighten the lead and to see when it *is* straight.

Lead fins may be covered with more than just fiberglass. Some custom-built keels are made relatively thin and straight in section, then built out to the desired "hydrodynamic" shape with foam and putty. Other mass-produced keels consist of lead ballast cast into fiberglass exterior half-shells with fillers of putty and foam. If the fairing has been chewed away and the lead exposed, you already know what I'm referring to. You may already have decided that the shell must be "husked" from its tip to a point above the bend before you can get at the lead to straighten it—like rolling up a pant leg to work on a wounded knee. Once the lead is as straight as you can get it, the fiberglass and other materials around it can be replaced.

While studying the problems with a damaged fin, look down the keel and boat from directly forward or aft to make sure the fin is coming straight out of the hull. Be sure that the keelbolts are not bent and that the fin has not loosened from the hull. As long as the keel-to-hull joint is not shaken loose or damaged, and assuming there is room to assemble the rigging used to apply pressure, I would attempt to straighten a fin in place. If a solid fin is badly dented and its lead locally displaced, you will also find that because of its great weight or inertia you can pound the locality of the damage quite hard with a hammer to flatten it while the fin is in place, without bending the rest of it.

A loose or tilted fin

If the fin is either loosened or tilted, it must come off so that the bolts can be checked for any loosening in the lead or fiberglass. The bolts must be straightened if bent, and then the lead must be refitted to the hull in its proper, perpendicular alignment.

Suppose the bottom of the keel is swung off to port or starboard when the hull is level. What does it mean in terms of damage or future trouble? One thing is certain: Your boat will have a permanent list in that direction if left unrepaired. As implied above, only by dropping the keel can you ascertain the nature and extent of the damage. The damage could include bent keelbolts, a mashed joint between the lead and fiberglass on one side, a slightly opened joint on the opposite side, some crushing of the fiberglass under the nuts and washers, or an outright fracture in the fiberglass of the hull or keel stub.

Dropping a fin keel

Removing a ballast keel is not a task you want to undertake unless you have to, but

sometimes it is necessary to drop the fin in order to get the bolts out of the way, or perhaps to straighten a bend in the fin or in the keelbolts. Just make sure that the bolt holes remain in the same position and of the same size through the original laminate, and slightly oversize in any new layers built up around them. Otherwise, shrinkage of the resin or a slight variation in the new part can prevent reentry of the bolts without "ovalizing" some of the holes. The easiest way to assure trouble-free reinstallation of the keel is to plug the holes with a snugly fitting waxed dowel. The dowel should extend into the boat a bit higher than the new laminate's thickness, and either be tapered or wrapped with a few turns of paper to a slightly larger diameter from the original laminate upward. When the fin is reinstalled, its upper face and the shanks or unthreaded part of the bolts that will reside in the laminate should be well coated with a bedding compound. Alternatively, a keel putty of filled resin can be used as long as the bolts and one of the mating surfaces, either the top of the fin or the bottom of the boat, are waxed to facilitate future removal. When the nuts and washers have been replaced and made up with bedding compound, keel putty, or a washer or two of wet mat under them, you can encapsulate them in fiberglass to seal off any water that might find its way up a bolt hole. If you decide to do so, you should wait until all the new fiberglass, including the keel putty, is cured very hard before you make up the nuts tight and cover them, for this will be the last time you *can* tighten them unless you want to chop off the covering. Again, don't forget the wax—just on the nuts, washers, and bolts, not on the surrounding fiberglass.

Straightening bent keelbolts

To straighten bolts that have been bent, you can rig up a press using a hydraulic jack to apply pressure. A piece of steel pipe or a piece of shafting with a hole bored in the end can be dropped over the bolt and used as a lever to apply a powerful bending force (Figure 8-10). To protect the threads of the bolt, and to allow a stronger, larger-diameter pipe to

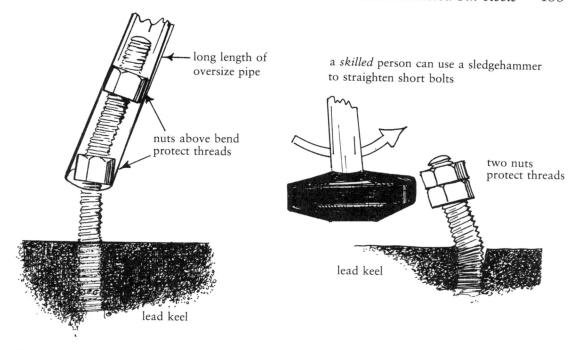

long length of oversize pipe

nuts above bend protect threads

lead keel

a *skilled* person can use a sledgehammer to straighten short bolts

two nuts protect threads

lead keel

Figure 8-10. *Straighten keelbolts with brute force (judiciously applied).*

be used, the pipe can be fitted over two or more nuts run onto the bolt above the bend. Sometimes, when the end of the bolt protruding from the lead is short, all that is required is a stout wrench fitted over a pair of nuts, and a piece of pipe on the wrench to act as a lever.

I hesitate to mention it lest some reader butcher the job, but a much favored and simple way to straighten bolts is with a sledge hammer. Don't, however, use a sledge hammer without nuts screwed on to protect the threads of the bolts. Also, to keep the bolt from enlarging the hole in the soft lead, a jig can be made to hold the bolt in place while it is hammered straight. The jig can be made from a piece of steel with a hole located so that when it is dropped over the bolt, the plate projects off the top of the fin far enough to clamp, bolt, or weld a piece of steel angle to it. The steel angle should rest against the side of the fin, making a flat, wide fence that will restrain the bolt as it is bent toward the opposite side (Figure 8-11). Should the hole already be enlarged, it can be filled with a strong epoxy putty such as Marine-Tex.

Repairing the hull or stub keel

Should the fiberglass through which the keel is bolted be damaged, you probably already have a good idea what to do based on the

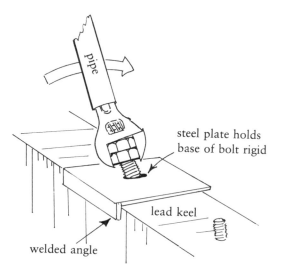

pipe

steel plate holds base of bolt rigid

lead keel

welded angle

Figure 8-11. *A steel jig can hold the keelbolt in place, preventing the bolt hole from enlarging.*

preceding discussion of fiberglass repairs. In short, the procedure is to grind away the fractured parts, then rebuild them with long, tapering joints of new laminate to the old. You will not find any core in the laminate where the keel is bolted on, just a thick, solid single skin. Not only should you make sure that your new laminate is laid up just as thick with alternating mat and biaxial roving, but if there's room for them, you might want to use some wider, slightly thicker washers on the keelbolts to spread the strains of the bolts on the fiberglass.

With so many bolts sticking out of the fin, it can be exasperating to try to align them all at once in tight bolt holes. Remember that you can enlarge the holes where the bolts are binding, and then fill in the holes with glass fiber-reinforced resin or with strong epoxy putty before installing the nuts and washers. You can also use larger and thicker washers over such enlarged holes.

Bolted-on iron fin keels

Iron fins come in three basic types: bolted on with an exposed bolted flange, bolted on with a covered bolted flange, and bolted on with the whole fin covered with fiberglass and fairing putty that extends onto the hull (Figure 8-12).

The simplest of these to remove is one with an exposed bolted-on flange. At the same time, the exposed bolt heads are often

the first thing to deteriorate; galvanized or not, the bolts eventually need replacement. The nuts and washers inside the hull may have been covered with fiberglass or a lump of filled resin putty. Once any covering is removed, with the nuts wound off or split with a ⟨nut splitter⟩, you can usually drive the bolts out easily. Two other ways to release badly rusted bolts are to cut through the nut with a metal cutting wheel on a grinder, or to bore out the bolt head from below with an electric drill pressed upward with a lever. When using a large electric drill, install a large handle to make sure you can keep the drill from turning if the bit gets jammed. Also make sure that your finger is free to release the trigger. Another way to say this is: Don't get wrapped up on the drill. A half-inch or larger drill powerful enough to bore out iron bolt heads is more than powerful enough to damage your hand, arm, or any other part of your body that gets in its way.

After installing new bolts, you might consider covering the flange with a couple of layers of mat topped with a coat of gelcoat or epoxy paint to prevent a corrosive attack on the new bolt heads. On the other hand, if it took 20 or 30 years for the first set of bolts to cause concern, perhaps a proprietary rust inhibitor will be good enough.

To guard against corrosive attack, most current builders of iron-keeled boats cover either the flange or the entire keel with fiberglass. Some are recessing the flange in a shallow box-like opening in the hull, so that the flange and the bolt heads are covered over with fairing putty and fiberglass laminate. Most keels with flanges are thin fins with

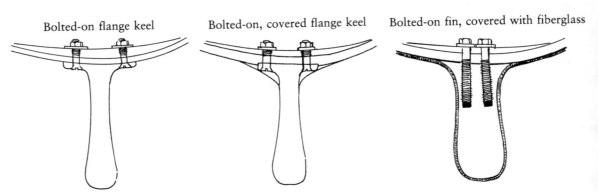

Bolted-on flange keel   Bolted-on, covered flange keel   Bolted-on fin, covered with fiberglass

Figure 8-12. *Three types of iron fin keels.*

bulbous bottom sections. Many of these are completely covered in fiberglass; in others, the covering stops at the thin part of the fin. A plain, tapered iron fin, bolted to the hull or to a stub keel, may also be covered completely with fiberglass. Whichever type of attachment your iron keel has, you will have to determine where to cut any covering of fiberglass or fairing putty if you need to remove it to repair the contiguous hull or stub keel laminate, as described above.

Centerboards and centerboard trunks

Although centerboards in early fiberglass boats were usually metal, wood, or fiberglass-covered wood, most today, even in the smallest boats and sailboards, are molded fiberglass or sometimes molded thermoplastic. Replacing a metal or wooden board, or even one that is covered with fiberglass, should not be a big problem if simply duplicating the original centerboard is satisfactory to you. If the original board is a metal plate in a close-fitting trunk, you'll have to be satisfied with it anyway, unless you want to build a wider case to contain it. A wooden board can probably be improved if it is covered with fiberglass, and it can certainly be made more durable. In this section we'll look at the common problems with molded fiberglass boards, and how to address them.

Repairs to fiberglass centerboards

Mold line splits

Molded boards sometimes split along the join of the two fiberglass half-shells. This problem is rare on boards having a good, solid filling of resin putty on the interior, but not uncommon on those filled with or built around core materials or a ballast casting. In the latter, there are more likely to be voids and a skimpy smattering of resin around the perimeter gluing the halves together. Unless the leading edge or bottom corner of the

board has been smashed or split by a collision, wetness along the lower edge may be the first sign that a split is opening. Splits may be caused by physical stress when the board is bent and twisted in use, but they are also often caused by water penetrating at some other point, settling to the lower edge (when the board is in the up position), and freezing.

Both causes call for a similar repair: First, grind a shallow depression in the edge of the board, continuing out onto the side faces and tapering off at a low angle. Then build up a strong patch of glass fiber materials, starting with a narrow, short piece and following with ever wider, longer pieces.

If the split was due to water penetration of the board, the entire board should be examined to find out where it is getting in. There may be other splits around the perimeter, but the hole for the pivot pin and the hole for the pendant attachment are prime suspects, too.

Random cracks or puffing on the face of the board

These may also be the result of water penetrating the interior of the board and bursting the skin. Often the expansion of rusting iron or steel reinforcement, given away by orange streaks running from the cracks, may be doing as much damage as ice. Again, one should investigate the source of the water getting into the interior or the trouble will continue.

The proper repair is to grind away the fractured fiberglass, cutting deep enough to make room for a good strong patch of laminate. Remember that the board has to fit inside its case loosely enough to be raised and lowered without jamming; don't make the board thicker than it was without first checking the existing clearance. If there is plenty of room, the board would benefit greatly from some added strength and watertightness.

Stress cracks in the board's gelcoat

Just as in the hull or other parts, the gelcoat of a centerboard can show stress cracks from being bent or twisted more than the relatively brittle gelcoat can stand. If the cracks are fine, if water does not weep from them after the board has been immersed for a long period, and if the cracks are confined to the gelcoat with no apparent wrinkles in the laminate itself, they might be safely ground off, and if no sign of fracture is found beneath them, painted over with a couple of coats of epoxy paint or resin to ensure watertightness. Nevertheless, if there is plenty of room in the case for the added thickness, a couple of layers of mat applied after the grinding would be better to add both stiffness and watertightness. If it is not possible to cover the area with a single piece of mat, bear in mind that two thin layers of mat with butted seams are better than one thick layer with overlapping seams. Overlapping seams will often open up when you grind them flat and smooth, but well-staggered butt joints in a two-layer laminate require little grinding and therefore should remain watertight.

Fracture of the fiberglass skin

Aside from collision damage on its leading edge, a board that has sustained blows to the side can have a fracture in the laminate on one or both sides. More than one centerboard has been broken off cleanly at the bottom of the slot in the keel, but a lesser blow can crumble the skin on one side while stretching open the skin on the other. Damage to both sides of the board is especially likely when there is a relatively tough interior core that does not absorb much shock. These fractures are different from stress cracks in that they are coarser, deeper, likely to remain wet long after immersion, and usually concentrated along a definite though sometimes jagged line. Of course, there is no question that the board is fractured if it is actually bent or creased along the cracks.

With this sort of fracture, start the repair by grinding down to the bottom of the laminate along the break, tapering the cut well out into the surrounding area. Build up a strong patch with plenty of unidirectional fibers running across the break. A warning: If the board is bent and there is a fracture on one side and apparently none on the other, you must be careful to straighten the board and clamp or weight it down securely before

fiberglassing. It must be held securely so that the shrinkage of resin as it cures does not create a new bend or worsen the existing one. For the same reason, it is not good to put a lot of layers on one side and let them cure before putting any on the other. A safer approach is to put an equal number of layers on each side, turning the board as soon as the first side has cured enough to permit it. Again, whenever possible clamp the board or weight it down on a flat surface before beginning to apply the laminate.

It almost goes without saying that in strengthening a board weakened by fracture, you should add at least as much fiberglass material as was contained in the original laminate. Further, use unidirectional roving if possible, and if there is ample room in the case, add a few extra layers.

Broken, worn or leaking hardware

Hardware is the biggest single cause of leaks into centerboards containing voids or porous cores. Holes bored for hardware will always leak eventually if they are simply filled with bedding compound, but even when they are properly lined with fiberglass, loosening of the fastenings and wear around the hole for the pivot pin can open paths for water. If water runs out of the fastener holes after the board has been immersed, it obviously ran in there, too.

To stop leaks or to prevent them when replacing worn or broken hardware, each bolt or rivet hole should be bored larger than the fastening by about half its diameter, and then filled solid with a strong polyester- or epoxy-based putty and rebored. This is also the standard cure when a pivot pin hole that is not lined with metal has been enlarged by the pin. In fact, even a metal liner can become worn, allowing the board to rattle on the pin. In this case, you can install a new metal plate on each side of the board, grinding recesses in the board if necessary to maintain clearance in the trunk. Bolt or rivet the plates into the recesses, bedding them in wet mat or filled resin putty. Once more, don't forget to first bore out the holes, fill them with resin-based putty, and then redrill them to the proper diameter.

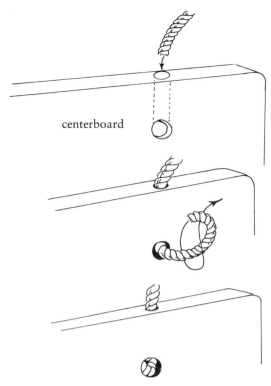

centerboard

Figure 8-13. *Reeving a knotted pendant for a centerboard.*

Usually, the only other hardware installed on a centerboard is an eye or bail of some sort for the pendant. In some boards, this function is served by two holes, one edgewise into the top of the board and a second one through the side of the board to intersect the bottom of the first. A rope pendant is then rove through and knotted (Figure 8-13). Whatever the attachment method, all holes should be sealed against leaking.

Replacing a fiberglass board

If your molded fiberglass board is destroyed, and you can't obtain a new one from the manufacturer, there's no reason why you can't build a new one by covering foam, wood, or metal with fiberglass. Your selection of one of these core materials depends on the nature of the board you're replacing, and will undoubtedly be influenced by your experience with the original board. If the original board was broken, you should thor-

oughly examine its construction, weigh it, and measure it. Not only is weight an important feature in a centerboard, but in combination with the measurement, the weight will set the limits of the construction features. Consider the four categories of boards according to weight: floating boards, neutral-buoyancy boards (more or less the same weight as an equal volume of water), sinking boards, and ballasted "drop keels." In practice, the floating board must be forced down and will bob up if released. The neutral board sinks gently until fully immersed, but it needs to be held down when the boat is underway unless a large part of it remains above the water. Obviously, the sinking board is heavier than an equal volume of water, and requires a certain amount of force to pull it up depending on how much heavier it is. The extra-heavy drop keel, whether it is a pivoted centerboard or a daggerboard, is designed to provide both righting ballast and lateral plane. Being so heavy, the drop keel requires a powerful hoisting mechanism, one which also prevents runaway lowering.

Thinking about these factors relative to your original board and the nature of your boat will help you understand why the original was built with the weight and the operating mechanism that it had. A floating board is especially suitable for a sailboard or open boat's daggerboard, because it won't sink if it goes overboard. A more-or-less neutral or a sinking-weight board bears positively against the water flowing by it when underway, but without being a great burden to raise. This type is best for centerboards or daggerboards that provide lateral plane only, such as those in light, unballasted boats or those which drop through a ballast keel. The drop keel or heavy board, however, is a necessity when the boat would be tender without it.

The point is to avoid any design changes that might spoil the board's performance on a given boat. Unless there was a problem with performance or the operation of the board, the prudent approach to building a new one would be to make it the same weight, size, and shape. If you do have reason to change the board's construction, you can easily predict its total weight by multiplying the volume of each material to be used by the corresponding weight per cubic foot, and adding up the results. Then, by comparing the projected board's weight with that of an equal volume of water (which weighs 64 pounds per cubic foot), you can tell how the board will act when immersed.

Repairing the centerboard case

The function of a centerboard case or "trunk" is the same, whether it houses a board the size of a cookie sheet in a sailboard, or a thick, hydraulically operated, several-ton board in a 90-foot motorsailer. That function is, of course, to provide a water-proof case around the board when it is pulled up into the boat, and a strong housing to anchor its upper end when it is lowered.

Watertight integrity is much more easily accomplished with fiberglass than with wood. It is therefore a very poorly built fiberglass centerboard case that leaks, unless it has been damaged. Of course, it's not uncommon to find the thin cases in light, open racing boats fractured and leaking from the leverage of the board after an extended period of hard sailing. Also, when the entire centerboard housing is below the waterline, the hardware through which the pendant raises and lowers the board or a pivot pin penetrating the case can easily develop a leak.

Following are the procedures for repairing some of the problems you may encounter.

An hourglassed case

Sometimes, when a centerboard boat is hauled, the center of the case and the slot in the keel can be squeezed together as the bottom of the boat is pushed upward by the blocking or poppets placed under the hull (Figure 8-14). The problem can also be caused by features that weaken the hull and deck structure, such as companionway hatches and quarter berths located near the middle of the case, if the weakness created by these openings is not compensated by supporting bulkheads, posts, or beams. In either instance, the consequent squeezing of the case can jam the board. An hourglassed case is more common on wooden boats, but the problem can affect fiberglass boats as well.

Grinding the board thinner is not the solution, and is likely only to delay further pinching. An effective repair starts with making cuts between the case and any joinerwork that is tight against it, wedging the case apart, and then strengthening the structure so that it can adequately absorb the external pressures. This may require strengthening the bulkheads or the sides or bottom of the boat; installing an athwartships "strong beam" in the way of a companionway; installing a fiberglass stiffener or bed log horizontally along the case under the cabin sole; or installing additional floor timbers. Which of these measures your boat needs depends upon what is causing the inward pressure on the slot, and only a careful study of the hull

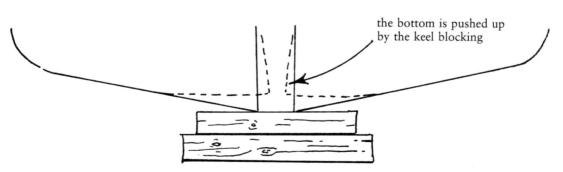

Figure 8-14. *An "hourglassed" centerboard case.*

can determine that. If the boat has been in production for some years, however, the manufacturer or other owners may know of solutions that have worked.

Another possible cause of hourglassing is a lead keel that has been pounded or has been struck on its side, bending the center of the slot inward. In this case, you might be lucky enough to be able to open it up again by simply driving wedges into the slot. If it is an external, bolted-on lead keel, the wedges are not likely to damage it in any event. If, however, the lead is covered with fiberglass or encapsulated within a hollow keel, one might drive the wedges between boards placed within the slot (Figure 8-15) in order to help protect the fiberglass covering.

Keep in mind when wedging open a centerboard case that the wedges will exert a more even pressure if they are used in pairs with identical slope. Put the large end of one

wedge in the slot, then drive the other up on it, large end down. The parallel outer faces of a pair press outward more or less evenly over the entire length of their contact with each other and the case. A number of pairs of wedges arranged along the middle portion of the case and pounded in rotation will distribute the spreading action evenly along the length of the slot. The wedges can be left in place to hold the hourglass curves straight while you fiberglass in whatever stiffening members are required.

Fractures or holes in the case

In unballasted or internally ballasted hulls, the centerboard case can be broken along with the hull or stub keel in which it is installed. To repair this type of damage one must do as much of the work as possible on the exterior surfaces, for working inside a centerboard case ranges from extremely in-

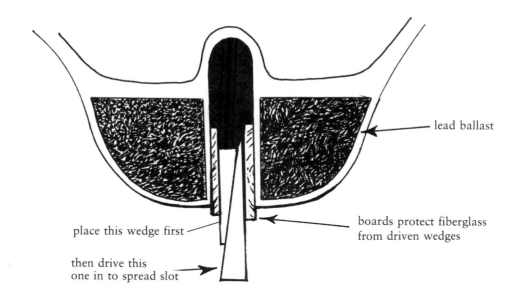

lead ballast

boards protect fiberglass from driven wedges

place this wedge first

then drive this one in to spread slot

underside of centerboard trunk

use enough wedges to hold the hourglassed curves straight until stiffening members can be added

Figure 8-15. *Bolted-on or fiberglass encapsulated keels that house centerboards are susceptible to hourglassing as well.*

convenient to impossible. Hopefully, the most one will have to do inside the slot is to slide in a waxed piece of backing material and wedge it tightly against the side that is holed. That surface will then remain fair and smooth while the repair is made.

Centerboard pivot problems

Eventually, the pivot pin, the bearing or hole in the centerboard, or both will become worn. How much wear has occurred can be estimated with the board in place by pushing, prying, or jacking its pivot end up and letting it down again. If there is excessive play, replacement of the pin is relatively easy in most boats. The pin is usually a plain piece of rod or shafting set in a hole in the case from inside the hull, or through the keel at the bottom of the case from outside the hull. The pin may be retained in its hole by a patch of fiberglass or gob of putty over each end, or over one end if the hole is blind. Occasionally, screwed-on, flush bronze plates are also used—a carry-over from wooden boat building—but these are only useful on a fiberglass boat with a bare, external ballast keel. After locating the hole, opening it, and taking off the weight of the board, the pin should slide or drift out readily. On older boats with many coats of bottom paint, locating the hole may be difficult. If you run into a problem, try to determine the pin's location by measuring with a rule shoved between the board and the wall of the case.

We have already discussed what to do if the hole or bearing in the centerboard is enlarged, but when the pivot pin is set in a fiberglass keel containing a metal ballast casting (or, if you will, a fiberglass-covered metal ballast keel), you may have other troubles. Obviously, the pivot pin hole in such a keel passes through the fiberglass skin on either side of the metal ballast and on each side of the centerboard case—a total of four intersections with the interface between metal and fiberglass, and four places where water penetration can cause trouble (Figure 8-16). If the pin should wear through the lining of the hole, or if it should fracture the lining as a result of a severe shock to the board, nothing will be isolating the interface from the water.

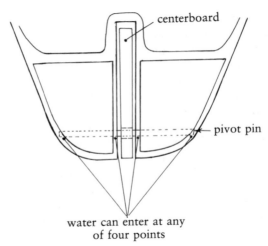

water can enter at any of four points

Figure 8-16. *Keel/centerboard assemblies are prone to leaks around the pivot pin.*

As one might guess, the greatest danger of breaking the seal is at the inside walls of the centerboard slot, the two most difficult places to reach. If the metal ballast is lead, the only problem with cracks in the fiberglass that are oozing water is that the area must be dried out and patched to prevent further propagation of the cracking when the water freezes. If you catch it early, you might accomplish this by chipping out the fractures and applying a strong epoxy putty such as Marine-Tex. Otherwise, you may have to bore out the hole in the lead and fiberglass and line it with a fiberglass tube. If you must resort to this method, make sure to countersink the fiberglass skin around the tube where it exits the keel so that you can lay in a series of fiberglass doughnuts made from mat and strand roving or a strong ring of resin-based putty to seal the joint.

The procedure for repairing a leaking pivot pin hole in an iron keel is essentially the same as in a lead keel, but catching the problem early is even more important. Lead is almost immune to corrosion from salt water, but rust growing on the inside of an iron keel can puff out and crack the fiberglass skin, with or without the help of freezing. The worst part of this problem is the difficulty of cleaning away the rust and boring out the hole in the iron, unless the hole is already large enough for a proper fiberglass lining that can be sealed to the fiberglass keel covering. Still, installing a fiberglass tube is the only satisfactory way I know of sealing the hole. The problem should be enough to make boatbuilders think twice about the idea of wrapping an iron keel with fiberglass and installing a centerboard pivot pin through it. Oh well, live and learn.

Rudders and skegs

All-metal spade rudders

Since these rudders are not in the domain of fiberglass repairs, we will not discuss their construction or repair. Nevertheless, I should remind you to provide a strong buildup of fiberglass reinforcement where the rudder stock enters the boat, and to supply an upper bearing for the stock whenever possible. Also, don't forget about the advantages of a modern fiberglass rudderport over the old-fashioned bronze stuffing box designed for bolting to wooden boats.

Metal-stock, fiberglass-blade rudders

Free-standing or skeg-hung spade rudders with fiberglass blades, commonly used in sailboats, are built in much the same way as attached rudders for long-keeled boats. Therefore, we will take up both as one type. These rudders, when mass produced, consist of fiberglass half-shells laid up in the halves of a mold that is split on the centerline. The half shells are left in the mold while it is closed around the metal stock and any reinforcements or core materials are added. A resin-based putty is also introduced into the mold to fill voids and glue everything together.

This construction is almost identical to the method used to mass produce centerboards. Its strength and durability depends heavily on the composition of the matrix and the adhesion of the resin putty. Leaks in the rudder shell, voids in the interior, and freezing of water that lodges within can eventually

cause the most common failure of this construction: splits along the centerline joint of the two fiberglass half shells. Grinding back the split and continuing around onto both sides of the blade several inches with a hollow in which a U-shaped patch of fiberglass can be laid up will tie the sides together while it seals the split. If there is a void behind a split, it should, of course, be filled with putty. The rudder should also be examined carefully for any other avenues of water penetration, which must be stanched.

Besides centerline splits, a rudder may develop cracks and puffed out areas in the sides of the blade due to extensive incursions of water into its interior. Rust bleeding out is an unmistakable sign of iron reinforcement rusting inside. If you have read this far, you know what you have to do—grind it and cover it with plenty of laminate to reseal it. Don't forget the minimum two layers of mat on the outside, which seals water out best. Also, as prescribed for centerboards, don't lay up a lot of fiberglass on one side of the blade without either weighting it down flat with a waxed, smooth surface against the new laminate, or laying up balancing layers on the other side while the first side is still green.

Tightening a blade on the stock

To keep the blade from turning on the stock, metal rods through the stock or metal tangs or plates welded to it are buried in casting putty (casting resin with a filler added). Sometimes—I know because it has happened to rudders built in my shop—these rods or "keys" break, allowing the rudder to swing on the stock like a weather vane rather than steer the boat. Unfortunately, it is often cheaper to buy a new rudder, or at least to build one, perhaps salvaging the original stock, than it is to try to repair the old one. The feasibility of repair depends upon the details of the original construction, which vary with different builders from a flimsy shell of fiberglass around punk-like foam on a puny stock to a solid-as-a-rock, matrix-filled shell around a sturdy stock.

If the broken rudder's stock is a stout one, and the blade seems a good solid one, I would not give up the idea of repairing or rebuilding it without some exploratory grinding, which will cost you little more than your time. Mark a line over the after side of the stock on either side, and holding the grinding wheel flat, grind away the fiberglass from that line forward until the side of the stock is exposed along its length on both sides (Figure 8-17). When (or before) that state is reached, the stock may try to fall off the blade, depending upon where and how completely the tangs are broken. Now you will be able to determine what type of tangs were used, the construction of the blade itself, and the practicability of reusing each of the parts. In one configuration a U-shaped tang is wrapped around the stock, its long legs terminating well back toward the trailing edge of the blade. In a boat I surveyed recently the loose blade needed only replacement of a large pin through the tang and stock.

Should the blade be solid enough, it could have new channels ground in the stock into

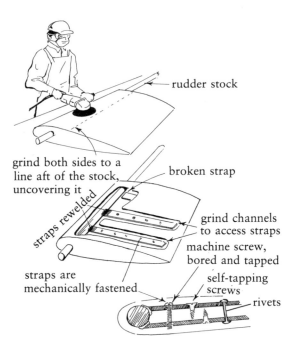

Figure 8-17. *Broken rudder stocks are more often replaced than repaired. If, however, the rudder was well-made, you may be able to repair it with little more investment than your time.*

which to weld new straps. The tangs should be set with their outside surfaces approximately flush with the outside of the rudder stock, and they should be riveted, bolted, or screwed to the blade. Then the tangs can be recovered with laminate, joining the new laminate that must be laid up around the stock. All of the new laminate added to the blade should be tapered out into the original laminate far enough to achieve the minimum 12-to-1 joint, or preferably more. This procedure is best even if the broken tang or tangs are in the center of the blade; you needn't bother to uncover the broken tangs, you'll save some grinding, and your fix will be stronger than the original.

This is but one way to repair the rudder. If the blade is not worthy of reuse, you can build a new blade with a wooden core notched for the straps as above, or laminate the core around new bolts through the stock if it was originally of that type of construction. Meanwhile, if the rudder stock was destroyed, or if you consider it unworthy of reuse, a machine shop can make up a new one for you to install in the original blade or to build into a new blade.

Skegs

If your damaged rudder is not mounted on the after end of the keel, it may be positioned at the after edge of a skeg. I say "positioned," because "mounted on" implies some support from the skeg, whereas on some models it is questionable as to which is supporting the other. You should not necessarily be alarmed if the skeg forward of your rudder has no apparent ability to protect or even steady the rudder. Sometimes a skeg is added after sea trials of a prototype or an early production model reveal steering problems. In this case, the original spade rudder, designed to be self-supporting, is usually left as it was except for providing a pintle at the heel to fit a gudgeon built into the skeg. With a rudder capable of supporting itself, great strength in the skeg could be considered redundant.

To determine whether a damaged skeg should be providing support to the rudder, you might study a few other boats of a similar size to see if your rudder is more like the spade rudders or keel-hung ones in ruggedness. The size of the rudder stock is the all-important factor. A rudder that can stand alone can stand with little or no support from a skeg, whereas a rudder on a strong keel has only torque to combat, since the keel supports it against bending. If you were to hang a keel-hung rudder on a skeg, the skeg would have to be strong enough to provide the same support.

Repairing a skeg

The repair of a skeg depends not only on whether it has to support the rudder, but on how it is attached to the boat. Many skegs on the sailboats of the past few decades have been built separately from the hull because they are so deep and thin that it would be impractical to include them in the mold. Such skegs are then bolted to the hull, to a stub keel, or into a shallow, box-like recess in the hull. As such, they are relatively easy to remove and replace with a new one from the manufacturer or to repair if badly mangled.

Unless you are anxious for the challenge of building a new one, buying a replacement skeg from the manufacturer should be much easier. Unfortunately, I can only say it "should be" easier, because the model may no longer be built, or there may be a long wait to have the part shipped if the boat is an import. Of course, if the original skeg was poorly built, it still might be worthwhile to have a new one from the manufacturer just for its shape, but you may feel compelled to add some additional laminate to beef it up. Don't worry about how to tell whether it needs strengthening; if you can't tell, it probably doesn't. Conversely, if the original skeg was wobbly, split and leaking, or broken off to expose a flimsy, foam-filled interior, then the new one possibly needs wrapping with some solid laminate. If your poorly built skeg is on an imported boat, you will have to agree with me that foreign builders do not always do everything as well as they could. (Here I go again, ever the cynic about imports.)

In any event, if you are stuck with such a skeg, there is no reason why you shouldn't wrap it with some layers of a glass fiber material such as biaxial roving, alternated (or backed) with mat. As always, you should end up with two layers of mat on top for water-tightness. There are two factors that you have to consider, though, when you cover a skeg: First, you must maintain enough clearance between the rudder and the skeg to let the rudder turn without binding. To do that may require you to grind back the original skeg laminate far enough to allow for the thicker laminate you want to build up around the trailing edge. Alternatively, if you feel that the after edge is strong enough with fewer additional layers than the sides and leading edge, you could reduce the number of layers on the after face and still go as heavy as you please elsewhere. The other factor to keep in mind is that while a little more thickness means nothing on most skegs, you still want to maintain the airfoil shape. I suggest that you do not overlap the additional layers; rather, use butted layers all over the skeg, working carefully to avoid creating lumps and hollows that will require a great deal of fairing. Of course, if the skeg was too skinny or poorly shaped to begin with, you may be able to improve it significantly by altering its shape.

Building a new skeg

It's not particularly difficult to build a new skeg for any boat. Even with nothing left but the shape of its base taken from where it was fitted to the boat, using the rudder as a guide to its shape along the after edge (and perhaps a picture of the hull taken when the boat was hauled out), one should be able to get by (Figure 8-18). Given those dimensions, one can draw the skeg in profile and determine its thickness at the trailing edge (the same as the leading edge of the rudder in most cases). The dimensions of the rudder will also determine the radius of the hollow in the skeg's after edge, how much clearance there should be between the skeg and rudder, and whether or not the sides of the skeg at the trailing edge need to be cut back to allow the rudder to turn to its stops (somewhere between 30 and 40 degrees). The thickness of the body will usually be fairly consistent; that is, the sides will be close to parallel or

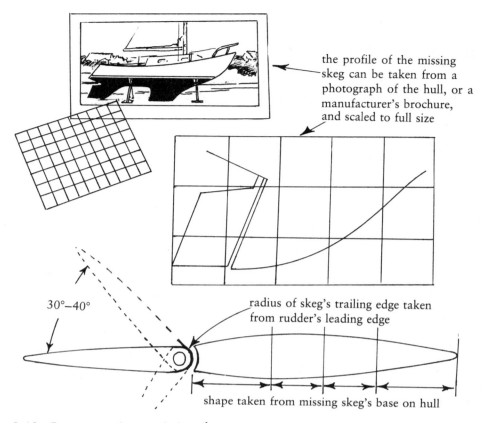

the profile of the missing skeg can be taken from a photograph of the hull, or a manufacturer's brochure, and scaled to full size

30°–40°

radius of skeg's trailing edge taken from rudder's leading edge

shape taken from missing skeg's base on hull

Figure 8-18. *Reconstructing a missing skeg.*

slightly convex, and the leading edge will not be sharp or flat, but a fairly lean parabola like the leading edges on most rudders. There will be plenty of other skegs in the boatyards to study.

The easiest core materials around which to laminate a new skeg are foam, plywood, and aluminum. Foam is the easiest to cut, fit, and shape, but it is weak and expensive, and you will have to build up a thicker laminate on it to get a strong skeg. Plywood is the cheapest, although you must remember to use an exterior, waterproof grade. Even when plywood is buried in a laminate, it should always be made with waterproof glue if used anywhere in a boat. Plywood makes a strong core; it is easy to anchor bolts in and easy to shape, and you can get any thickness you want by gluing it up in layers. It also has another advantage in that—in the manner of the contours on a topographic map—its glue lines guide you when you taper it to shape.

Aluminum is more expensive than plywood, but it is good for thin skegs because it's nice and strong. It makes a heavy skeg that has negative buoyancy, while a plywood-cored one tends toward the buoyant side of neutral and a foam-cored one is quite buoyant. Aluminum will get along alright with stainless steel internal bolts to the hull or hardware, but it shouldn't be used with bronze fasteners, just in case water penetrates the laminate along the bolts. Of course, if the bolts pass only through the fiberglass, away from the core, there'll be no galvanic corrosion.

I suppose I should mention steel, which makes the strongest, and the heaviest, core of all. If the original skeg was built of steel, if you think the weight is important ballast, or if the skeg is a particularly vulnerable one, what can I say. Just make sure you wrap the steel very securely in fiberglass with a large percentage of mat to seal out moisture. After all, you don't need strength as much as watertightness when the core is made of steel. Stainless steel bolts are the best for bolting a steel core to the hull, but here, too, think *seal*! As for hardware bolts, such as those for a gudgeon, it would be best to over-bore the steel and line the holes with an epoxy putty (such as Marine-Tex), then rebore for the bolts.

Whenever a skeg calls for bolts to fasten it to the hull, these must be anchored well. In a foam core, this is done by filling a large slot around the bolt with glass fiber–reinforced putty. The slot for the putty will need some sort of "fish hook" arrangement to keep it from pulling out (Figure 8-19). The bolts can be threaded stainless rod with several nuts and washers along their lengths, or if of smooth stock, short pieces of stainless steel can be welded to the shanks. Either type of stock can be bent to increase holding power; even one L-shaped bend at the end will do. Good attachment, in any case, means plenty of surface contact between the laminate of the shell and the glass fiber–reinforced material in which the bolts are bedded.

Although the original skeg may have sim-

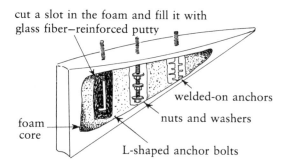

Figure 8-19. *Bolts used to reattach foam-cored skegs need extra attention to prevent their pulling out.*

ply been bolted, there is no reason why you can't tab your new skeg to the hull as well as rebolt it. If enough layers are used and the fiberglass is carried far enough onto both the hull and the skeg, the bolts will be entirely unnecessary. Certainly, the manufacturer's reason for using bolts is the convenience of building the skeg separately from the hull, and the absence of tabbing from skeg to hull is only to save the fairing and smoothing labor it would require. Your replacement is not a production job, however, so there can be real comfort in a good job of tabbing.

CHAPTER 9

Troubles on Deck

Leaks around fittings

Sooner or later every fiberglass boat's deck starts to leak. Seldom does the leak gain access through the laminate, unless, as we have discussed in other chapters, the laminate cracks. More often, water sneaks in around hardware or fastenings that pierce the laminate. Unfortunately, unlike wood, fiberglass does not swell when wet. Therefore, one ought to stanch any deck weep at the first opportunity, for it will always get worse as time goes by, never better. It's axiomatic that deck leaks are more common than hull leaks in fiberglass boats, and are their foremost geriatric problem.

It is the fastenings of the most frequently stressed items that are most likely to develop leaks. These include the fastenings for grab rails, chocks, cleats, sheet tracks, turning blocks, steering pedestals, rudderport collars, cowl vents, navigation lights, antenna brackets, hatch hinges, latches, and even flagpole sockets. Undoubtedly, chainplates are the worst leakers among hardware that extends through the deck of a boat; as for deck-fastened hardware, lifeline stanchion bolts usually cause more trouble than all the other offenders taken together.

Chainplate leaks

The tension on a chainplate can be enormous, equal in a knockdown to a substantial fraction of the displacement of the boat. Yet almost every builder prepares well for that stress on the plate's anchoring arrangement with many bolts through a tabbed-in bulkhead or knee, or with metal work that spreads the stress over a sizable area of laminate. As a result, the plate should not slip upward. At the same time, the builder will align the plate's axis as closely as possible with the shroud or stay orientation to minimize the horizontal pressure on the deck. For example, if the upper shroud chainplate is anchored to a bulkhead that is in line with the mast and shroud, the plate is tilted to become, in effect, an extension of the shroud's direction of travel (Figure 9-1). This way, an increase in tension won't tend to pull the chainplate in any other direction or try to loosen it in the deck. That's the optimum arrangement for a shroud chainplate, but it is more the exception than the rule. Forward and after lower chainplates are sometimes similarly aligned with the shroud, but backstays and headstays frequently are not.

What this means is that a very large percentage of stay and shroud chainplate bodies line up with the wire only where they are bent at the top to take the fork of the toggle or terminal fitting. As a result, every time the wire is tightened there is a horizontal pressure on the edge of the deck where the chainplate protrudes. No wonder they almost all leak sooner or later.

I don't mean to imply that chainplates that *are* lined up with the wire won't leak, just that they don't suffer a tightening and

146

relaxing of *horizontal* pressure on the deck every time the boat tacks or the rig is yanked by the boat's rolling or pitching. As we all know, any chainplate can be rudely yanked when the wire it anchors is hung up on a protrusion or serves as a fender when the boat is driven against a pier. On small boats it doesn't take a collision to overstress the chainplate fasteners; people hoist themselves aboard or steady themselves by grabbing the rigging. On any boat a boom will jibe against a shroud now and then, sometimes with enough force to break the boom.

Even those chainplates that are installed on the outside of the hull are not entirely leakproof. If heavy strains don't loosen the external bolts and cause them to leak, accidents that pull the wire out of line like a bowstring can easily loosen the upper bolt or two, long before any serious damage occurs to the plate.

Many of the factors that disturb a chainplate's watertight fit are aggravated by the boat owner or boatyard rigger who sets the rig up so tight that, with a big enough bow, one could play it like a violin. Riggers seem to get away with overtightening because fiberglass has wonderful strength in tension. As long as nothing creaks, splits, or crunches in the way of the chainplates, riggers continue to crank down the turnbuckles with strong twists of the marlinespike, screwdriver, or wrench. But while fiberglass is strong, it bends readily. Overtightening of the rig places stresses on the hull, causing bedding compound to crack and squeeze out (along with several more severe problems that we will discuss later). Once the hull has been pulled out of shape by the rig, it should come as no surprise to anyone if the chainplates begin to leak.

If it were not for the adhesive property of water, a chainplate would not leak more than any other poorly bedded deck fitting. But leaky chainplates are unusual inasmuch as rain and spray tend to gather on the surface of a shroud or stay, running down the wire and the turnbuckle to the point where the chainplate enters the deck. Only the mast with its larger surface guides more water to its base than the rigging.

What should we do to correct chainplate leaks? Dig out the bedding around them, clean the area with solvent, and apply fresh compound. Polysulfides (Thiokols), those excellent, sticky glues that turn to synthetic rubber, are the best kind. Polyurethane caulking might be alright too, but not those silicone leak-fixers that look less conspicuous because they are clear (but can be peeled off whole because they don't stick worth a hoot).

Some chainplates are fitted with little metal finishing plates that cover the hole in the deck (Figure 9-1). In time they loosen and need rebedding and refastening. Although you may not notice until you remove them, they might be made of aluminum and be all but rotted away. Whatever their apparent condition, water can and does leak by them, and the bedding under them should always be replaced when rebedding the chainplate. When you have dug out the old bedding, try to wiggle the chainplate. If there is motion edgewise, the bolts are loose; even if there isn't any looseness detectable from above the deck, from time to time you should inspect the bolts down below.

If a chainplate is loose, it is more likely that it can be moved "flatwise" (by bending it the way the flat stock would bend easiest, anyway). This is assuming that there is enough of the chainplate projecting above the deck for a good grip, and that there is enough play in the hole through the deck to allow movement. If the chainplate can be moved, working the fresh sealant all the way around it will be easier. There is nothing wrong with enlarging the space around a chainplate just a little if there is so little clearance that you can't really tell whether you're getting the sealant into it. Just don't cut into the deck too deeply. Neither is there anything wrong with building a tapered boot of the caulking up the chainplate, as long as there is no finishing plate that will interfere. The reason for not chopping the deck out too much around the chainplate is that you wouldn't want to cut all the way through the upper skin of a cored laminate, or far enough through a single-skin laminate to weaken it. You need a close fit of relatively incompressible fiberglass surrounding the chainplate

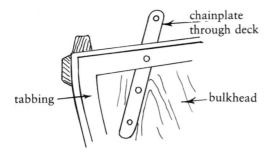

Figure 9-1A. *Typical inboard chainplate installation.*

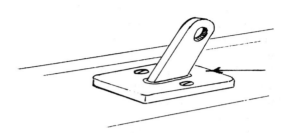

Figure 9-1C. *Chainplate finishing plate.*

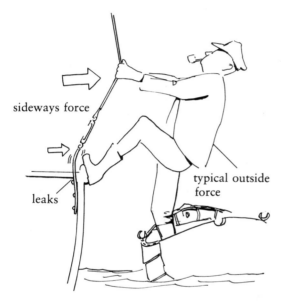

Figure 9-1B. *Outside forces can place severe strains on chainplate bolts.*

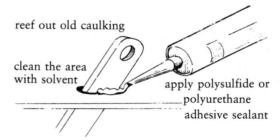

Figure 9-1D. *Deck-piercing chainplates are especially prone to leaks.*

below the caulking, or the caulking compound will be mashed unmercifully as the chainplate is yanked back and forth by the shroud. Of course, if there is insufficient support at the deck level, allowing the chainplate to move around too much to keep water out, you can build up a thick area of laminate around it. This could be a neatly tapered little hill atop the deck, or a thick fiberglass block built up in a recess in the deck. Such a recess should be made by chopping out some of the upper skin and the core around the plate and building it back with many layers of laminate. In either case, the top of the new laminate should be relieved slightly around the

edges of the chainplate to allow for sealing with bedding compound.

What are the consequences of not repairing leaking chainplates? Admittedly, a little water running down a chainplate would seem to be no calamity, as long as it doesn't drip off onto a berth, or a shelf filled with books or clothing. This attitude is typical of the position many of us take toward such a flaw in our boat: if it doesn't inconvenience us personally, it can wait. Nevertheless, surveying boats has taught me that there is no such thing as a harmless deck leak. In fact, I really believe that a deck leak is more likely to cause serious damage than a hull leak. In boats where leaking chainplates have been ignored, I have seen rot in plywood bulkheads, and I have seen fiberglass knees split open by water that has frozen inside their cores. In other boats with copious chainplate leaks I have seen bulkheads loosened from their tabbing along the hull and deck. In many cases I could not tell which came first: the leak, which then loosened the tabbing, or the loose tabbing, which set the bulkhead adrift and made the chainplate leak. What difference does it make, really? Either condition ought to have been attended to before both became that bad.

Stanchion base leaks

Like chainplates, the bolts of lifeline stanchion bases and bow or stern rails are also prone to leak. When the stanchions or rails are set up in sturdy bases of sufficient area, and when the bases are well bedded on a relatively stiff, unyielding laminate with a strong backing plate of equal or greater area below decks, they *might* stay watertight for a decade or more (Figure 9-2). Most don't, however, simply because they don't meet one or more of the above requirements. When the bedding turns brittle with age, or the deck crunches under the tremendous leverage of the stanchion, the bolts will loosen and begin to leak.

If the laminate is exceptionally solid and has remained firm, all you have to do is unbolt the stanchions and rebed them. Remember that it's the bolt holes through which the water intrudes, and these—as well as the underside of the base—must get some of the bedding. An old wooden boatbuilder's technique is helpful if you are using an oil-based bedding compound: Wrap a string of cotton around the bedding-smeared shank just below the head of the bolt before driving it into the hole. With modern synthetic adhesive sealants this step is not necessary.

If the deck laminate has not remained firm, you have a more serious problem than merely rebedding the stanchion base. You must see that the base does not compress the core or crack the fiberglass from above, and that the bolts and the backing plate do not

do the same from below. Before removing a stanchion base with leaking bolts, inspect the laminate above and below the deck for any sign of "give" when the top of the stanchion is yanked hard. If there are cracks in the laminate around the base of the stanchion, you will not need a hard yank to tell that the laminate is hurting. You might even be unpleasantly surprised by a bit of water that squeezes out when you rock the stanchion. Water coming out means a fracture of the upper skin, and a noticeable depression in the laminate around the edge of the stanchion base indicates compression of the core material. You can verify what sort of laminate is directly under the base by finding the ends of the bolts and observing their location relative to the telltale lump or ridge along the underside of the deck where the sandwich returns to a single skin. This is usually just inboard of the most common type of deck joint, an inward-turning hull flange which the deck overlaps under the toerail. Very often, the stanchion bases straddle the transition from cored to single-skin deck laminate; some of the bolts will penetrate the sandwich, while others pass through the solid laminate or through the deck joint.

We might as well have it out right now: Having seen what so often happens to the deck, I don't approve of bolting stanchion bases or any other heavily stressed hardware through the usual core materials. In my experience, nothing more compressible than a medium-density wood—such as fir, mahogany, or plywood made from these—will endure the punishment. When you must install hardware in a balsa- or foam-cored laminate, I suggest that you first cut out the core and insert a replacement of wood, aluminum, fiberglass, or glass fiber-reinforced resin putty. Then rebuild the outer skin and rebed the stanchion base.

I realize that this is a pretty stiff order; as we know from previous discussions, the outer skin will have a generous taper where the patch overlaps the original. This means that a larger area than what the stanchion base covers will be new laminate without the nonskid pattern in it, unless you can remove the core from the underside of the deck. If you must work from the top surface, one thing you can do is to draw a neat margin bordering the stanchion base, tape off any surrounding nonskid, and finish the margin smooth to match the smooth margin that the deck has, or should have, along its outboard edge. Another thing that you can do is to undercut the outer skin by scooping out the core for a good distance past the edge of the hole and filling it with a strong resin-based putty. This will keep the disrupted area of the deck's surface to a minimum, while still providing a wide, strong underpinning for the base. Such tunneling under the outer skin will require some ingenuity if the core is a tenacious, well-constructed one, and possibly some special homemade tools for hooking the balsa or foam and pulling it out. If this turns out to be too frustrating or time- and energy-consuming, I would quickly bite the bullet, abandon the digging, and cut out a bigger hole for the replacement core.

I hate to mention this lest it lead you into an ill-advised shortcut, but there is another approach to the cure of deck crunching *if* it hasn't progressed too far. Given only light cracking of the outer skin fairly close to the base and no widespread saturation, you can try distributing the pressures of the base and backing plate over a wide area by making them larger. Since a stanchion base is a relatively costly item to custom-make, the original base could be supplemented with a plain but larger plate on the deck under it. Or, if the base is stainless steel and you have access to a good welder, you could have it extended on one or more sides, although usually not on the outboard side because of the toerail or bulwark close by. Not only might this be a good way to handle a base that is already creating problems with the laminate, it might also be wise in some cases to install a larger base and backing plate as a preventative measure. The base of the stanchion next to the boarding gate, for instance, is often subject to cruel and unusual punishment. This is a good example of a base that could benefit from a larger base and backing, even if it has not yet caused a problem.

Now suppose that your deck problems are already severe and that saturation of the core is rampant around many of the stanchion bases where the outer skin has been broken. In that case, what we have said about replacing the core in the stanchion areas still goes, but you should also review the chapter on "Dealing With Core Problems." Unfortunately, we are not talking about a theoretical problem. It is doubtful that there is a large group of fiberglass boats anywhere that doesn't include several whose stanchion bases are leaking, and one or more whose deck is endangered by incipient core saturation.

Backing Plates

Any heavily loaded deck fitting needs a good backing plate to disperse the pressure on the underside of the laminate (Figure 9-2). Intense pressure on such small areas will not only compress and crush a sandwich laminate, it can distort and crack a single skin, too. Given enough force, a highly loaded fitting could even tear a chunk out of the laminate. One might think that only something like a bow cleat or a turning block needs a good backing plate, but though they certainly do, the place where inadequate backing plates are most often found is under stanchion bases. At the risk of sounding like a broken record, I keep repeating that builders don't realize how cruelly a lifeline stanchion pries on the deck. When a 200-pound man hoists himself aboard by pulling on the top of a 24- or 30-inch stanchion, you can imagine what the upward pull is on a bolt only 2 inches from the opposite edge of the plate. You can also imagine what the downward pressure is on the other edge.

The only way to handle such a force is to provide a relatively unbending, incompressible laminate between a sturdy base and a backing plate of adequate area. A big base alone won't do it, unless it is ridiculously large in area, nor will a big backing plate alone. It is essential that both base and backing plate be reasonably, but unobjectionably, large. I think they should be bigger than the current norm. But area alone is not enough. The base and backing plate should also be a relatively unbending, incompressible, and unbreakable material. Of course, the bases usually have these properties, the vast majority of them now being made of stainless steel. The older bronze ones were good too, but there have been some very bad aluminum, die-cast, zinc alloy and stamped nonferrous ones, and yes, there have been some thin and flimsy stainless ones, too.

It's most often the backing plates which are either lacking in strength and stiffness, too small, or missing altogether. For example, many builders use disks of fiberglass laminate for backing plates. If these are installed on your boat and your stanchions are leaking and wobbling around, get rid of them and install generous-sized plates of stainless steel. You could use bronze plate or aluminum of the corrosion-resistant type here, but except for a little difficulty in boring the holes, stainless steel is the best and is often the cheapest.

The problem with fiberglass for a backing plate is its flexibility, which doesn't let it distribute the pressure of the bolts as well as a stiffer piece of metal. If the fiberglass was very thick, it wouldn't be so bad, but that would mean a rather bulky slab of it, which wouldn't ordinarily be on hand or worth making up.

Hardwood backing blocks, which we used for years in wooden boats, are also much more bulky than metal plates by the time you make them thick enough not to bend. Thickness tends to make backing blocks obtrusive in fiberglass boats, which lack the deep deckbeams of wooden construction to hide them. Wood is also more compressible than metal and therefore less suitable for use under the small stainless steel washers that are generally available today. If you do use hardwood to make new backing blocks, it will be worth the trouble to obtain or make up some extra-large washers for the stanchion bolts.

With all the trouble we have today with stanchion bolts on fiberglass boats, you may be wondering how we ever got by in wooden boats. Well, we didn't. Stanchion bases have been a problem since they were invented, and they were always coming loose in wooden boats, too. As mentioned before, the leaking wasn't as bad, because properly driven bolts were watertight thanks to the wood swelling tightly around them. The swelling of the wood also helped them resist being pulled out more than bolts through clearance holes in fiberglass, and, of course, wooden boats weren't built with a core of balsa or foam.

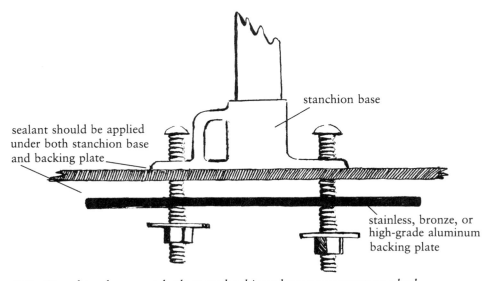

Figure 9-2. *Stanchion bases need adequate backing plates to prevent unscheduled dives over the side.*

Further, because of ribs, sheer clamps, and interior sheathing or ceiling, all of which tended to space the interior arrangement away from it, more of the drips in wooden boats found their way unobtrusively to the bilge than do those in thinner skinned fiberglass boats.

Leaks around deck joints, rails, and railcaps

Deck joints go with rails and railcaps because, to date, the standard way to build a decked fiberglass boat is to mold the hull in one piece and the deck in another, then install a rail to cover the joint and the row of fastenings in it. Figures 1-12 through 1-16 show various deck joints and the types of rails used to cover them.

Deck joints themselves don't leak as much as they used to. Most builders have switched to less leak-prone types of joints, and most are more conscientious about fastening and sealing them. This is not to imply that all older fiberglass boats have deck joints that leak. There are many perfectly sound, watertight joints today on boats built up to 30 years ago. Then, as now, good workmanship begat durability.

Still, if leaks along your deck joint indicate that the watertight integrity has been broached, the first thing to do is to trace the leaks carefully and find the source. The leaks have one of three sources, or a combination of them: the joint or interface of the hull and deck laminates; the mechanical fastenings used to hold overlapping laminates together; or the mechanical fastenings used to fasten a rail over the joint.

The rail fastenings

With a sort of "last in, first out" perversity, the mechanical fastenings of various rails tend to be the earliest source of leaks. This is not too surprising, as they usually pierce the deck joint after it has been assembled, and the fasteners get little or no benefit from the compound that was used to seal the joint. Naturally, the rail gets bumped and kicked, which helps to loosen the fastenings, and if it's a wooden rail, its alternate swelling and shrinking further assists the loosening process. I wish I had a penny for every tube of silicone applied along the corner of a toerail or a guardrail to try to keep their fastenings from leaking. It doesn't work; you must take the rails off and rebed them. Give each fastening its own individual shot of bedding—in the rail, under the rail, and in the hole through the fiberglass.

Hull-to-deck joint fastenings

After the rail fastenings, in order of their tendency to leak, come any fastenings used specifically to fasten the hull and deck moldings together. In some boats, these will be a sizable bolt every 6 inches or so around the entire deck edge. In others, the deck fasteners may amount to but a scattering of light screws or rivets as needed to hold the overlapping laminates together until the rails are applied and the rail fastenings take on both jobs. Regardless of how many they are, these fiberglass-to-fiberglass fastenings are often prevented from leaking only by bedding used to seal the toerail above. The problem is compounded by the fact that two single-skin fiberglass laminates are too thin to provide good holding for a screw without its point projecting through into the interior. Despite the fact that the joint, the fasteners, and the rail above may be bedded, a potential path for water is created through the laminate.

Because of the incredible ability of water to find its way through the smallest hole, in my experience at least, self-tapping screws are the least likely to leak of all the fastenings used in a deck joint. I have found tapping screws in older boats that were obviously original, without so much as a drop of moisture around them. I can't believe that screws would hold the joint together as well as bolts if the hull were distorted, but they have obviously never leaked for two or three decades. I presume that is because self-tapping screws are wedged into a predrilled hole so tightly that they tend to prevent the passage of water down the interface. This tightness is probably augmented by the fibers displaced by the threads of the screw, adding to the pressure around it. Of course, it is only the great strength of stainless steel that permits forcing a screw into a hole that tight without breaking it off. Nevertheless, self-tapping screws are virtually watertight when the hole is drilled to the right size.

This is more than you can say for most bolts, and I hate to even mention rivets, which, not surprisingly, are particularly bad from the standpoint of leaking. Rivets have to be made of a malleable metal, and malleability is not a desirable quality for maintaining the pressure against the fiberglass needed to keep water out of the interface. Rivets were used in the deck joints of many early fiberglass boats, but builders soon found that they could only be trusted for temporarily holding the two parts together while they were glued with a strong resin-based putty, or while the joint was tabbed with fiberglass laminate. As a permanent fastener, rivets (and riveted joints) are difficult, at best, to keep watertight—with or without caulking.

The deck joint

Fortunately, the modern deck joint itself doesn't often spring a leak except after accidental damage. Some very good adhesive sealants, mastics, and filled-resin glues and putties are available, so that only a careless builder who misuses these compounds or skimps on the mechanical fasteners is likely to produce a leaky joint. There are still some cautious builders who doubly seal the joint by fiberglassing over it, even though this is highly labor-intensive.

Despite everything that boatbuilders have learned over the years, you are not alone if your boat's deck joint has been worked open by hard sailing. Don't, however, emulate those owners who try to stanch such leaks by smearing various kinds of goo on the joint—especially on the inside of the boat! If water is coming through between the deck and hull laminates, then the bedding compound, has lost its "life"; it is dried out, cracked, or crumbling, or, if a hard resin-based glue/putty was used in the joint, it has lost its grip on one or both of the surfaces it's supposed to be connecting. If you have one of the few deck joints that has been sealed with a tabbing of laminate, there is another possibility that you will readily recognize: The tabbing has probably delaminated from at least one side of the joint or has been split open.

Boat owners rarely have a reason to check the mechanical fastenings of the deck joint unless, of course, it's leaking. If it is leaking, the owner can only hope that he won't be faced with a great gaping crack between the two laminates. Unfortunately, this is sometimes the case, because the mechanical fastenings that should be backing up the joint are too small, too widely spaced, or nonexistent. It goes without saying that any section of the joint that is leaking isn't stuck together anymore, and now is the time to find out what the problem is and to decide on an approach to solving it. The only good thing about a gaping stretch of the deck joint is that it removes any doubt that the joint needs refastening as well as resealing.

Let the repair suit the leak

It should also go without saying that a deck joint that has opened up must not only be refastened mechanically, but also rebedded, reglued, or sealed over with fiberglass to boot. This means that any rail covering the joint must be removed in all cases. From there on, the most practical approach depends on the construction details of the particular boat.

In a small boat with little or no interior bulkheading and without a hull or deck liner or other interference covering the joint, the procedure would be to open up the joint, clean it out, rebed it, and then refasten it.

This is how one might expect to repair many small, mostly open boats which, not coincidentally, are often in need of this type of repair. The deck on many small boats is shaped like a section of a shoe box cover, which can be lifted off if the boat comes down with the rubrail caught on a piling or on the gunwale of another boat.

In larger boats with more complicated construction, there can be so much interior joinerwork tied to both the deck and the hull that it would be a major operation to cast everything loose in order to open up the joint for rebedding or regluing. In that case, after removing the rail and installing any new mechanical fastenings needed, the joint could be sealed by fiberglassing over it, preferably on the outside.

It is a fact that nothing will seal a deck joint better or more durably than fiberglass. It is also a fact that a proper laminate spanning the joint would hold it together as well as or better than mechanical fastenings. Nevertheless, building a substantial laminate over the deck joint of most boats is not as simple and easy as it might seem. Let's review some of the conditions that could affect our ability to both seal and strengthen the joint with fiberglass.

If the joint has good mechanical fastenings (albeit leaking ones), but still leaks due to failure of the bedding compound, a few layers of fiberglass can be applied over the joint after sanding the original laminate surface to clean it and expose its glass fibers for the best grip. If you cover both the joint and the heads of the mechanical fastenings, both should be sealed against further leaking. In most cases, this outside covering laminate won't add anything to the physical strength of the joint. This is because you want to apply the laminate in a narrow strip so that the rubrail or toerail, when reinstalled, will cover it. The fiberglass covering replaces the failed putty or bedding compound and serves only to seal the joint. The strength of the joint still depends on the original mechanical fastenings.

If it is possible to gain access to the joint on the interior and build up a laminate of generous width across it, you can add a great deal of strength to the joint. In climates where freezing is not a problem, this approach would seal the joint from leaking into the interior, too. Unfortunately, in freezing climates you would still be faced with the problem of water creeping into the joint and possibly opening leaks along its length when it freezes. Unless the boat is used only in a tropical climate, it is still important to keep the joint and the fastenings sealed at the exterior surface, even if the interior is heavily fiberglassed.

Ideally, then, a generously thick, wide tabbing on the *outside* of a deck joint would be the best way to both seal and mechanically join the parts. This type of joint would last virtually forever, but would require extensive refinishing of both the hull and deck surfaces. As a repair to a deck joint that is merely leaking, it is not usually worth disturbing the surfaces beyond what can be concealed by the covering rail. Nevertheless, if you are confronted with damage that involves the hull and deck surfaces and requires widespread refinishing anyway, by all means, ignore the deck joint as joined by the manufacturer and fiberglass the hull and deck into a one-piece unit. Fair the new joining laminate into both the hull and deck with proper long tapering laps, doing it all on the outside. That's the sort of joint a builder would love to have made in the first place.

In summary, a hull-to-deck joint needs to be strongly fastened with mechanical fasteners and a sealing compound, with fiberglass tabbing, or with both. The joint, and any mechanical fasteners through the joint, must be sealed on the exterior. The ideal joint consists of a heavy fiberglass lay-up over the outside of the joint, well faired into both the deck and topsides. Almost as good is a heavy lay-up on the inside of the hull with a lighter tabbing to seal the joint from the outside. More often than not, neither of these ideal methods is practical for the repair of a leaky deck joint. In this case, the best procedure is usually to ensure that the joint is well fastened mechanically, and then cover both the joint and the fasteners with a light fiberglass tabbing concealed under the toerail or rubrail.

More about leaks

Damage to the deck itself

The damage to the interior of the boat from a deck leak obviously depends on what gets wet and for how long. Damage done to the deck itself, however, depends primarily on how the deck is constructed. A sandwich construction with a porous core suffers most, and as we mentioned in the chapter on core problems, will eventually be ruined if not repaired. Without question, the single-skin deck is least likely to be damaged by leaks, although in freezing climates, water sitting in cracks or voids will tend to propagate more cracks and can turn minor leaks into major ones. This is one of the reasons why a fiberglass boat should always be stored under cover. It's also a good reason for the expeditious repair of *all* leaks, whether the water drips on something dear to the owner, or simply runs into the bilge.

Liners don't help

If we only had leaks in single- or sandwich-skinned decks to repair, our projects would be fairly straightforward. Builders, however, like to install fiberglass liners in the overhead, which saves them many hours in finishing off the interior of the deck. Unfortunately, in addition to covering up the ridges and grooves and the rough underside of the deck molding, the liner also conceals important construction details like the wiring and the fasteners for the deck hardware. In solving *his* problem of putting a good face on the underside of the deck, the builder has created *your* problem of determining the source of leaks that drip off or out of the liner. Consider a constant drip from a portlight (see below). Where is the water getting in that drips from the frame? The only thing you can be reasonably sure of is that the source of leak is somewhere above the place where the water emerges. You will have to direct a high-pressure jet of water from a hose at each through-deck fitting or fastening, starting with the lowest one suspected (including the

portlight itself), until water emerges. Otherwise, you might as well rebed every bit of hardware from the leak up.

Liners give much less trouble when the fastenings are allowed to penetrate them, or when access plates are installed to facilitate repairs and replacements. As a surveyor who is hired to point out leaks to buyers or owners and to suggest repairs, I cannot forgive a builder who hides anything that might need repair with a liner—and neither will you if you have a leak that you can't get to. If the liner is spaced well away from the underside of the deck, builders should install covers to allow access to the fastenings. If the liner is tight up against the underside of the deck and headroom is limited, the builder should use a metal backing plate with rounded edges and corners. The backing plate can be bored and tapped for the fastenings, and the ends of the fasteners can be ground off flush and peened or covered with a cap nut. These are the ways I know you will want your fittings installed, once you have had to fight a deck liner in order to rebed or repair them.

Hatches and portlights: leaks, fractures, and other troubles

The gasketed types

Of the two basic types of hatches and portlights—those that clamp tight on a rubber gasket and those that depend on a lip or coaming to keep water out (Figure 9-3)—only the gasketed ones can be expected to stay watertight under all conditions. Although the gasket is the heart and soul of this type, it is surprising how many people will keep winding them tighter and tighter on a gasket that has been "dead" for years, until finally something is bent or broken. Unless the frame is distorted, all that is needed to keep them tight is to install a fresh gasket and keep the tightening screws or dogs working freely. A new gasket is easily installed in rubber cement or with a cement made specifically for the particular gasket material.

On the other hand, if you have a gasketed deck hatch or portlight that never has closed properly, it could have been improperly installed. I have run across a number of aluminum-framed foredeck or skylight hatches that were force-fitted to the crown of the deck; faint as the crown may have been, it was sufficient to keep them from closing properly. These hatches are made to be installed on a dead flat surface. If they are not, they may not only leak, but the light may crack as well. Even a light made of polycarbonate or Lexan does not take kindly to distortion of the frame into which it is bolted.

Another builder's mistake you may have inherited is a portlight or deadlight that was installed on the side of a curved cabin trunk. This situation often goes unnoticed until the light in it cracks. Sometimes, even the cast aluminum frame will crack, too. Preformed, curved deadlights and windows are available, and for smaller boats, there are thin thermoplastic deadlights in light, rubber-gasketed frames that were made to take these slight curves. The heavier, flat ports and deadlights should always be installed on a flat surface or they are sure to cause trouble. It won't look quite as neat, perhaps, but you can make one of these ports happy by building out the laminate or by inserting wedges under its frame—well bedded, of course.

The other common sources of leaks through gasketed hatches are their flanges and the fastenings used to install them. Here, rebedding the flange and the fastenings as described for other deck hardware should make them watertight again for many years. Running a bead of silicone around them, on the other hand, won't work for long, if at all.

Box hatches

Box hatches, those which fit down over a coaming or into a rabbet in a coaming, are usually watertight enough for pleasant summer sailing along shore. When strongly built, provided with gasketing, and secured with stout hardware, box hatches can go anywhere. Box hatches made of fiberglass can go unattended for years without splitting, rotting, or falling apart as wooden ones did unless they were faithfully and heavily refinished every season. Unfortunately, not all box hatches are maintenance-free, for some builders have learned at their customers' expense how lightly they can build a fiberglass hatch and get away with it.

Tough as fiberglass is, you may find that not enough of it was used to prevent a hatch cover from cracking underfoot or chipping when snagged by the sheet of a jibing sail. Nevertheless, armed with the information in the preceding chapters, I'm sure you can repair a hatch. While you will want to make cosmetic repairs in the top of a hatch, increasing its strength and stiffness and heading off worse problems will be done more easily by adding layers on the underside. With a single-skin hatch, you may be able to add core material and an inner layer, as long as you can maintain the same clearance between the hatch and the coaming. You don't want to add so much thickness to the underside of the hatch cover that the new material rides on the coaming top and lifts the bottom edges off their landing. You should also be careful not to turn reinforcing layers down along the inner face of the sides of the hatch if there is little clearance between the coaming and the inside of the hatch. In cases where the underside of the hatch cover is fitted with a gasket that presses against the top of the coaming, any reinforcing laminate laid up on the inside of the hatch will have to be confined to the rectangle inside the coaming. This means that in some cases the only practical way to reinforce a weak hatch cover will be to grind away the gelcoat and add new layers of laminate to its exterior.

Meanwhile, if you would rather have a new hatch and can't get one from the manufacturer, you should consider building one from scratch. Few fiberglass projects are more fun than building a female mold for a hatch cover and then laminating one inside it. To start, all you have to do is build a box with inside dimensions that match the outside dimensions of the finished hatch (Figure

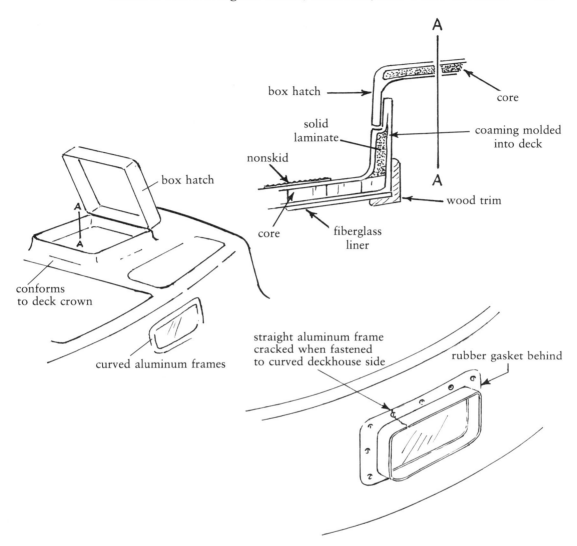

Figure 9-3. *Gasketed portlights and hatches generally remain leakfree, but the gaskets do deteriorate over time.*

9-4). Wax the interior of the box well, and then lay up the fiberglass inside, along with any core material you want to include for extra stiffness. For rounded corners on your hatch, you can "thumb" a radiused fillet of putty or wax into the corners of the mold. For nonskid on its top, rubber cement a piece of embossed material to the bottom of your mold. For a flush-fitting deadlight in the hatch cover, you can mold a hole with a rabbet for the light by gluing two disks or rectangles of plywood to the bottom of the mold. Make the first piece slightly larger in size and thickness than the light to allow for bedding and for lateral expansion, especially if the light is thermoplastic. Then make the second piece on top of it smaller by the width of the rabbet all around. When you do the lay-up, you will carry your laminate up over the first piece, stopping against the second to form the hole with the rabbet around its edge. After five coats of wax with an hour between to dry, you can coat the mold with catalyzed gelcoat and lay up the hatch as soon as the gelcoat has cured. Remember, don't fasten the mold together any better than you have to so that you can take it apart if the hatch won't readily pop out.

Cockpit seat hatches

Cockpit seat hatches in sailboats often take terrific abuse, not just because they are used as a cover for the lockers beneath, but because the crew tends to use them as a step. Typically, crewmembers will leap on and off the seat hatches when climbing between the main deck level and the cockpit sole, and they often stand on the seat hatches to gain better visibility, to reach the rigging on a boom, or to furl the mainsail. If the builder built the hatch cover to be used as a step, it will undoubtedly survive this treatment. If however, the builder thought of it as just another hatch cover, it is not likely to function well as a step for very long.

Cracks in the gelcoat are bad enough, but this is simply a cosmetic problem. Fractures in the laminate of the covers, on the other hand, may let water into the core material that is often used to help make them stiffer without adding weight. Fractures will lead to saturation of the core and eventually to delamination of the hatch. It is therefore important to promptly repair damage to seat hatches with sandwich reinforcement, even though they may not feel weakened underfoot. You will also want to repair and reinforce single-skin hatches that are developing cracks, simply because cracks are often a warning that the hatch is likely to fracture. Keep in mind that a hatch that is too limber is easy to repair. Once a hatch becomes fractured, however, the repair is much more difficult.

The majority of fiberglass seat hatches rest with the underside of the top bearing on the inner edges of a coaming around the opening (Figure 9-5). The sides of the hatch usually just hang in the middle of the gutter that drains water away from the coaming. In order for the hatch to close properly, you must keep any added reinforcing materials from overlapping the inner edges of the gutter, although, in some cases, it may be possible to grind the top of the coaming down enough so that a few of the added layers

could be extended out to the edges of the cover and down the sides.

Another way to strengthen hatches is to apply wooden slats to their tops. The slats can be fastened from beneath with screws, and should be set in a polysulfide adhesive sealant such as 3M 101. Many sailors would love to have teak slats on their cockpit seats; stiffening the hatches is a good excuse to go ahead and do it. Before you do, however, you should figure out how the hinges are going to be arranged, for you may have to move them to the surface of the wood or above it, lest the hatch jam when you try to open it. If moving the hinges is necessary, you might find that a different style of hinge would work better. A seat built with the slats spaced off the fiberglass on cleats would be drier than one with slats screwed tight to the fiberglass, even though the slats may be well spaced and scuppered. The only problem here is that too much added height may make the seats uncomfortable for children and shorter adults. If the seats are too high it may be necessary to add a cockpit grate to bring the sole up to a comfortable height for sitting.

Companionway sliding hatches

The most used of all hatches, sliding companionway hatches that are in a position to be walked on when furling sail are often badly abused as well. Yet with a width of only 20 to 36 inches and a pronounced crown to add strength, it should not be difficult to build one strong enough to last as long as any other part of the boat. Unless it was the victim of an accident like the boom falling on it, a companionway hatch cover that is broken was simply underbuilt to begin with. While cockpit seat hatches may be prone to fractures, leaking is the problem more commonly associated with companionway hatches.

The typical sliding hatch does not leak when ordinary rain and spray land on it, but it is almost impossible to keep tight against crashing seas and water driven by wind. Most of the time, it is more important to most of us for the hatch to slide easily when pushed by the user, yet even this requirement

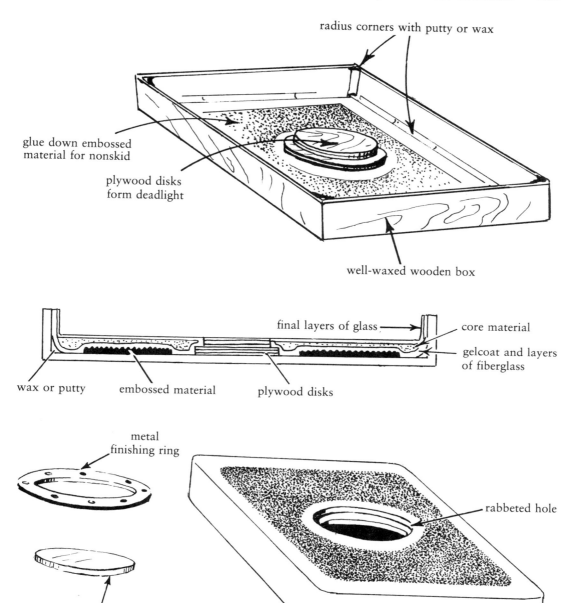

radius corners with putty or wax

glue down embossed
material for nonskid

plywood disks
form deadlight

well-waxed wooden box

final layers of glass

core material

gelcoat and layers
of fiberglass

wax or putty   embossed material   plywood disks

metal
finishing ring

rabbeted hole

plate glass or Lexan

Figure 9-4. *Building your own fiberglass hatch is an easy project that will not
only provide you with the forming and laminating skills needed to tackle bigger
projects, but also leave you with a custom-made hatch superior to (and cheaper
than) store-bought alternatives.*

is not always satisfied on all boats. To make
a hatch that slides easily while remaining
truly watertight would require a very so-
phisticated and probably expensive arrangement. As a result we often settle for a hatch
that is about as tight as a cover on a shoe
box, with an after edge that does not hang
down over the top edge of the doors or slides
in the companionway, but merely slides out
over them a little.

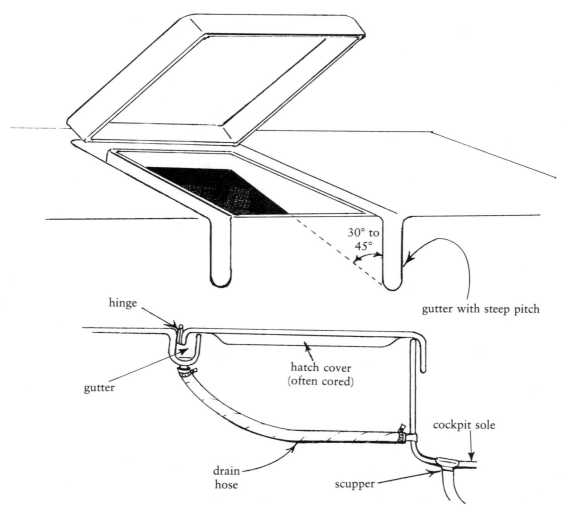

30° to
45°

gutter with steep pitch

hinge

gutter

hatch cover
(often cored)

cockpit sole

drain
hose

scupper

Figure 9-5. *Typical fiberglass cockpit seat hatches. Either configuration ensures drainage of water from gutter.*

The slight overhang on the after edge is often the source of your first leak, but only when the water is driven against it from astern. At the forward end of the sliding hatch, one has a better chance to weatherproof the crack between the hatch and the little athwartships rail between the hatch slides. This is usually done by attaching a part shaped like a small deck beam on the underside of the hatch cover on the forward side of the athwartships coaming at the front of the hatch (Figure 9-6). Now water has to be blown under the beam on the hatch cover, and then up over the coaming on deck in order to get inside. To make the water's path

even more torturous, one can also interlock the two members with a tongue and groove or put a gasket between them. As tight as this may be, however, water can still be driven along the slides on which the hatch rests at either side. Now one begins to see that no matter how carefully the forward end of the hatch is treated, it is not likely to keep out all hard-driven water. This is where the "weather cover" or seahood is brought into the design. A seahood (Figure 9-7) is a part similar to but larger than the companionway hatch cover fastened to the deck and covering the forward end of the hatch cover and its slides. The hatch cover slides into it when

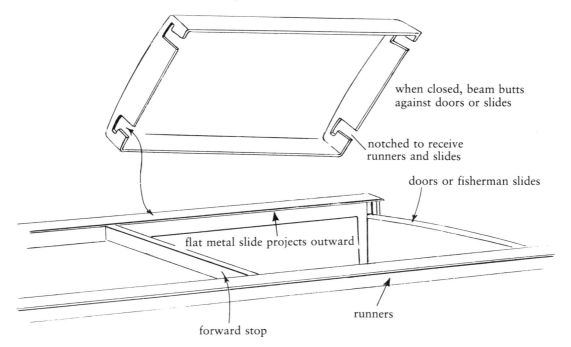

when closed, beam butts
against doors or slides

notched to receive
runners and slides

doors or fisherman slides

flat metal slide projects outward

forward stop

runners

Figure 9-6. *Typical sliding hatch.*

opened, and out when closed, yet not far enough to expose that forward end. With a weather cover, a hatch has to be almost underwater to let much of it in, provided that the other three sides are planned and built with reasonable care.

Two common features of some of the best companionway hatches are fairly tall slides to keep water from climbing over them, and a lip on the slide that projects outboard, around which the hatch cover curls or is rabbeted. High sides on the hatch cover that hang well down toward the deck, and a long overhang aft over the doors or fisherman slides are two other good features. Not all of these water-shedding features are included in the many different configurations that have appeared since builders started making hatches in fiberglass. As so often happens, the new material spawned attempts to reinvent the sliding hatch, or at least to adapt it to the strengths, weaknesses, and production advantages of the new material. If your companionway hatch slides easily, is held firmly in place, can be walked on, and only leaks in the worst of weather, it may be as good as there is. To shed hard-driven water, the

only improvement you may need to make is to add a weather cover.

Solving companionway hatch problems

The rule of perversity says that because we need them to slide easily, hatches prefer to stick until we feel like trying to open them with a martial arts kick. Except for the fear of stepping back off the bridge deck into the cockpit or falling down the companionway, I've often been tempted to do just that.

Many boats have a type of hatch that sits over the slides like a hat with its brim on the deck, and runs between two rabbeted wooden guides that hold it down and guide

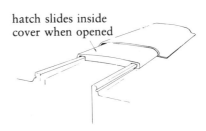

hatch slides inside
cover when opened

Figure 9-7. *A hatch pocket, or "seahood," provides an extra measure of security.*

it by entrapping that brim (Figure 9-8). This type of hatch can be jammed if the wood swells and closes in against it, or if the hatch is flattened by walking on it, spreading the two side flanges and jamming them in the rabbets.

In the case of swelling, you will definitely have to remove the guides and widen the rabbets. Widening or deepening the rabbets may also help the hatch to slide freely if it has been flattened or if it was distorted while it was still green. If the hatch was broken, however, you will have to restore its shape and repair it with fiberglass.

This type of hatch can also jam if someone steps on one of the guides and breaks the overhanging part of the rabbet. The broken piece can become wedged between the hatch and the guide, or can cause the hatch cover to ride up and jam against the broken remainder. You can solve this problem by making stronger guides of white oak, ash, or locust; if they must be teak, make them thicker, for teak is a bit brittle. The dark red Philippine mahogany is also a good substitute for teak as, in a given thickness, it is more resistant to splitting.

Another, more common type of fiberglass hatch slides on a metal track (Figure 9-8). On one or two brands of boats I have surveyed, a short length of sail track was used, with sail slides fastened to the underside of the hatch. Nevertheless, brass or stainless steel flat stock, fastened to the fiberglass run with flat-head self-tapping screws, is the most common track material used on fiberglass boats. The well-proven system is to let the flat stock project over the inboard or the outboard edge of the run so that it catches in notches or rabbets in the sides of the hatch. Wooden hatches had essentially the same arrangement for a century or more, except that the brass strip was usually attached to the hatch cover and rode in a rabbet cut in the guide rails, rather than the other way around. Wooden hatch covers had to have at least one hatch beam at each end to stiffen the top and hold its pieces together. When we started building hatches from fiberglass, the beams were unnecessary, but the rabbet was not easily provided in the side of the guide. Some

bright chap moved the metal flat stock so that it projected over the edge of the guide, allowing any notch of wood or metal spaced off the underside of the hatch to hold it to the slide.

If you have a problem with this type of hatch that requires removing it, you could easily find that the hold-downs are built into it, and that the only way to remove it is to unscrew the metal slides from the runs. Removing the screws will entail some logistics; you will have to push the hatch open to remove half of them and closed to get at the rest. On the other hand, you may find that a way was provided to remove the hold-downs at the aft end of the hatch cover. In this case, you will be able to slide the hatch forward, lifting its after edge over the coaming between the guides at the forward end of the opening. Once the hatch has been pushed this far forward, the hold-downs at the front of the hatch will have run off the metal slide, allowing the hatch to be lifted up. Unfortunately, if a weather cover has been installed over such a hatch, it will probably have to come off too, either to get at the forward screws in the flat stock, or to allow the hatch to be lifted clear of the coaming at the forward end of the opening.

The jamming of this common type of hatch usually involves the metal slides in some way. The metal can be worked loose due to abuse, accident, or poor installation, so that the hatch is adrift on one side and jams against the other; or the metal slide can bend so that the hatch binds on it.

I have also seen hatch guides that developed sag or curve at the forward end of the opening. The cabin trunk in these cases had become a bit sway-backed, bending the guides and jamming the hatch as it tried to bridge the curve. The simplest repair is to shim the metal slides up straight, for it is a much bigger project to straighten out or prop up a cabintop that has taken a set in the sagged position. If the coachroof is very limber, you might want to install a post or a strong deck beam at the forward end of this companionway opening. Nevertheless, most cabintops with sagged runs that I have seen appeared to have gotten that way early in the

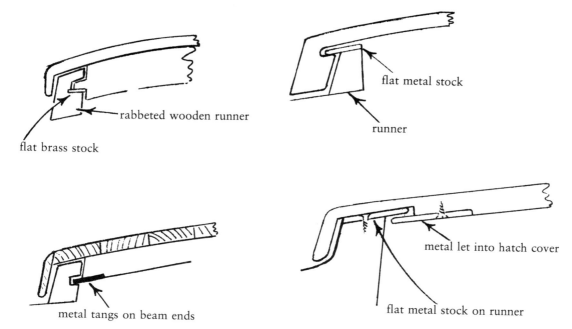

flat metal stock

rabbeted wooden runner

runner

flat brass stock

metal let into hatch cover

metal tangs on beam ends

flat metal stock on runner

Figure 9-8. *Types of hatch cover guides.*

boat's life, possibly before the laminate was fully cured; the condition seemed to be arrested; and the trunk top was amply strong, despite the restful attitude. In lightly built racing boats, this condition is often due to excessive rigging tension, which bends the hull the way a tightly drawn bowstring bends an archer's bow. In this case, a sticky companionway hatch may be a minor symptom of a much more serious problem.

Related to the problem of sagging guides is the problem of pinching the hatch due to settling of the bridge deck or cockpit sole at the companionway opening. This is essentially the same problem of the hull bending or flexing, but in the athwartship direction rather than fore and aft. This problem appeared much more often in wooden boats than it does in fiberglass ones. In fiberglass boats, the trunk top, sides, aft bulkhead and bridge deck or cockpit sole are all one molded unit with many angles, corners, and curves that resist distortion of its shape in most directions. The many pieces that make up the same structure in a wooden boat depend on their fastenings to maintain their relationship

in any direction, and age brings an inevitable relaxation at these stressed areas. Of course, the weak area we are talking about here is the companionway opening, the big hole in the after end of the cabin top and its after bulkhead. The deck and trunk cabin would be a sturdy box structure without the companionway opening; even a one-piece fiberglass molding tends to cave in here if there is too little support in the way of the companionway.

Openings for quarterberths and engine compartments often result in insufficient support in the bridgedeck area of the main bulkhead (the bulkhead that forms the after end of the cabin trunk). As the deck sags and the sides of the companionway opening lean inward, both the sliding hatch and the doors or fisherman slides (drop boards) may jam. Should this be the problem, you can jack the deck back up to its original position and install whatever posts, partial bulkheads, or deck beams are required to support it. This would be a better solution than cutting or grinding the hatch and the doors to accommodate the distortion.

Repairing a companionway hatch

There is no need to repeat the techniques of repairing damage that might have occurred to your hatch as a fiberglass part, as these are well covered in previous chapters. There are, however, some procedures and details to bear in mind. First, if the hatch is broken so that it can be twisted or warped, be sure to fasten temporary stiffeners to it or to prop it up level and secure it in that position with weights or clamps while repairing the fiberglass. If the hatch was damaged by someone walking on it or by some other force that is likely to recur, then you should consider strengthening it as well as repairing it. Here again, make sure that the hatch is not warped, and fasten it in a level posture before laying up more laminate. Further, do not apply too many layers at once, lest the new laminate heat up, shrink excessively, and distort the hatch. And finally, guard against any distortion in the fit of the hatch on its runs and on the metal slide pieces, for either could cause it to bind and make it difficult to slide.

Replacing a companionway hatch

I have to mention replacing companionway hatches because they have been known to break up too much to be worth repairing, and even to get loose and be lost overboard. If the manufacturer can supply a new one, purchasing one will certainly be less bother for you than building a new one. Even if the original hatch was ill-conceived or poorly constructed, since the manufacturer's mold already exists, it might cost less to buy the hatch and build it up or improve it than to make a mold and laminate a new one. That approach failing, you can build a new one as described previously for box hatches, by building a throwaway female mold of wood for the sides and hardboard for the top. If your original hatch still exists in good enough condition, another alternative might be to alter or repair the hatch temporarily, and then take a fiberglass mold off it. That may sound like the long way around the problem to you, but a temporary fiberglass mold need not be difficult to build. Two layers of 1½-ounce mat for a small hatch mold, say 18 inches by two feet, or four layers for one as big as 30 inches by three feet should be sufficient. Stiffen the mold with a few wooden stiffeners lightly glued or tabbed to it before you take it off the original hatch being used for the plug. Just a reminder: Put a strip of corrugated cardboard between the newly built mold and any stiffener before tabbing it on; otherwise, shrinkage of the tabbing might pull the mold and stiffener together hard enough to produce a ridge in the mold surface, which will "print through" as a groove in the new part. Also, don't forget to level the original hatch before making a mold, and the mold before laying up a part, lest you come out with a warped or twisted piece of work. If necessary, fasten the plug or the mold to the top of a workbench, making sure that the edges of all four sides lie in the same plane before laminating. Then, when the part is finished, let it cure well before popping it out and letting it lie around unsupported.

Strengthening a companionway hatch

Whether you purchase or build a new hatch or repair the original, you will want to strengthen it if it was flimsy. It is possible to strengthen a hatch that simply bends too much when you step on the after end by installing a wood or metal stiffener athwartships across the top near the after end. In addition to acting as an external deck beam on the hatch, a rail such as this can be used as a handle for pulling the hatch closed and, incidentally, will keep water on the hatch from running off the after end if you push the hatch open too rapidly. This type of external stiffening rail could keep one's foot from slipping off that end, too, although all hatches that might be walked on should have a nonskid surface. At the same time, if there is a weather cover over the hatch, be careful that the beam does not prevent the hatch from opening far enough to clear the heads of people using the companionway steps or ladder. If crewmembers went below facing aft and holding the grab rails the way they should, companionway hatches wouldn't need such a long opening.

Two other ways to strengthen a hatch are to install a core, making it a sandwich construction, or simply to add more layers of fiberglass to the present construction, whether it is single-skin or sandwich. Your first preference, of course, would be to add the layers on the inside of the hatch, to avoid having to refinish the exterior surface of such a prominent part. Adding a core on the inside would be less trouble for the same reason, but it would also make the hatch heavier, because additional laminate would have to be added to both sides of the core. Remember, in most cored fiberglass parts, the outer skin must be heavier than the inner skin because of the need to resist impact and other abuse, and because fiberglass is not as strong under compression as it is in tension. Also keep in mind that whatever laminate you add on the interior must clear the guide rails and the coaming that runs athwartships between them. If clearing the guide rails and coaming means that the hatch must be raised higher, also remember to check its fit with the doors or fisherman slides and with the weather cover if one is installed. After studying all of these details, you may find that adding material on the inside creates more problems that it solves. If this is the case, you might decide to strengthen your hatch by laying up added materials on the outside after all.

Treating the overstressed boat

A frequent cause of non-accidental damage to fiberglass sailboats is overtightened rigging. The effects can be as conspicuous as a pronounced hollow in the top of the cabin trunk under a deck-mounted mast step, or as subtle as turnbuckles that must be taken up a little closer to their limit each year. The signs of overstressed rigging can stare you in the face, like cracks in the cabin trunk, or they can be as imperceptible as a downward bulge under a keel-stepped mast. Should you be one of those owners who likes to keep his rigging tuned to a high note, you should be on the lookout for problems developing in the structure of your boat.

While we usually consider these problems to be the result of overtight rigging, they could also be considered the result of a weak structure. Fiberglass is strong under tension and flexible under bending strains, however, and most fiberglass boats are capable of withstanding considerable abuse of this type. To counteract the tendency of upward-pulling shrouds and downward-thrusting masts to deform boats, builders have learned to place bulkheads in line with these parts. As a result, the most popular interior arrangement in a small production sloop, for example, is one in which the mast is stepped between a head and a hanging locker opposite. In this arrangement, the aft bulkheads of the head and the locker are in line with the after lower shrouds, the forward bulkheads are in line with the forward lowers, and a knee or divider in each line up with the upper shrouds. The fore-and-aft bulkhead of the head either supports a deck-stepped mast, or ties the deck and hull together alongside a mast stepped on the keel. Tab these bulkheads to the hull and deck, mount the chainplates close to or directly on them, and you have an extremely well-braced structure.

Nevertheless, not every arrangement is as resistant to deformation, and even with an ideal arrangement, overconfident builders often cut back their scantlings or laminate schedules until problems develop. Therefore, I do not wish to accuse every owner whose boat develops problems related to the rig of overtightening it. On the contrary, hardening up the headstay and forestay is the way to make a boat move to windward, and a reasonable tension on the shrouds and running backstays keeps the rig from pumping or slamming back and forth when the boat is rolling and pitching. Any boat buyer, especially a racer, has a right to expect his boat to withstand the rigging tension required for good performance. If the builder fails in that regard, the racer's not going to let his competitors leave him behind; he's going to switch to a different boat.

In treating an overstressed hull, your first concern should be to strengthen the boat wherever it is beginning to deform or break. Don't just repair it—beef it up. That done, easing off the tension on the rig as much as practicable without losing performance will help to prevent a recurrence of the structural problems. Most sailors with whom I have discussed rig tension do not think extremely tight shrouds improve performance. As long as they hold the mast straight and hand it from side to side without a jerk when she tacks or jibes, the shrouds are doing their job. Nevertheless, all sailors agree that keeping the luff of the jib straight is the name of the game when going to windward. To accomplish this, some very powerful devices are employed to tighten up the backstay, which results in increased tension on the luff of the headsail. Judging from what they are capable of doing to the hull of a boat, backstay tensioners might have been developed during the Spanish Inquisition. They tighten the rigging over the mast, forcing it against the deck or keel enough to bend the boat like a bow. Some hulls can withstand this tension without permanent damage; some cannot.

The effects of overly tight backstays

When the mast is forced downward, it pushes down on the deck or hull, depending on which is supporting it. In canoe-bodied hulls fitted with a compression post under a deck-stepped mast, both the deck and the bottom of the boat are bowed down a bit. In one such case, the owner drove more shims under the heel of the post each year, preventing the trunk top from losing its crown in the area of the mast step. Eventually, when the bottom had stretched down about an inch, the fiberglass cracked near the heel of the post, producing the leak that alerted us to what was happening.

In boats with deck-stepped masts over a door or passageway, the lintel (a strong deck beam) or the internal reinforcement in the deck laminate may be sprung downward. The lintel or reinforcement is likely to crack if it is of wood, or to bend if it is of metal. Similarly, when the mast is stepped through the deck, it can stretch the hull bottom down,

damaging the mast step and any parts that are supporting it.

Another result of too much tension in the backstay is that some types of backstay and forestay hardware may be pulled up, broken, or have their bolts sheared off, depending upon how the hardware was constructed and fastened. At the same time, despite all the problems I have seen with stemhead plates, padeyes, and such pieces (especially some cast aluminum ones), I have yet to see a stemhead fitting or a chainplate fastened with a row of stainless steel bolts that was pulled out of the deck or transom.

In a few cases of damage that I have not been able to attribute to other causes, it was my opinion that the upward pull of the stays actually bent the ends of the boat upward enough to cause structural damage. This damage includes cracking or delamination of the fiberglass tabbing of forepeak and lazarette bulkheads; delamination of cored foredecks and side decks; the lifting of the after deck, splitting the hull-deck joint from the transom forward to the cabin trunk; and the creation of stress cracks at the corners between the deck, the coamings, and the cabin trunk.

The effects of overly tight shrouds

Overly tight shrouds can, of course, force the mast down in the same way that the fore-and-aft components of the rig do, causing or contributing to the same kind of damage to the hull and deck. Overtightening of the shrouds also adds to their normal upward and inward pull when the sails are heeling the boat, hastening the onset of distortion, delamination, and breakage in the way of the mast and chainplates. Bulkheads tear loose from their tabbing; foredecks or cabin trunks with masts stepped through them are forced upward; side decks are forced inward, tilting the cabin trunk side; and the gelcoat cracks at the bending points. Any or all of these symptoms warn that the laminate will fracture next.

Repair damage first, then add strength to the boat

It bears repeating that merely to restore damaged parts to their predamaged condition would leave the boat vulnerable to a repetition of the same damage. Any relaxation of the rig's tension notwithstanding, in order to have confidence in the boat's ability to be driven hard and to handle heavy weather, the hull must not only be repaired—it must be strengthened.

It is possible that stronger materials are available now that were not available when the boat was built. Using the new reinforcing fibers and fabrics and employing a few more layers in the laminate, or installing strengthening members such as knees, beams, ribs, or floor timbers, are all good ways to build resistance to rigging tension.

Strengthening the structure is a good move in any repair where it can realistically reduce the repetition of an ever-threatening type of damage. Strength is as axiomatic in boat repairing as it is in boatbuilding: As long as it doesn't lead to disappointing performance, no boat can be too strong.

Index

Note: Italicized page numbers indicate captions.